Windows
of Faith

Muslim Women Scholar-Activists
in North America

Edited by

Gisela Webb

Syracuse University Press

Epigraph calligraphy by Elinor ʿAʾishah Holland
The paper used in this publication meets the minimum requirements of
American National Standard for Information Sciences—Permanence of
Paper for Printed Library Materials, ANSI Z39.48-1984. ⊗

Library of Congress Cataloging-in-Publication Data
Windows of faith : Muslim women scholar-activists in North America /
edited by Gisela Webb.
p.   cm. — (Women and gender in North American religions)
Includes bibliographical references and index.
ISBN 0-8156-2851-X (cloth : alk. paper). — ISBN 0-8156-2852-8
(pbk. : alk. paper)
1. Muslim women.   2. Women in Islam.   I. Webb, Gisela.
II. Series.
HQ1170.W52   1999
305.48'6971—dc21   99-40405

Manufactured in the United States of America

In the Name of God, the Merciful, the Compassionate

Contents

Introduction

"May Muslim Women Speak for Themselves, Please?"

GISELA WEBB

꿈 The purpose of this book is to give evidence of, and voice to, the diversity of expressions that constitutes contemporary Muslim women's scholarship and activism in the United States. What makes this collection of essays unique and of critical importance in understanding the current situation of Muslim women's studies in America can be understood by looking at the genesis, methodology, and goals of this volume. In summary, these women's writings can be seen as the product of the gradual but steady emergence of a movement among many—perhaps a critical mass of—Muslim women who insist that their religious self-identity not be dismissed and that, in fact, it be affirmed in the midst of their acknowledgment of and strivings toward solving what they see as serious problems that have faced and continue to face women in both Muslim and non-Muslim societies and communities around the world. This approach to Muslim women's scholarship and activism has been designated Muslim women's *scholarship-activism* because it originates in the conviction that to look at women's issues *from within* the Islamic perspective must include, and indeed unite, issues of theory and practice. This means that any analysis or theory of women's nature, role, rights, or problems must include attention to the practical, immediate issues involved in actualizing the Qur'anic mandate of social justice and, concomitantly, that any considerations of "practical" solutions to problems and injustices faced by women must have sound theological grounding in the Qur'anic worldview.

The chapters in this text can be seen as evidence of the lively, creative, critical, and self-critical discussions currently taking place in the academy and in Muslim communities and professional organizations in the United States, raising issues of religious pluralism, democracy, gender, and modernity as they relate to Islam and Muslim identity. Although these discussions reflect the overall current situation of heightened awareness and political self-consciousness of groups that constitute the increasingly diverse ethnic, cultural, and religious nature of contemporary *American* society, they also reflect, when seen from within the Islamic historical perspective, the contemporary living out of the Islamic legacy of *ijtihad*, or ongoing interpretation of traditional texts and law in light of changing social and cultural contexts. Most of the rapidly growing Muslim population of the United States, and academics in the field of Islamic studies as well, lament the fact that the media ignores this vigorous and progressive dynamic of Islam in the United States while it focuses attention on the more sensationalist and fear-generating sectarian, extremist-political, or ultraconservative Muslim movements inside and outside the country.

In its current presentation of Muslim women, the American media and cultural imagination tend to focus on "Muslim woman" as an oppressed or mute victim. Less-apparent is the work that has been undertaken by Muslim women scholars seeking critically to examine issues affecting women's lives in Muslim communities. Those issues include the convergence of historical, cultural, religious, and ideological forces at work (past and present, Muslim and non-Muslim) that have defined the nature and role of women. The field of "Muslim women's studies" has until now included (1) anthropological and sociological work, which spoke to the particularity and diversity of women's experience in differing social, political, and ethnic climates (e.g., Erika Friedl, Elizabeth Fernea, Valerie Hoffman-Ladd, Fatima Mernissi, Sherifa Zuhur) and (2) the revisiting of normative historical accounts of the development of theological, legal, and cultural traditions regarding women and the feminine (e.g., Leila Ahmed, Fatima Mernissi, Riffat Hassan, Azizah al-Hibri, Sachiko Murata).

More recent on the horizon—and the work to which this book is dedicated—are a number of newly emerging clusters of "scholarship-activism" that have developed alongside of, and in part as a result of, the formation of interdisciplinary networks of (mostly) Muslim women involved in grassroots work on issues of jurisprudence, theology, hermeneutics, women's education, and women's rights. The methodology of these Muslim women scholar-activists is neither monolithic in style or content nor isolationist with respect to debate and discussion across discipline, religious, or cultural lines. It includes, as these chapters make evident, the retrieval, investigation, scrutiny, criticism, reinterpretation, and use of classical Islamic texts, methodologies, and cultural traditions to address the problems Muslim women face. It marks a stage where, as Amina Wadud puts it, "Muslim women are subject and object of their own discourse." The approach is a frontal challenge to a perceived chauvinism, a new patriarchy, that "Western" feminists—perhaps unwittingly—did not see developing in their own ranks toward Muslim women (and other non-European women and their cultures), whose assumptions were crystallized in the "universalist" assumptions underlying the United Nations platform on women's rights. This approach is also a frontal challenge to the established Muslim cultural patriarchy in its use of Qur'an, *sunnah* (the example, or tradition of Muhammad), and *shari'ah* (Islamic law), which these women see as having moved away from the essentially egalitarian thrust of the Qur'an and the model of participation of women in the public sphere set during the early Islamic period. These Muslim women scholar-activists see conservative neo-traditionalist elements in the Islamic community as trying to silence or dismiss their work by simply labeling them as "followers" of secular Western feminism. The approach of these Muslim women scholars is *activistic* in its attempts to find both short- and long-term solutions to the mental and physical suffering of Muslim women who find themselves pawns in the global political, economic, and ideological confrontations between East and West, North and South, Muslim and non-Muslim worlds.

A heightened visibility of and, indeed, impetus for this new merging of scholar-activist activities coincided with work preceding the 1995 World Conference on Women in Beijing. A number of discussions took place among (mostly) Muslim women scholars, activists, and lawyers to think through the idea and content of a United Nations platform on the status and rights of women and to determine whether there should be a platform reflecting particular concerns of Muslim women (in contradistinction to a platform determined solely by Western assumptions and Western feminists). One such discussion meeting was the 1994 conference in Washington, D.C., "Religion, Culture, and Women's Human Rights in the Muslim World," sponsored by the Sisterhood Is Global Institute (SIGI) and American University's Center for the Study of the Global South. Presenters and attendants represented a wide range of perspectives from "Islamist" to "Islamic modernist-secularist" to "Western feminist" and "womanist." The meeting, in fact, brought to light the work of existing research and activist organizations, such as KARAMAH: Muslim Women Lawyers for Human Rights, founded by Azizah al-Hibri, and the North American Muslim Women's Retreat and Dialogue on the (U.N.) Document (on the elimination of all forms of discrimination against women) organized by the North American Council for Muslim Women and the American Muslim Council. The conference also spawned new women's groups that would venture into the area of cooperative scholarship and activism, such as the Muslim Women's Georgetown Study Project.

Clearly, for students of contemporary Islam, contemporary religion in America, and women's studies to ignore this sort of grass-roots Muslim women's activity, including the rapidly increasing networking of these women in a variety of disciplines, academic and professional, would be to ignore issues of *development of Islam in America* and its inevitable impact on Islam globally.

The event that served as the final catalyst in the development of this volume was the enthusiastic audience response and near mandate to publish the papers delivered by the panel "Self-Identity of Muslim Women," Nimat Hafez Barazangi presiding, at the 1995 Annual Middle Eastern Studies Association (MESA) Meeting. This response echoed the enthusiasm generated by papers delivered by the panel "Muslim Women's Scholarship-Activism in America," Gisela Webb presiding, at the 1995 Annual American Academy of Religion Meeting. There was a particular sense of urgency in the comments of some women in the MESA meeting audience, who spoke of their involvement in grass-roots educational, political, and other social service organizations in various countries and who saw the papers as "practical scholarly resources" very much needed right now in their work as Muslim women educating other Muslim women. They saw the papers as offering both historical information regarding the development of traditional attitudes toward women within Muslim societies *and* as practical approaches to solving present-day situations of injustice and abuse (such as women not being allowed in the public sector—even the mosque in some places—in the name of Islam.) Others in the audience saw such discussion as critical in the increasingly diverse cultural climate of America's communities and universities. A number of Muslim men, too, expressed feelings of "privilege" in seeing and being a part of a new turn in discussion on Muslim women's issues. The spirit of lively engagement of the panels with the audiences was only matched by the spirit of solidarity and the manner of respectful, open dialogue and debate among panel members themselves. A number of those papers have been included in this volume.

This book, therefore, brings together some of the leading Muslim women scholar-activists in North America, placing into the academy's and the public's purview the work, the concerns, the goals, and the methods of participants in the most current phase of Muslim women's studies.

I am particularly appreciative of that early encouragement from Amina Wadud, Maysam al-Faruqi, and Nimat Hafez Barazangi to begin the "gathering of voices" for publication. Indeed, it must be said that the entire process of producing this volume was quite unique for an anthology of essays: from beginning to end, the project was much more of a collaboration than a collection.

The first chapters in this volume are focused primarily on theoretical issues related to the rethinking and recontextualizing of classical Islamic sources and literary traditions whose interpretation, usage, and silencing have led to attitudes fostering second-class status for women or the exclusion of women in the public sphere in Muslim communities. The first two chapters set the stage by critiquing the current approaches to Muslim women's rights (both within and without the Islamic community) and opening the boundaries of discussion.

These chapters are followed by four that deal with Islamic law, as Islamic law (*shariʿah*) and jurisprudence (*fiqh*) form the element of Islam most directly responsible for the definition of woman's role and the boundaries of woman's activities in Muslim communities. The issue of Islamic law and its interpretation is also the element most responsible for many contemporary problems Muslim women face daily as conservative political "Islams" reinstitute "Islamic" laws pertaining to women and family.

As evidence of our commitment to a multidisciplinary approach to the issue of gender-justice in Islam, we include a chapter on Muslim women's literary (traditions by or about women) history and an example of contemporary Qur'anic spiritual exegesis, each of which tackles the problem of the relationship between knowledge and authority in very different ways.

Finally, in the last two chapters we focus on more singular "on the ground" experiences that Muslim women scholar-activists in America are monitoring and attempting to illuminate and ameliorate through their work.

Each scholar brings a unique contribution to the text.

Amina Wadud, from Virginia Commonwealth University, Qur'anic scholar and author of *Qur'an and Woman*, made news when she accepted the revolutionary invitation by a South African mosque community to deliver a "pre-sermon sermon" (*khutba*) at Friday congregational prayers. This highly symbolic move—an African American Muslim woman speaking/standing *before* a congregation—(not without protest in the streets) was a signal of the direction many Muslims across the globe want to take in terms of religious and social boundaries. Wadud discusses contemporary developments in the process of self-naming and identity-development in which Muslim women are currently engaged, proposing a dynamic, process-oriented alternative exegesis of the Qur'an as a strategy of identity development.

Nimat Hafez Barazangi, from the Cornell University women's studies program, long-time researcher and activist in Muslim women's education in the United States and internationally, begins her discussion on Muslim women by presenting a propaedeutic argument not simply for women's right to education but for the right of Muslim women to higher religious education (active participation in the ongoing "reading" and interpreting of the Qur'an) as the foundational means to becoming the spiritually and intellectually autonomous person *mandated* in the Qur'anic view of the individual, male or female, as "trustee" of God.

Azizah Y. al-Hibri, law professor at the T. C. Williams School of Law, founder and current president of KARAMAH: Muslim Women Lawyers for Human Rights, well-known for her work on gender studies (and on Islam and democracy) and more recently for her participation in the Bill Moyer's Public Television series (now book) *Genesis*, gives an overview of the major areas of Islamic law affecting women's lives, raising the question of meaning and application of a system of law conceived in the midst of past patriarchal structures.

Maysam J. al-Faruqi, from Georgetown University and founder of the Muslim Women's Georgetown Study Project—a grass-roots women's *ijtihad* (legal interpretation) research group—explains the internal logic and methodology of classical *shariʿah* and juridical interpretation as envisioned by early jurists, arguing for the retrieval of its original flexibility and balance against the present day rigidity, inconsistencies, and misuse in application. She presents a detailed, striking argument against, and a correction of, the interpretation of the early jurists of two critical verses in the Qurʾan that have led to many problems for women in Muslim societies, maintaining that for Muslims, juridical problems can and must be approached from within the "rules" of Islamic jurisprudence itself.

Asifa Quraishi, an S.J.D. candidate at Harvard Law School, with an LL.M. from Columbia Law School (with training in U.S. and Islamic law), and vice-president of KARAMAH: Muslim Women Lawyers for Human Rights, presents an eye-opening, disturbing, enlightening case study of the application of *shariʿah* rape laws in contemporary Pakistan. She uses this case to examine the original intentionality of texts used to legitimate the laws, showing the distortion of *shariʿah* by local cultural patriarchies.

Aminah Beverly McCloud, from De Paul University, author of *African American Islam*, brings her first-hand knowledge of issues facing Islamic communities in United States, particularly those in urban areas of the country. She discusses emerging issues in the application of Islamic law in the context of a mushrooming Muslim population in America (of converts and "born Muslims"), including the problems women face in *not* knowing their rights under Islamic or U.S. law and the precarious situation of the Muslim university professors as they face demands to give "official legal opinion" in the context of young Islamic communities not familiar with classical Islamic law and jurisprudence.

Mohja Kahf, from the University of Arkansas, discusses the work that she has begun—and that needs to be done—in the retrieval of an Arab/ Muslim women's literary tradition and the immense implications of this type of work for the reconstruction/reinscribing/revisioning of woman's place and voice in Muslim history and society, past and present. Her chapter is a refreshing, ground-breaking demonstration of how literary history can reveal much about women's role and gender relations during the paradigmatic formative period of the Islamic community. One must, however, first take the posture of *khabirini*, that is, be willing to listen to the self-generated discourse of Muslim women.

Rabia Terri Harris, American-born founder of the Muslim Peace Fellowship, exemplifies the grass-roots work of Muslim women educators to stop violence and implement the concomitant values of compassion and justice necessary for any sustained peace, whether in the sphere of the home and family, mosque, or international politics. Her rich commentary on the Qur'anic exhortation to "read the signs on the horizon" (Surah 51) bears the stamp of the Islamic spiritual (Sufi) tradition, which—with its attention to the psychological dimension of human experience—has historically maintained that the quest for human justice (for human integration and healing at the societal level) must be accompanied, perhaps preceded, by integration of the disparate, hidden-to-oneself, aspects of the self that are the sources of fear, intellectual stagnation, misuse of power and authority, and ultimately, violence.

Gwendolyn Zoharah Simmons, doctoral student at Temple University, a civil rights activist in the South in the sixties, and a convert to Islam through a Sufi teacher in the seventies, has worked her entire life in peace/justice and women's advocacy work. Her chapter is an overview of the wealth of activist work Muslim women are undertaking globally at the grass-roots level—in the name of a Qur'anically based gender justice—but it is set in the context of her personal journey from confronting racial inequality in the American South during the sixties to confronting gender inequality in American Muslim communities in the nineties.

Riffat Hassan, from the University of Louisville, is one of the true pioneers of Muslim women's studies in the United States and has written extensively on the subject of women's role and rights in the Qur'an and in Muslim societies (including her native Pakistan). She argues the necessity of, and a methodology for, Muslim women dealing with the issue of family planning *from an informed Islamic perspective*, one sorely missing in most of the debates between "Western development programs" and conservative "neo-traditionalist" discourse on birth control in Muslim countries. Dr. Hassan has also contributed an appendix section that forms an overview of fundamental *human* rights grounded in the Qur'an.

ᴄ୬ʳ

We believe that this text will provide academics with an interdisciplinary approach to contemporary Muslim women's studies and that it will
serve as a useful resource for students and teachers faced with the challenge of integrating gender studies into religious (including Islamic) or
interreligious studies. It is also our intention that this book will serve as
a practical resource guide for women who wish to become involved in
the women's research and activist organizations through which Muslim
women are working to correct abuse, injustice, and subordination of
women.

Finally, it is our hope that this volume will communicate both the
spirit of supportive, open dialogue on Muslim women's issues among
women of faith that was the inspiration for its genesis and the spirit that
sustained its development.

Special gratitude goes to our families, friends, and colleagues for their
patience and encouragement, to our friend Kareema Altomare for providing much of the women's organizations material in our appendix section,
and to Patricia Lauch, my administrative assistant, whose help in the final
stages of editing was invaluable.

Contributors

Nimat Hafez Barazangi has received several awards for her participatory research, including the Glock Award for her doctoral dissertation "Perceptions of the Islamic Belief System: The Muslims in North America" (1988) from the Department of Education at Cornell University, a Visiting Fellowship from Oxford University's Centre of Islamic Studies, a scholarship from the International Council for Adult Education, a three-year Serial Fulbright Scholarship, and the United Nations Development Program 1999 TOKTEN Fellowship. Currently, she holds a research fellow position at the Women's Studies Program at Cornell University. She specializes in curriculum and instruction, Islamic and Arabic studies, and adult and community education. Her most recent publications include her guest-edited volume of *Religion and Education* (vol. 25, 1/2, winter 1998), entitled *Taqwa, Issues of Islamic Education in the United States*, in which she has an article, "The Equilibrium of Islamic Education: Has Muslim Women's Education Preserved the Religion?" and her edited volume *Islamic Identity and the Struggle for Justice* (1966), in which she has a chapter entitled "Vicegerency and Gender Justice."

Maysam J. al-Faruqi teaches Islamic Studies in the Theology Department of Georgetown University in Washington, D.C. She received her Ph.D. at Temple University in 1987, having concentrated in the area of economic theory in classical Islamic law. She helped complete a number of works left unfinished by the death of her late uncle and aunt, well-known Islamic scholars Drs. Isma'il and Lois Lamya al-Faruqi. She is founder of the Muslim Women's Georgetown Study Project, a grassroots *ijtihad* (legal interpretation) research group based in Washington, D.C., that focuses on women's issues and Islamic law. She is completing a volume on the subject of women and Islamic law.

Rabia Terri Harris came to Islam in 1978 through the Jerrahi Order, a 300-year old traditional Sufi teaching order headquartered in Istanbul. She is assistant editor of *Fellowship*, the magazine of the Fellowship of Reconciliation, the world's oldest and largest international, interfaith peace and justice organization. Harris founded and serves as coordinator of the Muslim Peace Fellowship, an open gathering of Muslims dedicated to Islamic intellectual renaissance and nonviolent transformational politics. She received her bachelor's in Religion from Princeton University and her master's in Middle Eastern Languages and Cultures from Columbia University. In 1989 she was granted a Fulbright scholarship to study unpublished manuscripts at the Suleymaniyye Library in Istanbul. She has translated a number of works on medieval Islamic spirituality and lectures widely on progressive understandings of Islam.

Riffat Hassan, a native of Lahore, Pakistan, received her Ph.D. from St. Mary's College, University of Durham, England, on the subject of the Philosophical Ideas of Muhammad Iqbal. She is Professor of Religious Studies and Humanities at the University of Louisville in Kentucky and has been an international lecturer and author on Muslim women's rights in the Qur'an since the 1970s. More recently, she served as plenary speaker at the United Nations International Conference on Population and Development in Cairo in 1994, representing the Religious Consultation on Population, Reproductive Health, and Ethics at the plenary session at the nongovernmental forum of the Fourth World Conference on Women in Beijing in 1995. She is founder and president of the International Network for the Rights of Female Victims of Violence in Pakistan (INRFVVP). Recent publications include "Muslim Feminist Hermeneutics" in *In our Own Voices: Four Centuries of American Women's Religious Writing* (1995), edited by R. S. Keller and R. R. Ruether, and *Setara di Hadapan Allah* (Equal before Allah), a book consisting of the writings of Riffat Hassan and Fatima Mernissi translated into Bahasa Indonesian (1996). Her most recent monograph is *Women's Rights and Islam: From the I.C.P.D. to Beijing* (1995).

Azizah Y. al-Hibri teaches corporate law and Islamic jurisprudence at the T. C. Williams School of Law, University of Richmond. She is a former professor of philosophy, the founder and president of KARAMAH: Muslim Women Lawyers for Human Rights, and a member of the Advisory Board of the Public Religion Project (University of Chicago), the Pluralism Project (Harvard University), and Religion and Ethics NewsWeekly (PBS). She is also a member of the board of directors of the Interfaith Alliance Foundation, a member of the Virginia State Advisory Committee to the United States Commission on Civil Rights, and a member of the Virginia Religious Task Force for the Prevention of Family Violence.

Azizah al-Hibri has authored, edited, or contributed to several books and journals, including *Women and Islam, Technology and Human Affairs,* and *Religious and Ethical Perspectives on Population Issues.* Among her recent articles are "Islamic and American Constitutional Law: Borrowing Possibilities or a History of Borrowing?" in the *University of Pennsylvania Journal of Constitutional Law* (forthcoming 1999) and "Islamic Jurisprudence and Critical Race Feminism" in *Global Critical Race Feminism,* Adrien Wing, ed. (forthcoming 1999). Al-Hibri is founding editor of *Hypatia: A Journal of Feminist Philosophy* and is currently on the editorial board of the *Journal of Law and Religion.* She practiced law on Wall Street for many years before her return to teaching.

Mohja Kahf is assistant professor in the Department of English and the Middle East studies program at the University of Arkansas, Fayetteville. After receiving her Ph.D. in comparative literature at Rutgers University, she taught in the Rutgers Women's Studies Program for one year. She has published her first book, *Western Representations of the Muslim Woman: From Termagant to Odalisque* (1999). Born in Damascus and raised in the United States, Mohja Kahf is a poet. She participates in U.S. Muslim community work.

Aminah Beverly McCloud is associate professor of Islamic studies in the Department of Religious Studies at De Paul University and is author of *African America Islam* (1995) and *Questions of Faith* (1999). She is an internationally known lecturer on Islam in America, a Fulbright scholar, an Islamic expert witness, and the founder of the Islam in America Conference and the Islam in America Archival Project.

Asifa Quraishi is an S.J.D. candidate at Harvard Law School. She holds an LL.M. from Columbia Law School, a J.D. from the University of California, Davis, and a bachelor's in Legal Studies from the University of California, Berkeley. She is the vice president of KARAMAH: Muslim Women Lawyers for Human Rights and an associate of the Muslim Women's League based in Los Angeles, California. Previous publications include "From a Gasp to a Gamble: A Proposed Test for Unconscionability" (*U.C. Davis Law Review* 1992) and "Essence and Existence in the Philosophies of Hegel and Mulla Sadra" (*California Legal Studies Journal* 1988). Asifa Quraishi has held clerkships with the United States District Court for the Eastern District of California and the United States Court of Appeals for the Ninth Circuit, specializing in death penalty law and policy. She has also been active in American Muslim youth and community education all her life.

Gwendolyn Zoharah Simmons is assistant professor of religious studies at the University of Florida in Gainesville. She was born during the "Jim Crow" era in Memphis, Tennessee, and was the first member of her immediate family to attend college, being awarded a four-year academic scholarship to Spelman College, a prestigious traditional black college for women in Atlanta, Georgia. She withdrew after two years to work full time in the black freedom struggle of the sixties and seventies, including two years in the project directorship of the Student Non-Violent Coordinating Committee's Laurel, Mississippi, project. She deferred her college career for several years, receiving her bachelor's degree from Antioch University in 1989 in human services and her master's degree in Islamic studies in 1996 from Temple University, where she continues doctoral studies. Simmons received Fulbright and American Center of Oriental Research Fellowships for dissertation research, "The Contemporary Impact of Shari'ah Law on Women's Lives in Jordan and Palestine," and was based in Amman, Jordan, for that period. She has served on the staff of the American Friends Service Committee, a Quaker-based international peace, justice, and development organization, for twenty years. She is a Sunni Muslim and a member of the Sheikh Muhammad Raheem Bawa Muhaiyaddeen Mosque and Fellowship in Philadelphia.

Amina Wadud is associate professor in the Department of Philosophy and Religious Studies at Virginia Commonwealth University in Richmond, Virginia. She received her Ph.D. in Islamic Studies and Arabic at the University of Michigan in 1988 and is an internationally known author and lecturer on the subject of women and Islam, particularly for her work on alternative Qur'anic hermeneutics and her critique of secular feminisms, "In Search of a Pro-Faith Feminism from an Islamic Perspective." She wrote *Qur'an and Woman* and has worked in grassroots women's human rights organizations and in academia globally, including Africa, Asia, and North America.

Gisela Webb is associate professor in the Department of Religious Studies, director of the University Honors Program and faculty fellow of the School of Diplomacy and International Relations at Seton Hall University in South Orange, New Jersey. She teaches in comparative religious studies, Islamic studies, medieval studies, and women's Studies. Her dissertation, which she completed at Temple University in 1989 under Seyyed Hossein Nasr, was a study in classical Islamic philosophy, mysticism, and angelology. She has since written in the areas of both medieval and contemporary Islamic spirituality, including "Tradition and Innovation in Contemporary American Islamic Spirituality: The Bawa Muhaiyaddeen Fellowship" in *Muslim Communities of North America* (edited by Haddad and Smith), "Islam and Muslims in America" in *Islam, Muslims, and the Modern State* (edited by Mutalib and Hashmi), and chapters on Islam and Islamic-inspired movements in *America's Alternative Religions* (edited by Miller).

PART ONE

Qur'anic/Theological Foundations

1

Alternative Qur'anic Interpretation and the Status of Muslim Women

AMINA WADUD

🌑 Since the end of colonialism, Muslims have been engaged in a significant process of identification, renaming the self in light of modernity and
a global community that includes non-Muslims (Esposito 1993; Mehmet
1990). The role and status of women are among the topics of concern
in this process. Views on the status of women symbolically reflect the
strength of the Islamic identity in various Muslim contexts. Where Muslim
identity is strong over against externally set colonialist standards, there is
greater flexibility toward women's development and greater public acknowledgment of women's valuable contributions inside and outside of
the family. When Muslim identity is weak in the face of external pressures,
women are more closely guarded not only from perceived and real external threats but also from internal flexibility and change. Changes in the
role and status of women seem to occur more within the context of a
stable group identity (Haddad 1985).

More than any other time in Muslim history, women themselves are
directly involved in the process of self-naming and identity development. I
address here a recent but crucial strategy of identity development—alternative exegesis of the Qur'an. Alternative Qur'anic exegesis, like other alternative interpretations of the primary sources of Islam, emphasize both
Islamic legitimacy and agency. By redressing the paradigmatic basis of
Islam, alternative interpretations succeed in developing an autonomous
and authentic Islamic identity. Although the sanctity of the primary

3

sources is maintained, the hermeneutics of those sources—how they are understood, interpreted, and then applied—reflect new levels of understanding and human participation.

Background

At its most fundamental level, Islam is built upon two primary sources: the Qur'an, with the Muslim consensus maintaining its status as the revealed word of Allah, and the *sunnah*, or normative practices of the Prophet Muhammad (pbuh). At another level, the complex and detailed Islamic intellectual legacy was built upon these two sources to form a number of sciences and disciplines: *shari'ah* (law), ethics, exegesis, dialectics, philosophy, and aesthetics. At a third level, Muslim people within their cultures draw from the first two levels and from their environment to bring about various permutations and complex configurations. Between scholars of Islam and Muslim laity, notions of Islam are sometimes haphazardly drawn from all three levels. No distinction is made between the "Islam" defined through cultural nuance and a wide range of Muslim practices, the "Islam" legitimated by authorities (usually male) of the intellectual legacy, or the "Islam" that reflects the primary sources. Is "Islam" what Muslims do, what governments establish, what the intellectual legacy articulated, or what the primary sources imply? In this chapter I refer to Islam only as a genuine reflection of the two primary sources. Although these reflections do occur within lived "Islam" and the "Islam" concluded in the intellectual legacy, ultimately the standard of evaluation must make a direct link between those standards and the two primary sources.[1]

These various configurations of "Islam"—primary, intellectual, and cultural—also influence developments in the discourse concerned with the status of Muslim women. Several strategies for addressing the issue of women have emerged. Each strategy implies, or results from, certain underlying notions or perceptions about women and about Islam. At the 1995 World Conference of Women in Beijing, Muslim women from various countries formed a noticeable and articulate presence. There were repre-

---

1. The Prophet's *sunnah* is believed to be a living embodiment of the Qur'an. Hence, both primary sources are reflections of the text: one, its words, the other, its embodiment. This means that *shari'ah* is not a primary source.

sentatives from these major strategies and from several others not considered here. I briefly define the major strategies in order to establish the significance of alternative interpretation of the Qur'an as a method for addressing the identity of Muslim women and men as they face the complexities of modernity and a global culture. My treatment of these strategies is not intended as an analysis of Muslim women's activities.

Three major strategies seem to have emerged: two neotraditionalist approaches and one secular approach. Thus far, a number of minor strategies might be located between these three. They, however, could be viewed as offshoots from, or reactions to, the three major strategies. Although alternative interpretation is also a strategy that falls between these three, I demonstrate how it poses a significant reconciliation between the disparate strategies because it addresses the concerns over developing and maintaining an authentic Islamic identity in the complexity of the new global communities.

Three Major Strategies to Address
Concerns of Women

At one end of the spectrum are two neotraditionalist strategies: one conservative and the other reactionary. They are "traditional" insofar as they both uphold the pristine honor attributed to women as articulated within classical texts such as al-Ghazzali's book on marriage and sexuality (1984).[2] Traditionally, a woman was dependent upon a male member of society, usually her father or husband, for establishing her legitimacy and maintaining her social honor. She was not considered an autonomous agent. In both of the neotraditionalist strategies, the Muslim woman is perceived only in terms relative to the man's home: a pious or recalcitrant wife, mother, daughter, or homemaker. In the context of the mass urbanization affecting many Muslim countries, both of the neotraditionalist strategies have grown in importance.[3] Both, however, might be considered responses to the misrepresentation of Muslim women and Islam through-

2. This section of al-Ghazali, *'Ihya' ulum al Din* has been translated by M. Farah (al-Ghazali, 1984).

3 As resources and job opportunities dwindle in the rural areas because of the demands of the new economy, Muslim populations are immigrating to the urban areas, thus affecting social, cultural and familial traditions and constructs.

out the colonial period. This misrepresentation continues to be projected by Western academia and popular media.

Much of Western scholarship and media coverage asserts or implies that Islam itself oppresses women. Muslims have responded to this portrayal by defending the name of "Islam," even to the extent of defending practices that are harmful to women. These responses and the dominant Western perspectives on Islam make no attempt to address the disparities among Islamic primary sources, intellectual developments, and Muslim cultural practices. Some Muslim response is called for in the context of Western hegemonies and their political and economic monopolies for they pose a threat to the preservation of an autonomous Islamic identity. When Muslim responses, however, begin to defend inhumane practices that do not genuinely reflect the objectives and spirit of the Islamic primary sources, it seems to be a situation of opposition against the West at all cost. When that cost is the loss of Islam as a reflection of the primary sources, then the defense cannot be deemed Islamic.

The more conservative neotraditionalist perspective seems ill prepared to face and accept the effects of the new global economies on local lifestyles. The effort to preserve the dignity of Islam from the disintegration of the encroaching Western culture and secularism often proves only to create a rigid barrier between what is perceived as Western modernity and what is perceived as Islam. In this conservative approach a strong emphasis is placed on a symbolic return to the Madinan model. The Prophet established a comprehensive Muslim community at Madinah based on the Qur'anic ethos.[4]

Today's conservative strategy concretizes those symbols by literally mimicking the original community at Madinah. Women may be heavily veiled, including the face veil, and they are rarely called upon to perform competitive public duties such as wage-earning employment outside the home. In some cases, the women in the groups who adhere to this perspective may also fall below the national trends toward higher education because educational institutions themselves are viewed as vehicles of corrupt

---

4. At Madinah the Prophet Muhammad established the first comprehensive and active Islamic community. The basis of its operation was the Qur'anic ethos. This Madinan period and the sahabah (those who lived concurrently with the Prophet) are believed to epitomize the true Islamic experience.

Western or un-Islamic values. As the women retire to a more secluded lifestyle, the men continue their education and employment to fulfill the traditional male responsibility to provide for and protect women.

Although the over-all income of such families might tend to fall below that of other urban Muslim families that maintain the benefits of the woman's additional income, the appeal of the conservative neotraditional-ist approach is that it prevents the double bind that is experienced by women in the more reactionary neotraditionalist approach discussed below. Despite this limited appeal this perspective is not only extreme but also unlikely to have long-term success except for that elite class of women who can afford not to work outside the home. Given the new global economy, such a luxury is untenable for most Muslims.

The second neotraditionalist perspective might be seen as a reaction to the consequences of the global economy. Paid employment for women is no longer simply necessary for the lower classes. More Muslim women leave their homes for paid employment than did directly after the end of colonialism. A decent and comfortable lifestyle increasingly depends on a woman's contributions to the family income. In addition, as women increase their levels of education and their professional capabilities, they become better informed and more active participants in the public sectors of society. Some Muslim governments support women's valuable contributions in the interest of greater national productivity and development. This in no way indicates that national interests are Islamic.

As women continue to increase their part of the trend toward higher levels of education, professional training, and valuable public contributions, they face a contradiction in their lives. Women continue to fulfill the bulk of household duties and child care. The notion that the honored woman does not have to compete in the public domain because it is the Islamic duty of the male to maintain and protect her creates a double bind: her professional life offers little or no relief from domestic duties, whereas her fulfillment of home and family responsibilities does not relieve her from providing the additional income. As a further reaction to this double bind, symbolic forms of Islamic dress imply that a woman maintains tradition and should be honored as such. Although the dress symbols are present in both neotraditionalist perspectives, here there is less rigidity and little or no confinement. I include professionally trained Muslim women who direct, organize, and provide Islamic social welfare and relief services in the context of day care, health clinics, food drives, fund raising, and educational and religious institution activities in this last category.

Both of the neotraditionalist approaches address the issue of Muslim women's identity, experiences, and concerns over equitable rights and responsibilities by asserting that "Islam" provided women their full rights more than fourteen centuries ago. They offer little concrete consideration or analysis of the innumerable instances when those rights are denied to women in the real contexts of lived Islam. Such a consideration would require a critical examination of the way the word *Islam* is used. When "Islam" is applied to the status quo, it makes it difficult for women to address this ambiguity of usage without being seen as recalcitrant.

Whereas both neotraditionalist approaches might be considered right winged, at the other end of the spectrum is a perspective also clearly articulated by Muslim women and various women's groups at the world conference. I consider this left-winged perspective a secularist approach because the women who represent it are adamantly opposed to all considerations of religion in the discourse over women's human rights. In their quest for rights they have become pro-Western, pro-modern, and anti-tradition, even though they fail to distinguish between lived Islam, the intellectual legacy of the Muslims, and Islam as a reflection of the primary sources.[5]

Furthermore, the secularists express little or no concern over the centrality of Islamic spirituality to Muslim women nor over the importance of Islam as a dimension of identity. The tendency instead is to accept the determinations of rights, liberation, and agency promoted in many Western women's groups. Although they address serious infractions of the rights of Muslim women in the context of some Muslim governments and conservative religious thinkers, they ignore the negative consequences of this approach. Adherence to internally generated notions of self is crucial in the quest for identity. In the secularist perspective not only are many of the standards of measurement external to Islamic cultural ethos but they also bear no resemblance to the primary sources of Islam. Although these

5. At the "Women, Law and Religion" workshop I attended in 1992, sponsored by the Asia Pacific Forum of Women, Law and Development, I met several Asian human rights activists and lawyers who claimed they had tried the alternative interpretive method and it had failed. Yet, they indicated no direct knowledge of Islamic primary sources, only knowledge as it had been passed down by male Muslim intellectuals.

standards are promoted as "universal," they continue to support other ethnic, class, and gender-based stereotypes. Of particular concern is that these standards of measurement continue to participate in the sexist dichotomy that grants greater value to men and what men do. Under the guise of "equality," women are offered opportunities to do the same as, or be like, men. No distinction is drawn between men as males and men as human agents setting the standard for what is considered most valuable or normative (Apter 1985). Ideally, Islam promotes an equitable experience of complementarity between women and men, who enhance the humanity of each other through sharing experiences and perspectives.

Despite my criticism of this secularist perspective, I cannot ignore the important strides made by these women as intellectuals and activists. Women who follow this approach are most likely to pursue the United Nations Convention to Eliminate All Forms of Discrimination Against Women (CEDAW). But while they herald it as a universal document encompassing the rights and dignity of all women—irrespective of religion, culture, or nationality—one of the most frequently asked questions in countries with a sizable Muslim population is whether CEDAW can be applied to Muslim women. Is CEDAW a genuine reflection of the Islamic ethos as projected by traditions and established in the *shari'ah*? Those engaged in answering this question do not always stop to analyze critically the gender biases that have developed alongside Islamic jurisprudence and *shari'ah*. Such a critique requires a clear rethinking of the term *Islam* as proposed here.

The relevancy of CEDAW to Muslim women similarly reflects the various strategies for postcolonialist identity development. Both neotraditional approaches are popular because they maintain that Islam is perfect, whether rhetorically or substantively. By aligning themselves with "Islam," no matter how it is understood, their discourse grants them the romantic essentialist security of authority and autonomy. For the neotraditionalists, everything that could possibly be done to honor, respect, and promote women's well being already exists within the historical and intellectual development of the Islamic tradition. No external "international" document is better able to govern Muslim women or to determine the true rights of Muslim women than those founded in "Islam." Humans are not more fit to construct laws and policies than Allah, whose sovereignty is ultimate and eternal, and the Prophet Muhammad, whose *sunnah*, or normative practices, are perfect and without error. External documents, such as CEDAW, are not only deemed un-Islamic because of their Western origins but also deemed anti-Islamic because of their self-proclaimed secularist basis.

It would follow then that secularist groups are most willing to endorse CEDAW and to take the dominant Western position that the document ensures equal rights for all women. The secularist position, however, contrasts with the position that predominates among Muslims, which is most clearly articulated by the neotraditionalists: "Islam is perfect and complete." What went wrong with the Muslims was the colonialist encroachment of the West, and what is needed now is a return to the Madinan model. A tension is created among Muslims between pro-West and anti-West sentiments, which little considers the postmodernist self-critique in the West. This tension is further exploited by conservative intellectuals who equate anyone who refutes their position as pro-Western and by implication un-Islamic, even heretical. Being anti-Western has become a basis for legitimacy in "Islam."

Islam as a Process of Engaged Surrender

Despite opposition and backlash from both sides, a new and forceful perspective has developed in response to the issue of Muslim women and human rights. Those that adhere to this perspective claim that Islam is a dynamic relationship of engaged surrender between Allah and the *khalifah*, or trustee, on the earth. Allah is known by the articulations of the Qur'an, its embodiment in the *sunnah* of the Prophet, and through the hearts of those engaged in surrender. Islam can never be reduced to any mere historical development, intellectual debate, or other limitation of its adherence no matter how much authority they might wield and how much legitimacy they might claim over Muslim sentiments, resources, and institutions.

Paramount for this new perspective is the definition of Islam. Islam is not a historical phenomenon that came into being at one place and time, like Madinah, which must then be followed blindly by one who adheres to notions that one has not experienced. Rather, Islam is a dynamic process within all creation that is in accord with the cosmic order established by the Creator, articulated in the Qur'an, and embodied by the Prophet. This engaged surrender perspective is not new or unique in one sense. It has historical precedent among the sufis, or Muslim mystics. Before the current era, however, mystics chose more ascetic lives in social retirement and were mostly unconcerned with issues of social justice.

Today there are spiritual activists whose pro-Islamic perspective does not restrict the definition of Islam to only that which was practiced, popularized, and legalized by the elitism of non-esoteric thinkers, past or present. All who are engaged in surrender to the divine order would find violations of human dignity and oppression in any situations that maintain a fragmentation between that divine order and the lived experiences of the people. Situations that arbitrarily maintain male privilege and gender hegemony comprise one such oppressive violation of the divine order.

Whereas those who advocate this perspective are adamantly pro-Islam, they recognize the historical and ongoing oppression experienced by Muslim women. It is because their definition of Islam is not static that they can contend that no one class, gender, nationality, or historical association, irrespective of profession or training, can maintain a fixed definition of "Islam" to the exclusion of the dynamic experience of the people who believe. In other words, they reject the privilege heretofore held predominantly, and in many cases exclusively, by male 'ulama to define Islam and to determine legitimacy within it.

The Islamic traditional sources are useful tools that can assist the inward experience of Islam. First among such sources is the Qur'an, which is considered the articulation of the divine will. What proceeds from the text, however, in the name of *tafsir*, is not one and the same as the divine will. *Tafsir* is (hu)man-made and, therefore, subject to human nuances, peculiarities, and limitations. This natural limitation is unlike the divine will, which cannot be contained, explained, or even maintained by any one such limited being or community, even though that is the aspiration. Because the divine will is always in the process of becoming, humankind can only hope to gain direction toward that will by likewise being in process, never complete.

This notion of Islam as a dynamic process of engaged surrender is essential to the perspective taken in this chapter. It understands that the Qur'an must be continually interpreted because dynamic manifestation of Qur'anic guidance is not only a form of interpretation but also the only way to actually attain the lived state of Islam. Although previous interpretive efforts offer many insights into that guidance, when they become the exclusive means of understanding the divine will, they also reflect certain blind spots. One significant blind spot was the complete voicelessness of women in the historical legacy of *tafsir.*

The Qur'an and Its *Tafsir*

The historical movement of Islam began with *iqra'* (recite), the first word revealed to the Prophet Muhammad. The revelatory process continued for twenty-two years after that, until his death. What the Prophet bequeathed to his community of every generation was a substantial text: the Qur'an. The text itself was the force that ignited the revolutionary (historical, political, and intellectual) development of the community, which led to all the definitions of Islam mentioned above.

The Qur'an has been the most important impetus behind the historical and intellectual development of Islam for more than fourteen hundred years. At one level it retains the same centrality in Islamic intellectual thought as it did in the formative period of Islam. In the formative period, however, there was a proliferation of interpretive efforts and methods to help with the consideration of textual meaning and significance. The impact of the revelation on the development and principles of Islamic *fiqh,* or jurisprudence, was undeniably profound. Although now both Muslim scholars and laity profess that the Qur'an is central to Islam, today's claim lacks substance and reflects a loss of dynamism. It lingers in the background instead, as a romantic notion, referred to haphazardly in the debates over Islamic legitimacy and identity.

Such a nonsubstantive notion of the Qur'an, the major source of Islam, is perhaps linked psychologically with the illusion that a perfect *ummah,* or living community, was founded in Madinah and that actions performed at that time and in that place should become the eternal basis for the Islamic process. Thus *doing* has taken the place of *being,* as signified by the intense development of Islamic law. Islam cannot be conclusively legislated at any one time since it is a dynamic process. In addition, it could be argued that the genuine Madinan model with regard to the Qur'an and the development of an Islamic ethos consisted of a complex, holistic, and multivalent relationship with the revelation. Not only did the companions of the Prophet memorize the text verbatim, they strove to comprehend the nuances of its implications. Most significantly, they strove individually and collectively to attain a living embodiment of the Qur'anic worldview as epitomized at that time by the character and *sunnah* of the Prophet Muhammad himself.

It would seem obvious that this process was equally significant to believing women as it was to believing men during this formative period. Because, however, there is such a great disparity in the Muslim intellectual legacy with regard to the record of women's and men's experiences of, responses to, and ideas about the text, it may appear otherwise. The legacy is extraordinarily silent about the female voice and this central Islamic source. This silence has left a tremendous gap in the intellectual legacy and has come to be equated with silence of the text itself on the necessary correlation and complementarity of both male and female experiences to Qur'anic holism.

For example, one feature of the postcolonialist Islamic resurgent movements and quest for identity is the reexamination of the basic Islamic paradigms in light of postmodern discourse. When Muslims grapple with notions of equality for women here, the historical silencing of the female voice creates a gap. Understanding both the effects of this gap and the nature of the missing female voice are useful to any consideration of how to correct the gender imbalance in Muslim practices.

Furthermore, the gap that results from the voicelessness of women in *tafsir,* a major Islamic intellectual discipline, cannot be closed with the mere rhetoric of equality in Islam. Closing this gap will be a major contribution to the current debates over the status of women in Islam. A vision of authentic Islamic development is predicated upon the historical struggles of Muslims who participated fully in that development. The absence of the female voice with regard to the Qur'an has severely affected the very notions many Muslims hold of the Creator and, consequently, of the notion they have about the purpose and role of humankind in creation.

This particular gender concern with regard to the Qur'an is part of my overall consideration that for Islam to remain vital and dynamic, the Qur'an must be continually interpreted and reinterpreted (Wadud 1999, 5–6). If the tradition of Islam has been generated primarily by male *'ulama* of the past, then "Islam" is mutable and subject to change. If Islam is what Allah intends, then Muslims can only attain Islam through the relative means of being human. Limitations of humankind bounded by time are a consequence of being human and of being subject to continually changing circumstances. Although any particular experience of Islam is limited, when Islam is viewed as a dynamic process of being human, engaged in surrender, each community of believers comes forth with change and adaptation. Consequently, change itself becomes an inevitable feature of Islam. Even when "Islam" is viewed as the culmination of traditions predicated upon the text (predominantly generated by male thinkers of the past), it is still mutable and subject to change.

Although many Muslim males may not perceive their privileged status as a disadvantage, those Muslims most comfortable with previous interpretive methods and conclusions are adversely affected by the gender disparity that was the consequence of the exclusive participation of men in *tafsir.* For all are constrained from experiencing a fuller breadth of the Islamic potentiality as a result of this absence of the important dimension of the female voice. Continual interpretation of the Qur'an and continual critical examination facilitates both the comprehension and actualization of Islam in a plethora of new contexts. It would also expand the perception of the role of women, which could lead to the implementation of a social system with genuine justice and equity between the women and men.

The closest word for religion in Arabic is the word *din.* It is a way of life or living tradition. The sources of Islamic orthodoxy have an impact on Islamic praxis. Right actions, in Islam, must be genuine reflections of Islamic primary sources. If justice and equity are clear principles of the Qur'an, then justice and equity must also be manifest in any real social system that would be considered truly Islamic. What needs more dynamic and critical consideration today is the historical application or restriction of justice and equity when applied to the social contexts of women in Islam.

Justice and the Qur'an

General discussions of social justice in Islam need to be clearly linked with specific discourses over the rights and well being of women. An interesting historical precedent was set between Islam, the Qur'an, and global notions of justice with the case of slavery. In the late nineteenth century, the global communities were engaged in a discourse over the injustice of slavery. This discussion included the Muslim world as well. There is, how-

ever, no textual prohibition of slavery. Although the Qur'an does not advocate slavery, all of its discussions about it take the institutions for granted
and focus on fair and just treatment of slaves. The text also includes incen-
tives for free men and women to grant freedom to slaves as part of the
duty and spirit of Islam or for the expiation of certain religious infractions.

Although Muslims entered into these global discussions, no claim was
made that a Qur'anic precedent existed for the rights of all human beings
to live free from slavery. Neither did Muslims resist this global trend toward recognizing freedom as an aspect of human dignity by maintaining
that the absence of a Qur'anic statement meant the institution should not
be abolished. When slavery became virtually obsolete, globally, it did so
with no particular assistance or resistance from Muslims. This is a strange
paradox. Despite the absence of any Qur'anic argument in favor of abol-
ishing slavery, the Muslim world responded positively to its abolition and
recognized it as a significant movement toward human dignity.

Meanwhile, Muslims remain paralyzed against the grossly inferior status experienced by women in the context of many Muslim nation-states
despite extensive textual precedent for establishing the full human dignity
of women. Consequently, the strongest arguments given for establishing
unconditional human dignity for Muslim women have come from outside
the primary sources. Although I do not consider the arguments at length
here, I include CEDAW as one such extra-Islamic method. The stress of
this chapter, however, is on the significance of continual Qur'anic interpretation as a strategy to assist in the fulfillment of women's human rights
and dignity.

The aim of the Qur'an is to lead humankind to establish and sustain a
just and moral social order. "Second only to the existence of the One God,
no other religious or moral principles are more emphasized in the Qur'an
and Tradition than the principles of uprightness, equity and temperance;
partly because of their intrinsic value but mainly because of the reaction
against the pre-Islamic social order which paid little or no attention to
justice" (Khadduri 1984, 10). Despite the consensus among Muslim scholars
and laity over the significance of justice to Islam as emphasized in the
Qur'an, there are not "specific measures to indicate what are the constituent elements of justice or how justice can be realized on Earth" (10–11).
This task was taken up by Muslim thinkers who drew from the text
and commentary to identify standards of justice. Certain constraints on

the breadth of such standards were imposed by the social-cultural circumstances of these thinkers and by the "public pressure . . . to renounce doctrines seemingly inconsistent with the literal meaning" of the Qur'an (11).

One major constraint was the near total absence of female articulations as a necessary aspect in the foundational discourse that established the paradigmatic basis and methodological consideration of Islamic thought. Consequently, much of what the Islamic intellectual legacy has left for understanding social justice in Islam comes from an androcentric perspective and does not adequately reflect female experiences and perspectives.

Two questions beg to be asked. What difference does it make? and Can we correct this error at the present time? One can never sufficiently recreate the historical female voice with regard to women's experiences of the Qur'an; the record is simply too sparse. The text still exists in its original form, however, and critical thinking still manages to be a component of human intellect. It could be possible to begin a critical consideration of the significance of the female voice in the text and the female perspective on what it means to follow the guidance of the text, that is, what it means to be Muslim. Both these important tasks—considering the female voice within the Qur'an and female responses to the text—are in their initial stages.[6]

The Qur'an has the overwhelming consensus of the historical and current Muslim *ummah* as *the* primary source of all that might be considered Islamic. No other development in Islamic thought can claim equal significance. For although the *ahadith*, or sayings, of the Prophet are considered second only to the revealed word of Allah, they have never had the same level of consensus among Muslims as the Qur'an has (al-Na'im 1990, 22–23). Meanwhile, *fiqh*, or the historical development of Islamic jurisprudence, and the *shari'ah* resulted from the application of these two sources through a process of human analysis and reasoning. As such, historical *shari'ah* itself could only be viewed as a third and certainly more fallible source.

The significance of Muslim consensus over the authority of the Qur'an is that it may lead them to reconsider the conclusions and perspectives they have drawn heretofore if sound textual arguments can be pro-

6. See Wadud-Muhsin 1992, 23.

posed. Part of the definition of *guidance* in the text would be to use it as a vehicle for ideological, spiritual, and intellectual growth. When Muslims perceive that the goal of the Qur'an is to establish human dignity and apply that perception equally toward women and men, they could facilitate the actual experience of that dignity whereever it is amiss.

Perhaps Muslims have not fully understood the principles of human dignity established in the Qur'an because they are finite beings attempting to embrace ultimate meaning. In turn, they have constrained the progress of human civilization by continuing to build upon certain convenient familial constructs and hegemonies that seem inflexible to change. To challenge such convenience is not only uncomfortable it is potentially disruptive in society until equity is fully obtained. There are some who would blatantly resist equity in the first place. Yet the precedent for such a challenge is the historical record of the psychospiritual developments of individuals and collective communities on the basis of their struggle to internalize the Qur'anic worldview. Not only does the Qur'an act as a transformative but also the effort to live in accordance to the revelation was a key feature of the companions of the Prophet in Madinah.

A Question of Perspectives

The perspective of an individual with regard to a particular circumstance is affected by his or her relationship to that circumstance as in the familiar analogy of four blind persons feeling different parts of an elephant and coming to different conclusions about the nature of the animal. Still, the whole of the animal is more than its constituent parts. Adding all four perceptions together still leaves a blind spot because the animal's totality is greater when integrated with the elephant's animate and dynamic nature. A similar metaphysical component is essential to the Muslim ethos. The Qur'an states, "Perhaps you hate a thing in which Allah has placed much good" (2:216). This implies that one's personal perspectives on an issue should not be the sole means for evaluating its worth. Yet, one's perceptions are powerful enough that one sometimes elevates them to objects of worship: "Have you not seen those who take their desires as gods (objects of worship)?" (Qur'an 25:43). Although strongly influenced by their perceptions, humans must temper those perceptions with the wisdom of guidance and the discipline of physical and metaphysical experience.

Like all inconstant things in creation, perceptions are mutable. The hearts and minds of humanity were meant to evolve as they were propelled along the path of guidance. When the Qur'an states that "Allah does not change a condition of a people until they first change what is within their own souls" (13:11), it indicates the human potential for higher and more dynamic levels of perception and consciousness. In turn, these changes must lead to and be led by social, cultural, and moral developments. Growth and development in technology demonstrates that human awareness has been transformed into new vistas, so likewise human systems of social justice must be transformed.

Just as women and men are equal in Islam, so are they considered distinct from one another. Not only is the female experience considered unique from the male experience but for all the centuries of Islamic history it has been considered both sacred and temptational, requiring close guardianship (Sabbah 1984, 25–97; Malti-Douglas 1991, 54–66). Despite this distinction, the overwhelming tendency in the Islamic historical legacy has been for men to tell women how to be women! Men have evaluated what it means to be Muslim not only for the Muslim male but also for the Muslim female. The standards of evaluation used, however, were based on male experiences and perceptions. This is an evident flaw. How can the male be given such precedent over the female to establish what is just for all without being supplied with direct and explicit personal information with regard to her being and perception? On the contrary, even women's voices have been branded *awrah* and hence prohibited from public discourse (the discourse arena predominated by men). The confusion and mistreatment of women that proceed from this flaw are not surprising.

Current Islamic Resurgent Movements

One major component of current Islamic resurgent movements is the quest for Islamic identity and for an authentic voice: a paradigmatic basis that stems from the center of the tradition and not just from the historical, intellectual, and ideological legacy that proceeded from that tradition in previous generations. This is a rather urgent quest, necessary to counter the effects of the hegemony of Eurocentric paradigms that continue to dominate well after physical colonialism.

In this context a self-generated notion of identity becomes indispensable. Despite the unofficial consensus over this important goal, Muslims have been unsure how to achieve it. Cultural, local, and regional variants have been haphazardly linked to "Islam," further complicating the matter. Nothing that actually counters the Qur'anic worldview would or should ever be considered "Islam." Yet a clear and precise articulation of how to conceptualize that worldview with its own mutable quality is still missing, leaving educated lay Muslims unsatisfied about the notions formed by leading 'ulama. How do Muslims form an adequate notion that takes into consideration the realities of time and place? As general levels of education increase in the Muslim populations, including among women, those who participate in this identity development will also increase.

As women grapple with the historical silences regarding their concerns and experiences, it is becoming more evident that an ideological link must be made to a spiritual and theological basis that can articulate female experiences and offer ideas unattainable by other means. Those who propose that *all* that can be said about Islam, about the Qur'an, or even in shari'ah has been said already intentionally or unintentionally support this historical absence of women's articulations, rendering women as objects of men's fancy and utility. Yet, nowhere in any text of the Qur'an or in *ahadith* is such a demeaning notion portrayed above the obligation for women to fulfill their *khilafah,* or trusteeship, on the earth for the sake of Allah.[7]

A blatant violation of this trusteeship has resulted from the silencing and prohibition of the female voice, the only legitimate articulation of female experiences. This violation undermines a holistic understanding of what it means to be Muslim by leaving the intellectual legacy with only the male voice to determine legitimacy. To increase the legitimacy of female-centered perceptions would create additional formulas in the generally accepted patterns of Islamic thought and fill certain gaps in the standards of Muslim perspective on gender equity and women's equal human rights. As general levels of education increase and women join the ranks of those involved in determining what is an authentic Muslim identity, there is no option more readily in need of articulation than the one that reexamines the primary and ultimate text of Islam to unravel the mysteries that have resulted from the silencing of the female voice.

7. When the Qur'an discusses the origins of humankind, it states that Allah's intended to create a *khalifah,* or vicegerent or trustee on the earth (2:30).

Intentional inclusion of female experiences and perspectives into the formation of basic Islamic paradigms would, therefore, facilitate efforts to eradicate all forms of discrimination against women in the context of Muslim societies. The center of this eradication effort, however, does not lie within nor necessarily contradict the efforts of international bodies such as the United Nations forming CEDAW. The center lies within the sacred text, the Qur'an, and the movement that grows out of that center consolidates the notions of fundamental human dignity.

Continual reinterpretation of the Qur'an sustains the integrity of the Islamic worldview but challenges any and all intellectual developments of the past and present that have violated any aspects of women's honor and dignity as human beings. That these violations have become encoded through jurisprudence, with the resulting laws being taken as complete and true reflections of Islam, indicates the limitations of the new jurisprudential methods if the *ijtihad* does not reexamine the ethical basis of the Qur'an in its totality and its potential implications. One of the alternative strategies for Muslim women's authentic Islamic identity development and quest for human rights is the new *ijtihad* approach. I agree with Abdullahi Ahmed an-Na'im's thesis (1990, 1–68) that much of what is considered *shari'ah* and held as divine and immutable was itself the results of an intellectual process historically. Hence, alternative *ijtihad* is a tenable strategy only if it includes the radical and continual rethinking of the Qur'an and *sunnah* proposed here.

The attempts to address the question of Muslim women's autonomous agency and authentic Islamic identity in the context of Islam and modernity can only be successful when a complete reexamination of the primary sources of Islamic thought, praxis, and worldview is made that intentionally includes female perspectives on these sources and that validates female experiences. This rethinking must begin with the Qur'an because of the unprecedented historical significance of the text intellectually and morally. This precedent of the Qur'an is also currently felt at the level of Muslim laity although it is sometimes unsubstantiated. When it can be clearly seen that Qur'anic interpretation is a process that is never complete, then continual interpretations will become legitimate and necessary, regardless of how variant they might be from interpretations concluded in the past. More significantly, it is in the very nature of the text itself to encourage and implement greater experiences of equality and equity between women and men (Qur'an 4:32; 33:35).

The success this endeavor can achieve would best be understood in the context of current and ongoing struggles of Muslim women: the struggle to realize their greatest potential before Allah as *khalifah* unhampered by the history of inequitable consideration or by the limitations of Muslim cultural practices. All that remains is to facilitate the legitimacy of the Muslim woman's perspective on the basis of her experiences. When this dimension is added to the foundational paradigm of what the word *Islam* means and, hence, what it means to be Muslim, it provides for new and widely variant considerations of how humans live in the shadows thrown by divine light. It is an inspiration toward fulfilling the duty that the Qur'an articulates: achieving wholeness as a spiritual being through the confirmation of the inward and outward experience.[8]

The strategy I have proposed here might be called a spiritual moral existentialist perspective addressing the question of being. Because the goals of historically formed *shari'ah* sidestepped the matter of *being* as incompatible with its methods of codification that concentrated on *doing*, it was not a process-oriented method. The results of this development have not sufficiently answered the questions that now arise about authentic Islamic identity development in the context of modern complexities. One such question is the nature of full human dignity of the Muslim woman. In her "being" she was granted that dignity by Allah. What women need now are ways and means of sustaining that dignity by removing whatever impediment prevents the actualization of their primary duty: surrender to Allah as a *khalifah* on the earth. This actualization cannot occur when their experiences and perspectives are marginalized for the utility of male experiences and development. The Qur'an provides the guidance. Muslim males and females are individually and collectively held accountable for following that guidance and establishing a just and moral social order.

8. Such an approach has been taken by Sisters in Islam, a Malaysian Muslim women's organization, who in 1991 published *Are Muslim Men Allowed to Beat Their Wives?* and *Are Women and Men Equal Before Allah?* (Kuala Lumpur).

2

Muslim Women's Islamic Higher Learning as a Human Right

Theory and Practice

NIMAT HAFEZ BARAZANGI

🌱 Limited access to Islamic higher learning is argued to be the basis for the Muslim woman's inability to emancipate and to self-identify as *khalifah*, a trustee—a Qur'anic mandate (or potential) of human existence. The Muslim woman's reliance solely on others' interpretations to guide her spiritual and intellectual needs, whether those of Muslim or of non-Muslim men and women, is by itself evidence that the Muslim woman's right to understand, consciously to choose, and to act on her choice of Islam is being compromised. Full access to the *din*, the Islamic belief system, calls for the Muslim woman to participate in the interpretation of Islamic teachings of the Qur'an and the *hadith* and to maintain the pedagogical dynamics of Islam, rather than being limited to maintaining human reproduction, the Muslim family structure, or individual human rights as suggested by others.

My understanding of woman's gender justice vis-à-vis "liberation" within the Islamic worldview is based on epistemological reading (the philosophy of knowledge) of the Qur'an. The rationale behind the demand

This chapter and the research that led to its conception would not have happened without the North American Muslim women and their daughters, among them my daughter, Nobl Barazangi. Her dialogue with me and the comments of Shirley Samuels and Gisela Webb were invaluable.

for woman's access to knowledge is derived from the Islamic framework. The methodologies of the discipline of education and learning and the struggle for human dignity that define the parameters for Muslim woman's emancipation are grounded in that framework. To examine her role as a human entity in the Qur'an does not merely concern the Muslim woman's "freedom of expression"; it concerns the woman as an autonomous spiritual and intellectual human being who can effect a change in history.

The intent of this chapter and of my overall research is to contribute toward an educational and pedagogical interpretation of the Qur'an for women living in the postmodern era and thereby to produce an action plan for the Muslim woman to regain her identification with Islam. My analysis of empirical data concerning North American Muslim women's perception of Islam in a historical context serves to clarify the meaning and the implications of Islamic higher learning regardless of these women's educational levels. Preliminary observations suggest that the majority of Muslim women's movements do not aim to eliminate the tension between the two sexes by claiming sameness in the struggle for equality. Rather, their goal is *taqwa,* to balance the tension back in favor of woman, as the Qur'an intends in the first place when human beings, male and female, were entrusted with individual rights and responsibilities toward themselves, each other, and the universe. I argue that one of the basic principles of Islamic justice is gender justice. The interpretations of these "equal" rights and responsibilities, however, stem from different perspectives of Islam. Muslim women groups are scattered on a continuum from the idealized polemic Muslim to the idealized static Western perspectives. Few make an effort to exact the balance between these perspectives.

The pedagogical implications of this research lie in: (1) intervening among Muslim men by coaching them to rethink and to act within the balanced perspective of Islam and its first source, the Qur'an, away from both the many layers of Muslim *taqlid,* following precedence, and from Western interpretations of Islam, (2) facilitating for Muslim women the environment and the means to realize their identity as autonomous spiritual and intellectual beings and to realize the vastness of their task to educate themselves and others in Islam, including changing the entrenched paradigm of understanding "Islam studies" and its practice, and (3) integrating human-rights activists' concerns within the Qur'anic concerns for a just human society where justice means balance and fair play in ideals and realities among all humans.

Muhammad Arkoun (1994b, 62) asks: "How many women, either in the Third World or in Western societies have mastered the biological, anthropological, historical, and sociological genesis of the condition of women in order to lead the battle for emancipation at the appropriate levels and in the interest of promoting the human being?" Arkoun offers his ideas on the role of women in Islam as a "man who learned and retained a great deal from my illiterate mother."

As invaluable and challenging as his ideas might be, and despite his valuing of women's sacrifices of self-realization to ensure the survival of the human species, I find it difficult to accept Arkoun's rationale for why women's role under Islam has not changed. His assertion that the Qur'an "could not modify two essential aspects of entrenched and centuries-old conditions: elementary kinship structures and control of sexuality" (Arkoun, 1994b, 60) is not a satisfactory explanation. It is particularly unsatisfactory because history indicates that these two conditions were indeed changed by the Prophet Muhammad and among early Muslims. Given that the Qur'an clearly indicates such a change in women's role when it asserts that human creation comes from, or is made of a *single* soul and grants human trusteeship for all, why do Muslim societies and male intellectuals condone the social practice of those contemporary Muslim men who do not control their sexuality even as they demand such control on the part of Muslim women? Why is it that only the female is expected to sacrifice her self-realization as a person for the survival of the species when the Qur'an clearly entrusts both sexes to carry the burden of the trust (2:30) in a mutual consultation (62:38)? Finally, if women in Muslim societies are expected to sacrifice their self-realization for the good of society, why is it that deterioratation in the moral and social relations of Muslim socities coincides with males claiming guardianship responsibility over women?

On another plane, Hanna Papanek (1984) wrote on the question of "women's emancipation": "Future work on issues concerning women and development requires an internationally oriented scholarship on women that is closely tied to both research and practice. American universities have not served us well in building that scholarship—both because of failures to include international orientations and teaching and research concerning women."

Just as Arkoun's *Rethinking Islam* brings fresh air to the understanding of Islam outside the Western and the Muslim "reason," Papanek's evaluation in *Women-in-Development and Women's Studies* (1984, 5) was still largely valid in 1995, the year of the Fourth World Conference on Women. Papanek points to the lack of a link between forces to develop a "body of research on both theory and policy." Although some work has been done since the late 1980s toward this end, there is no link between the general advocacy for women's rights and a thorough investigation about how different women, individuals and groups, perceive these rights. It is not only essential for women in development to realize that "women's issues" have arisen as a result of vast changes brought about by development, as Papanek suggests, but is as necessary that women in "area studies" and women in "human rights" realize that "international women's issues" have also arisen amid the one-sided views within the academic "area studies" and within a generic human rights advocacy. Orientalism and its related missionary and colonial movements made major contributions to these one-sided views both by perceiving Islam as frozen in the thirteenth to the sixteenth centuries and by explaining the pedagogy of Islam largely with Greek philosophical tools and within the framework of Christian missionary and colonial policy. The challenge before the Muslim woman is not limited to changing policies or legal status but includes changing the entrenched paradigm of understanding Islam and its practice. Thus, the focus on policy changes, as suggested by Papanek, should be combined with a focus on "what policy?" in "whose interest?" and "with which paradigm and methodology?"

The need to develop research paradigms that make gender central to analyses of social change, one area of the common ground suggested by Papanek, implies a continuous reflective process that assesses the application of such paradigms across the international body of women. Papanek sums it up: "We cannot have it both ways: arguing for a universally applicable set of explanations for the position of women while taking universal applicability as a given and, therefore, failing to take the trouble to check ideas against empirical fact" (1984, abstract).

To this end, developing research paradigms that make the Muslim woman central to the analyses of social change within Muslims societies and Muslim minority communities calls for historical understanding of the orientalist-missionary movement in Muslim countries during colonial and postcolonial periods and their lasting effects. The goal of this historical analysis is not to be apologetic but to understand the nature and development of the idealized, frozen-in-time Islam created by this movement. Such a historical analysis and understanding will allow one to free Islam both from its static and dogmatic codified law and to reopen the dialogue within its flexible pedagogical system. Arkoun (1994a, 49) points out and laments the fact that it is in imitation of this idealizing movement that "countries like Saudi Arabia and Libya have encouraged missionary activities previously unknown to Islam." In fact, it was in imitation of European institutionalized religion and its biases toward women that predominantly Muslim male leaders were encouraged by colonialists to impose more restrictions on Muslim women, particularly concerning Islamic higher learning, restrictions that were unknown in Muslim societies until the Spanish Inquisition. This effect is evidenced in the sharp drop in the number of scholarly or influential females reported in Muslims biographies.[1]

I am not invoking here the centuries-old reciprocal exclusion and "otherness" between the three monotheistic religions, Judaism, Christianity, and Islam, nor the postcolonial dichotomy between Islam and the West. Rather, I draw the attention of the academic and "scientific" community and human rights advocates to the fact that their claim for intellectual separation of "reason" and religion, as Arkoun (1994a, 51) put it, "ceases to operate once [their Western thought] is confronted with Islam." I also draw the attention of the *imams*, or male Muslim religious leaders, and ʿ*ulama*, religious scholars, to the fact that their claim for authority on "authentic Islam" ceases to be plausible once their polemic, fixed-in-time interpretations are confronted with awareness of the Qurʾanic intention that it be open for continuous interpretation at all times and places by both sexes.

I use the above arguments and historical analysis here to address the issue of applicability of the "universal" human rights document, the United Nations Convention on the Elimination of All Forms of Discrimi-

1. For example, in Al-Zirkili (n.d.), the number of notable women reported in Islamic history dropped sharply after that era.

nation Against Women (CEDAW)[2] to Muslim women in general. I specifically address the rights to education, as charted in the document, and how CEDAW has overlooked the Muslim woman's rights to Islamic higher learning (i.e., deeper knowledge of Islamic primary sources—the Qur'an and *hadith*) as a priori for regaining her natural endowments as a human and as a Muslim. As evidence for my arguments, I use examples from the Muslim males' generated imitation of the perceived rights to education as outlined in the document "Universal Islamic Declaration of Human Rights" (UIDHR)[3] that was prepared by the Islamic Council.

Examining the role of woman as a human entity in the Qur'an does not merely concern a Muslim woman's freedom of speech and sexuality or access to balanced education; it concerns woman as an autonomous spiritual and intellectual human being who will change history. The task of my research entails more than an examination of the related parts (verses) of the Qur'anic text vis-à-vis the above two documents. My intention in analyzing empirical data concerning Muslim women's perception of Islam is to make an epistemological "reading" of the Qur'an that will be meaningful to women living in the postmodern era and that will produce an action plan for the Muslim woman to regain her identification with Islam.[4]

The North American (American and Canadian) Muslim woman is the case-in-point here. I have been specifically interested in whether these women were and are able to benefit from the North American environment to further their Islamic higher learning as defined earlier. Those who view it as ironic that a secular environment could benefit the understanding of religion and of Islam as a worldview and belief system may also see it as ironic that these Muslim women expect to contribute to their new environment and to the historical change in the reading of Islamic sources

2. The United Nations 1994.

3. The Islamic Council 1994.

4. See Nimat Hafez Barazangi 1997. This 1997 work was conceived as a sequel to the original topic of the present chapter. The topic was presented first under the title "Muslim Women's Islamic Higher Learning Is a Human Right" at the Middle East Studies Association Annual Meeting in Washington, D.C., Dec. 6–10, 1995. The subtitle of this chapter "Theory and Practice," was added when the sequel was developed. Certain concepts overlap in the two essays, no doubt.

despite the Western and Muslim male views of them as passive, dependent beings.

Given the variety of social and economic applications of the Islamic worldview, is my general theory and policy making as premature as that of the universally claimed documents? To address this concern, I first outline the metaphysical (philosophy of principles and values) and epistemological background of this study. Second, I discuss the discrepancy between the Islamic worldview, on the one hand, and the "universalist-secular-humanist" and inherited Muslim religious views of education as a human right, on the other. I specifically examine the implications of these views for gender justice as proposed in both the CEDAW and UIDHR documents. I have explored elsewhere the inconsistency between the ideals of Islam concerning education and woman and their practice in contemporary Muslim societies and communities (Barazangi forthcoming). I discuss here their implications in two cases drawn from my field work with North American Muslim women and their daughters in the historical context of the Orientalist/missionary hegemonic influence and the Muslim limiting interpretation of the "text." I conclude by elucidating the relation between Islamic "universalism" as stated in the Qur'an and plurality in application. The shortcomings of the "universal" human rights of education will be evident as I argue for Islamic higher learning as an a priori human natural endowment that needs to be objectified.

Philosophical Concepts of Education, Feminism, and Islam

It would be a mistake to analyze the Muslim woman's education in isolation from what is happening in other relevant fields of study, such as feminist studies of education and *Islamization of knowledge*,[5] or without taking into consideration the effects of economic policies of the structural Adjustment Programs (SAPs) in developing countries, and the "Religious Right" movements in many Western countries and the reassertion of conservative morality around the world. Particularly instructive is the contemporary

---

5. The term *Islamization of knowledge* was first used by Ismaʿil Raji al-Faruqi (1982) to indicate the need of Muslims to integrate contemporary knowledge within the Islamic framework. At later stages, it has taken several meanings and applications throughout the Muslim world.

Muslim emphasis on women returning to a "traditional" form of dress, regardless of whether it satisfies the Islamic dictum of a modest public appearance, and returning to the "home," irrespective of whether that home satisfies the Islamic conditions of mutual expectation and consultation.

Madeline Arnot (1993, 1) states that after "twenty years of feminist education research, policy development and innovative school practice, it seems appropriate to evaluate the impact and significance of this world-wide struggle for social justice."

Similarly, after two hundred years of missionary education and more than fifty years of "universal" compulsory schooling in the Muslim world, it seems timely to evaluate the results of these systems of education and their actual impact on the Muslim woman. At the same time, the recent global economic restructuring policies and the consequent political unrest and educational reforms also require a considered response from those committed to promoting greater social equality and from those who are promoting the return to "Islamic education."

Although feminist studies of education "[have] managed to cross [their] national boundaries and [have] constructed a common agenda for the English-speaking academic world" (Arnot 1993, 1) (in, e.g., New Zealand, Australia, the United Kingdom, the United States, and Canada), few studies, to my knowledge, have constructed a common agenda for Muslim women. Even when an agenda has been proposed and/or constructed, it has been produced by Muslim males who deal with education from an idealistic, dichotomized (between religious and Western "secular") perspective, or by Westernized feminists (Muslim or non-Muslim) who operate from an "area studies" framework.

Peggy McIntosh (1994) wrote: "As a girl or woman learns to read, she learns to imagine alternatives to her situation. But if what she reads leaves her out, she may see these alternatives as unreal—making her more, not less, disempowered, the more she learns.'" The dichotomy between the ideals and practice in Muslim female education persists even in the most recent agenda developed by organizations in the East and the West, Muslims and non-Muslims (Barazangi forthcoming). This dichotomy and the agenda are explained, respectively, by my definitions of Islam, education, and Islamic education and by relating them to feminist studies and feminist views of education.

Islam and Education

Islam and education are linked in a shared process because, on the one hand, Islam as a worldview may not be realized without its pedagogy (the arts of teaching and learning) and, on the other hand, education has no meaning if it does not penetrate the individual's worldview and invoke change in perception of human relations. Through this change in perception education is expected to bring equality among humans, particularly between the sexes. I believe that only when education succeeds in effecting social change and social justice will it actualize the reality that justice is as fundamental to the Islamic worldview as the existence of a Just Supreme Being, Allah. Such an education is what I call "Islamic education." Thus, education does not become Islamic when it is taught by Muslims nor for Muslims nor when its content is the subject of Islam as a "religion." Rather, education becomes Islamic only when it fulfills the premise of producing an autonomous individual who intellectually and spiritually makes the choice to be *khalifah* (trustee, vicegerent) and to follow the course of action toward achieving social justice described in the Qur'an and objectified by the Prophet Muhammad.

Feminist Studies and Islam

Feminist studies and Islam struggle with and against each other in that both are oriented toward a better future for the female by rejecting human hierarchy. From the normative Islamic perspective human hierarchy is rejected as counter to the Qur'anic view of creation and human beings. Feminism here is used in its broadest sense as a creative theory of human relations that aims to transform social structures that do not consider the individual contribution, particularly of females. Yet because Islam and feminist studies appear to struggle against each other as a result of both the projection of Islam as a patriarchal religion and the projection of feminism as anti-Islamic in its values, one of my tasks is to show that the bases of feminist thinking are implied in the Qur'anic concept of justice as objectified by "the autonomous trustee" of the Qur'an, "Allah said to the angels: I will create a *khalifah* on earth" (2:30). My claim that the basis of feminism lies in the Qur'an is not intended to read history backward, as Arkoun (1994b, ix) describes the Muslim apologists, nor to invoke an upheaval among Muslims who do not accept the use of "feminism" to describe the Qur'an. I am merely reinterpreting what Rahman (1996:17–18) stated: The basic principle in the Qur'anic view of Islamic justice is the equality between the sexes. My frequent reference to the Qur'an instead of Islamic ideals is intended to distinguish the Qur'an and the prophetic model (documented in the authentic *hadith*) as primary sources of the ideal and practice, respectively, from their interpretations by Muslim males and Orientalists as secondary sources.

Feminism and Education

Feminism and education share one history because females are the cradle of education, and education is organically connected to feminism. Education here is defined as the process of conceptual change that transforms individuals' societies from one state of affairs into another, hence, not propagating that education is a woman's "territory," that females are only suitable for a career in education. Rather, I am emphasizing this organic connection between females' struggle to change concepts and education as a conceptual change process that enables females to realize themselves as the trustees in the Islamic educational process.

I argue here that the tension between Orientalist and contemporary Western ideals of Muslim societies and the ability of Muslim societies to build stable social organizations is a by-product of Westerners' and Westernized Muslims' insistence on "liberating" Muslim women from their Islamic culture instead of helping them emancipate from within their own worldview of Islam and the West.

The compounded effect of the historical deterioration of Muslim women's education in general, and Islamic education in particular,[6] seems to result also in another tension, namely, the contemporary tension between Muslim ideals and their practice, such as the contemporary claims of "Islamization," on the one hand, and between the West's ideals for itself and its ideals for others, on the other. This tension has resulted in dismissing the Islamic perspective of religion and its meaning of social construction in the understanding of the Muslim woman's role and the meaning of

---

6. Nimat Hafez Barazangi (1995a:420–25) argues that missionary and colonial education contributed to the dichotomy in women's education.

her Islamic higher learning. Achieving Islamic education and gender equality in Islamic higher learning becomes a priority because otherwise, the balance between individuals remains threatened by the non-Islamic attitude of superiority of one human being over another and by the one-sided (male) interpretation of the text and the word of the Qur'an and the *hadith*.

Islamic View of an Autonomous Individual

My reading of the Qur'an and the *hadith* indicates five basic principles—outlined in the Qur'an and extrapolated in the *hadith*—that were to permeate the life and thought of the autonomous individual who could make moral and intellectual choices in a just society:

1. The creation of male and female of a single soul (*Al-Nisa'* 'women' 4:1).[7]

2. The individual right and obligation to learn and be educated in the teaching/legislation (*Al-Alaq/Iqra'* the 'clot/read' 96:1–4). 'A'isha, the Prophet's wife and major transmitter of early Islamic history and values said: "Modesty did not prevent the women of Ansar [the people who supported the prophet's message] from learning").

3. The individual right and responsibility to take the oath of accepting or rejecting Islam, voting (*Al-Mumtahana* 'the woman to be examined' 60:12). The Prophet Muhammad dedicated a special day for women to discuss with him and to vote on his message and accept him as a Muslim community leader. He did this to establish women's freedom of choice.

4. The individual's ability to receive and dispense of inheritance (*Al-Nisa'*, 4:7).

5. The individual's membership in the Islamic sisterhood and brotherhood with no distinction of gender, race, class, or color (*Al-Hujurat* 'inner apartments' 49:10).

These principles explain not only the need and priority for Islamic higher learning but the unity of the Islamic philosophy, despite its theological and historical diversity, as explained by Renard (1994, 32). Within the above perspective of social organization and of education as a means

7. By citing the names of the Qur'anic *surahs*, (chapters), in addition to their numbers—the customary practice in quoting from the Qur'an, wherein the first number refers to the chapter and the second refers to the *'ayah*, verse—I am emphasizing the relevance of the name of the chapter to the content in addressing gender issues and its importance in the Qur'an.

to approximate the ideals of a just society, one can specifically affirm the role of woman and woman's education for gender justice in a Muslim society or, for that matter, in a Muslim community within a pluralistic society such as the United States and Canada.

The universal woman may also benefit if she chooses to realize that the realities of Muslim women's lives do not always represent these principles and that these principles are not limited to faithful Muslims nor any ethnic/national group because God is beyond particular faith and ethnic association and beyond gender. Allah is called "He" because of the nature of the Arabic language, which assigns male or female to all nouns and pronouns (Cornell 1994:63). The concept of absolute transcendence has profound implications for one's understanding of both divinity and human dignity.

This awareness of the unitary truth of God was deemed by early Muslims so important that it constituted the essence of knowledge itself (Cornell 1994, 64). Such a realization makes Islamic higher learning not only essential for but preliminary to human understanding of one's own nature and reality in relation to the universe. Islam's strongest argument in favor of *tawhid*, the theological claim of the Oneness of God, is that the believer does not have to resort to the abandonment of logic in order to maintain his [her] faith." Furthermore, if Allah created the world in order to be known, as Islamic teachings assert, then "it is necessary that human beings be given the capacity to recognize and understand the Truth that brought about their existence" (Cornell 1994, 66). The Qur'an—"the reading" that never ceases—came down from Allah as a mercy for humankind and continually informs the human being so that she can better serve her role as a changer of history as she realizes her identity as a person who consciously chooses to be a Muslim and creatively acts on this choice.

CEDAW, UIDHR, and Gender Justice

The title and the intent of the CEDAW document, "The Convention on the Elimination of All Forms of Discrimination Against Women," is not in tune with the Islamic worldview of gender justice that calls for universal social, economic, and political justice on two grounds. First, the "elimination of discrimination" does not necessary result in gender justice because it only constrains certain practices by legal acts. Second, the document emphasizes the role of the state in the implementation process. To assign the state as the guardian of such elimination of discrimination is problematic, given that the present Muslim states do not govern according to Islam yet act as authorities protected by "Islamic law."

Gender justice in the Islamic view means the regaining of equality between the sexes beginning with birth (Qur'an 4:1) and ending with membership in the Islamic sisterhood and brotherhood where there is no distinction by sex, class, race, and color within any form of social organization (Qur'an 49:10). CEDAW provides practical steps, spelling out in ARTICLE 10 the specifics of how discrimination might be eliminated in the field of education. I am, however, concerned with the ambiguity of legal changes when "Islamic law" is addressed. As long as Islamic law (*shari'ah*) is defined as the "totality of ordinances derived from the Qur'an and *Sunnah,* Prophetic tradition" (Islamic Council 1994, 149), the Muslim woman has no hope of becoming part of this process of legal change. There are two reasons: first, women are considered by many of these ordinances as dependents rather than as partners in the interpretation process. Second, even though "Islam" and "Islamic" indicate the worldview of one of the world's largest populations, which encompasses a unity of principles and plurality of practice without excluding membership of those whose faith is not Islam or those who are not males, the general practice in Muslim societies, especially in the last fifty years, is that more and more groups, especially women, are being excluded from this process by the *muqallidun,* followers of precedence, who use the *shari'ah* as an excuse (Barazangi 1996). The real issue then, is how do we expect male legislators to enact items a–h in ARTICLE 10 of the CEDAW document (e.g., [a] the same conditions for career) when the whole idea of a career for Muslim women is dismissed under the disguise of *shari'ah.*

The Islamic concept of "gender justice" as outlined above is not discussed in the CEDAW document or in any previous U.N. or "human rights" documents; the development of those documents apparently did not and does not consider the Islamic concept of human existence, purpose, and rights and responsibilities. The prevalent philosophy guiding the whole concept of a universal organization (the "United Nations") is by itself an indication that human beings and human relations are viewed within the philosophy of the secular "nation-state" concept (Sonn 1996, 69). Although by "secular," the ecumenical philosophy is assumed to be separate from the mundane human functions and the political governing, as Sonn argues, the underlying Judeo-Christian philosophy that accepts and postulates the separation of church and state is part of the guiding principles of the U.N. document. This claimed separation in the Western view is central to the problem at hand. As Arkoun (1994a, 51) observes, this separation of the "intellectual and psychological within Western thought ceases to operate once the West' is confronted with Islam—then people slip into a consensus which on the one hand presupposes all the values [of democracy, liberalism, etc.] as achievements and on the other sees them rejected and menaced by fundamentalist barbarism."

Understanding Islamic gender justice from this "supreme Western thought" point of view is not only problematic for the Muslim woman—as she finds herself at the crossroad between Muslim and Western "reason"—but, more importantly, it offers neither religious nor secular mental instruments of emancipation, as Arkoun (1994a, 53) asserts. I am not implying here an intrinsic gender injustice in both Christianity and Judaism. Rather, I am pointing to both the theological foundational assumptions as discussed, for example, by Hassan (1994, 19) and the influence of Judeo-Christian traditional practices on Muslim practices as apparent in some Muslim writings—following Christian separation of the science of theology and the practice of ethics—wherein "Islamic ethics has generally been ensconced in Islamic law rather than ethical discourse" (Sonn 1996, 65).

The example of ordinary Muslims repeating the ordinary Christian belief that Adam was God's primary creation and that Eve was created from Adam's rib (Hassan 1994:20) indicates the central problem here when attempts are made to understand Islamic views on gender from outside the Islamic framework (the story does not exist in the Qur'an). Compounded with this is the fact that many scholars, Muslims and non-Muslims (e.g., Smith and Haddad 1982), use the concept of Eve (Hawwa', the Hebrew/Arabic counterpart) when discussing women in Islam despite the nonexistence of this concept in the Qur'an, thus preventing an understanding of the Islamic view on gender. Ironically, other scholars who claim to interpret the Qur'an as a primary source use these secondary sources as the basis for their interpretations. Barbara Freyer Stowasser (1994), for example, bases the views of Eve in her *Women in the Qur'an* on Smith and Haddad's discussion of Eve. She further relies on their concept of Eve to understand gender justice in Islam.

The educational implications of such foundational misunderstandings become more dangerous when Muslim women on both ends of the continuum, between rejecting and defending Islam, believe and reiterate these concepts as "Islamic." This is why Islamic higher learning is needed to bring out evidence against these myths about women's creation. It would enable Muslim and non-Muslim women to change attitudes about women and gender relations and, as Arkoun (1994b, 53) suggests, to by-pass the arguments and divisions maintained in Western Christian contexts.

Because Islam, in the words of Fazlur Rahman (1996, 11−12), intended first and foremost to establish justice in the social order among all humans (realities) that would approximate the natural (intrinsic, ideal) justice of the creation, the first priority of a universal document is to address "gender justice" instead of "human rights." In Islam, the right to choose the Islamic worldview is an individual responsibility that is objectified only by a conceptual and attitudinal change of human relations on the part of the individual. The universalists' human rights philosophy may never approximate natural justice because human biases contained in national, socioeconomic (development), race, faith, and most of all gender identities have not actually changed the individual attitude and concept of gender.

Furthermore, the idea of gender justice is not limited to Muslim women nor to women as a subgroup of humanity but is intended for all humans. That is, only when human society changes its concept of male-female relations will it become closer to being in tune with its propagation of democratic, egalitarian principles and human rights for all. That is, unless the present attitudes about male-female relations are changed, any democratic system or process will fall short of addressing gender justice. The Qur'an, in a way, is a primary source to feminism in changing the concept of male-female relations from what was practiced before the inception of Islam (beginning with the rights to vote, the rights of inheritance, the protection against being the victim of infanticide, etc.). Yet to claim that the type of Islam taught in establishments controlled by male religious authorities and studied in the departments of Oriental and Near Eastern studies is the liberator of human dignity and the restorer of gender justice is a grave mistake. A critical examination of the discrepancy between these types of "Islam" brings one back to the reasons behind the opposition between the Enlightenment "reason" and religious "reason" that, in Arkoun's (1994a, 55) words, has spilled over into the twentieth-century Muslim world. During the seventeenth to the nineteenth centuries, that opposition was projected in the form of opposition between Islam and modernism, and in the twentieth century it is projected in the form of confrontation between Islam and the West. This opposition is at the heart of the "Muslim woman question."

The second shortcoming in the CEDAW document lies in the emphasis on the role of the state in implementing the articles of the document. That is, to assign to the state the role of the guardian in eliminating discrimination is problematic, given that the present Muslim states do not govern according to Islam yet act as authorities protected by "Islamic law." Without standards that are outside the human domain to reinforce the appropriate measures proposed to eliminate each form of discrimination (e.g., item [c.] "elimination of any stereotypic concepts of the roles of men and women"), how can one guarantee the elimination of these acts? One does not have a means to examine the change in actual policies and attitudes, nor can one bring balance back into the social order, as intended in the Qur'anic concept of Islamic social justice, because the standards of the United Nations do not consider the Islamic concept of justice. In other words, one may be able to resolve the tension between the sexes or between nations on one level but often may end up offsetting the balance on another level.

For example, the humanist and feminist perspectives that see the goal as empowerment might succeed in taking away the authority from male patriarchs and giving it to females, but females might act in the same authoritarian way once they become "empowered" because—in the case of Muslim women—they were not trained in the Islamic higher knowledge that would enable them to counter accusations of blasphemy or preaching of the *shari'ah*. Nor would these women be able to govern without the political backing of a military regime or a Western government. Using the concept of empowerment could be misleading if it is not joined by the questions of who is being empowered, in whose interest, and with what. Empowerment, excluding the power of persuasion (Papanek 1984, 8), will not be different from the quest for eliminating independent personalities, a goal pursued both by the church since 1960 and among democratic states, but with negative and sometimes scandalous results (Arkoun 1994a, 55).

Similarly, as long as those who wrote the UIDHR use the rhetoric that

God is the legislator while they accept human interpretation of God's legislation as part of the sacred law, the *shariʿah*, there is no hope for gender justice even if these leaders execute all the items under ARTICLE 10 of the CEDAW and under ARTICLE 21, "Right to Education," of the UIDHR (Islamic Council 1994, 149).

As long as the attitude of human superiority over another human is not changed, it will be almost impossible to achieve gender justice. Gender justice becomes a prerequisite to achieving such a change in attitude because the purpose of human existence, according to Islam, is to be the trustees for approximating natural, intrinsic justice on earth.[8]

In accordance with this perspective of gender justice, the above five Islamic principles could serve as a basis for a theory to support Muslim women's education (secular and religious) and for Islamic higher learning. These principles, although established by the Qur'an, are intended to develop an autonomous individual human being who can fulfill the trust only by choice. Sophistication of the human ability to recognize her autonomous intellect and her moral obligation to choose a choice of a course of action is the only means by which education can result in social change and social justice. Through this course of action, one can expect or, at least, hope that education will bring equality among humans, particularly between the sexes, because without education individual human potential cannot be realized. An essential part of this education is to understand and deploy the Islamic principles of human dignity that cannot be attained without Islamic higher learning.

The Case in Point in Historical Analysis

The romantic views of popular culture and literature in America and the West in general are not the only sources that portray women in Islam as "dependent, ignorant." Rana Kabbani states that the "Victorian imagination [of Orientalists] could not conceive of female eroticism divorced from female servitude and dependency" (1986:80–81). With all the conflicts between the power of the colonial and the powerlessness of the colo-

---

8. In the Islamic worldview natural, intrinsic justice includes animals and other beings as part of the balance of things, of naturally surrendering to the Divine Will. But the human being (Ibn Adam) is distinguished from the animal (*haywan*) by virtue of reason and consciousness, a prerequisite for justice.

nized, Muslim women's emancipation was conditioned by their liberation from their culture.[9]

My research on Muslim women's education indicates that globally the concerns for Muslim women's Islamic education and Islamic higher learning are particularly lost between the contemporary polarized Western negative image of a practicing Muslim woman and the Muslim propagation of differentiated function that calls for limited "religious" education.[10] None of the Western scholarly and activist groups raise the issue of Muslim women's inclusion in the religious, juristic, and scholarly ranks of Muslim communities.[11]

Meanwhile, Muslim women in the United States and Canada, as generally is the case in other Western societies, are not as free to practice certain aspects of their religion as are women of other religious groups such as conservative Jews, Mennonites, Mormons, and so on. The often-cited rationales are either that Muslim women are being oppressed by Islam and are coerced by their male guardians or that there is no place in secular societies for asserting the religious identity and symbolism of Muslim woman's modesty.[12]

While Muslim women are trying to build their own agenda for emancipation, they are being torn between "secular humanists" who discourage them from the development of their own reading of Islam and the Muslim males and some females who think that a woman's Islamicity is expressed by wearing a headdress and seclusion and that her Islamic education should be in an all-female school and university and should focus on domestic subjects such as home economics.[13] Ruth Roded rightly questions "the extent to which alleged seclusion of women actually prevented them

9. See "Bengali Women" 1995, 48.

10. For further distinction between "Islamic" and "religious" education, see Nimat Hafez Barazangi 1995b.

11. See, for example, papers presented at the Sisterhood Is Global Institute's conference, "Religion, Culture, and Women's Human Rights" (Washington, D.C., Sept. 1994). Some of this work is published in Afkhami 1995.

12. See, for example, Johnson 1989; and "Behind the Yashmak" 1989. See also papers presented at the Sisterhood Is Global Institute's conference "Religion, Culture, and Women's Human Rights" (Washington, D.C.; September 1994), some of which are published in Afkhami 1995.

13. See Lucy Carroll's (1982, 74–76) discussion of education.

from engaging in a variety of endeavors that were important by Islamic and external standards" (Roded 1994, 12). What is being discussed here, however, is the contemporary Muslim trend of measuring the Islamicity of a woman by her practice of wearing the conservative form of dress, the jilbab, mistakenly called the *hijab*,[14] and by her returning to her home and assuming only domestic chores.

Knowledge, particularly religious knowledge, means authority, and religious authority is power. Yet, this power may not be meaningful for the Muslim woman unless she is knowledgeable about the basic principles of Islam—other than what is generally taught as the belief in God, the Prophets, the angels, the Scriptures, and the hereafter—in order to realize her self-identification as a trustee (*khalifah*) within Islam.

I undertook my analysis of the polarized position of Muslim women in the context of the educational history of Muslim women, beginning with the intensified interaction between Western and Muslim societies, for the following reasons. First, Ruth Roded's work (1994, 11) presented the impact of Western culture/colonialism in actually reducing the number of women included in biographical collections in Islamic history. I view this phenomenon as a contributing factor to the dichotomous views on Muslim women's education and emancipation. Second, because the concept of education in Islamic societies does not seem to fit utilitarian Western theories of education (Barazangi 1995b), Muslim contributions to religious scholarship are considered marginal by Western educators. In addition, Western societies, still largely influenced by the concept of limiting religious leadership to male clergy, have minimized the importance of Muslim female religious scholarship. Third, the separation of "religious" and "secular" education among North American Muslim women, and among Muslims in general, seems to result from the dichotomy between the Western and Islamic worldviews on education, on Islamic education, and on women's role.

This dichotomy resulted, and results, in a tension between Muslims and Westerners in which Muslim women's education suffered and continues to suffer the brunt. Combining this dichotomy and the resulting historical and contemporary discrepant practices suggests not only that there was, and there is, "a constant tension in Islamic society between an

14. See Barazangi 1989 for explanation of the difference between *hijab* and *jilbab*.

egalitarian ideal and the realities of social, political, and economic inequal-ities," as Roded (1994, 8) suggests but that a discrepancy also exists within Western ideals for the self and for others.

As a case-in-point, two examples of a series of focus-group interviews are reported here from a sample of twenty-five Muslim immigrant mothers and their twenty-five youthful daughters aged fourteen to twenty-two. These women and female youths represent a subsample of a larger group of Muslims who participated in the author's study of North American Muslim adults' transmission of the Islamic belief system to their offspring.[15] The youth are first-generation children of immigrants who came to North America during the phase of immigration in the 1960s and 1970s.

The way in which mothers and daughters attempt to resolve cognitive conflicts suggests a number of related but different problems: (1) the Mus-lim mothers try to adjust an existing belief system and a particular attach-ment to the "Islamic" heritage to their living experience in the secular West; (2) the Muslim youth had to find ways to integrate the belief system (transmitted by their parents), the Islamic sentiment (enforced by the com-munities), and the "secular" system (enforced by society at large); and (3) the female Muslim youths in the West had to attempt to relate their expe-rience to the experience of their mothers in the mothers' country of origin under Western colonization and during the postcolonial upheavals in Mus-lim societies. The mothers' and the daughters' experiences seem to reflect an identity at the crossroad between the ideals and practices of the East and the West.

Case 1

A Mother's Response. I asked an active and respected leader in her com-munity whom I named "Safia" (a middle-aged mother of Indo-Pakistani origin who teaches religious education to the community children some afternoons and on the weekends) the following question: "How do you expect your children to relate between the two forms of guidance: the school's and the home's?" She responded that the three religions (Judaism,

15. See Barazangi 1988. In her dissertation Barazangi used generation as the unit of analysis. In this later analysis (forthcoming) of the same data, partially reported here, she used gender as the unit of analysis.

Christianity, and Islam) are similar and that she tells her children that Christians and Jews have changed what is in their books and put some human things in them. She added, "One time we were talking about dress and I told them [my daughters] to look at the statue of Mary. Do you ever see her without a covering on her head and body? But look at the Christians and Jews; they are changing their dress."

The use of such a parallelism between Mary's garb and a Muslim woman's modest dress might be used to bring a better understanding of common teachings among the three monotheistic religions. The response, however, clearly disregards the difference between Western and Muslim attitudes toward religious symbols. S. H. Nasr (1993, ix) asserts that the first thing a Muslim is dazzled by in the West is the dissonance, the compartmentalization between religion and everything else. I would also add that North American Muslims tend not to recognize that a similar compartmentalization is happening among them and in the Muslim world although not as explicitly expressed as in the West.

The mother's comparison is an example of how Muslim institutions can fail to integrate the two aspects of knowledge: the "religious" and the "secular." History relates the emphasis that Judeo-Christian religious institutions placed on compartmentalization and on the idealization of women in the persons of Mary or Rachel. These institutions have, at the same time, neglected to provide just solutions to the social realities of women in their societies, which eventually resulted in women's revolt against religious institutions and, often, against religion in general. Furthermore, the mother's use of the figure of Mary, with its historical association in Christianity with the idea of celibacy and ambiguous attitudes toward sexuality, transmits ideas that do not communicate and, in fact, contradict the Islamic concepts of modesty and encouraged mutual sexual satisfaction in marriage.

These parallels are, knowingly and unknowingly, frequently reiterated among Muslim parents and educators. Some sources suggest that Muslims began emphasizing female strict dress and seclusion after their contacts with the missionaries. Because I have no conclusive evidence yet, I am only drawing attention to the fact that not only the Orientalists may have shaped Islamic studies and philosophy for Muslims in the last three centuries, as Mahdi (1990, 72) suggests, but also that the missionaries and colonial forces may have shaped the pedagogy and practice of Islam as well.

The Daughter's Response. When I interviewed "Sana," the nineteen-year-older daughter of this mother, I asked, "Do you find any difference between the guidance you receive from your parents and the guidance you receive from school or non-Muslims?" She answered: "I think schools place more emphasis on your studies than they do on religious issues. Maybe they believe it is the responsibility of parents if they need to tell anything to their children—that they should be doing it and not the school." When I asked, "But how do schools expect you to relate the morals of learning other subjects and of dealing with other people in the school environment to each other if they do not teach general concepts about religious and moral matters, leaving it for the home?" Sana answered: "Well, the thing is, if they start teaching general concepts about religion, they will be teaching what they believe, and, you know, here the majority of people believe that Jesus is the son of God. We believe Jesus was a Prophet. Then there are other religions that don't believe in God. So you really can't teach general concepts of religion because there are so many different concepts of religion." When I probed further about whether there was really a basic difference between religions, Sana retracted by saying, "Not in the main religions: Jews, Christians, and Muslims. But when you go into other religions, especially the Orient, they are very different; they believe in idols. But if you set aside the belief in One God, most religions are similar because they teach you to love your neighbor and that you have a purpose in life. I guess schools can teach that, but it's very vague, and I don't know [how you would teach about a general concept of religion]." Such a response suggests that the young female was not only confusing the teaching of religion with the teaching about religion, but she was also not equipped spiritually and intellectually to relate the meaning of, and belief in, the One Supreme God to her practice of certain Islamic principles, such as understanding the purpose of life and loving one's neighbor.[16] This confusion seems to result from one of the very basic failures in Muslim religious education—that it is often mistaken for Islamic education. It is also a failure to think to teach the practice of a religion, in this case Islam, without understanding and relating the meanings of each practice to the concept of God as the source of knowledge

16. Islam and Islamic here are understood in their broadest sense as explained by Isma'il Raji al Faruqi (1986), intending the overarching peace with the concept of One God.

and value. Compounded with modern Western views of religious beliefs as superstitions and the practice of rituals as irrational and irrelevant to intellectual growth, Muslims and non-Muslims accepted the argument that religion has no place in the "objective, neutral, rational" educational process.

Discussion of Case 1. Confusion and uncertainty, it seems, often result from parents' well-intended attempts to shield the girls from the reality of their new culture instead of helping themselves and their children to understand and to practice Islam in the context of the new environment of which they are now part. These young peoples' statements about questioning and striving to know indicate a deep belief and an ability to realize that there is a difference between Islamic and non-Islamic life and education. But the ideals of parents and educators in and of themselves provide no means for these offspring to have a deeper understanding of the "why" that would enable them to negotiate their environment as autonomous individuals. Muslim parents and educators often miss the basic element of Islamic pedagogy: to prepare the next generation of women to realize themselves and to be agents of change while preserving "their" worldview, rather than simply making women instruments for transmitting certain rituals and social customs. Such shielding does not differ much from what Muslim societies practiced with respect to women's education in the face of European colonial and missionary, military and cultural invasion, namely, secluded, segregated education.

Case 2

To compare the views of the above mother-daughter case to those of the following case, I asked another group of mothers, "What do we mean by practicing Islam?" without pointing to any specific practice.

A Mother's Response. A mother of European descent in her late thirties, whom I name "Ella," answered by explaining how she has dealt with the question of her children going out with friends. Contrary to another mother in the group who answered, "by following the *Sunnah,*" Ella stated: "Usually the understanding among Muslim groups is that girls go out with girls and boys with boys. If we are in a group, Muslims in a study group, we sit in a circle, men and women. Who are we to say that it is wrong when youth do the same?" She also alluded to the fact that the Prophet (pbuh) taught early Muslim males and females together.

By realizing that idealizing the Prophetic tradition would not enable her to translate his fourteen-century-old behavior into today's terms, Ella decided to address the principles behind the Prophetic practice and to provide a somewhat detailed example. When I asked her about how she dealt with other social activities, she answered: "[For] going to a film, I would like to know what it is about; if it is suitable."

It seems that this Muslim woman of European origin has escaped the Orientalists' view of Islam and the missionaries' pedagogical practices of Islam that left a dent in Muslims' perception and practice throughout the Muslim world. The basic message of Islam has been transformed from a belief in One God into the rituals of prayers, fasting, and so on. Muslims raised in Europe (not affected by missionary and Orientalist work but, nonetheless, raised in a society in which "secularized" Christian concepts are prevalent) before their contacts with recent immigrants from the Muslim world may have developed simple and less-confused views of Islam, and educators should investigate such views further. These findings have further implications for understanding contemporary Muslim youth needs. My observation does not only concern the tension among Muslims' discrepant views of Islam and its pedagogy but, more importantly, the tension between the West's view of religion and its practice in Western society vis-à-vis "other" societies.

The Daughter's Response. The seventeen-year-old daughter of Ella, whom I named "Ema," answered the question about the difference in guidance between home and school by saying: "The guidance you receive from parents, you usually assume it's like an Islamic kind of guidance. It's within the Islamic perspective. But the one at school is not. And to look deeper into that kind of thing, like you check it on your own. You can look it up in the Qur'an or the *hadith*, or ask somebody [who knows] what is the right way to do it."

When I asked what the youth discuss in their youth dialogue group, she said: "Everything is actually discussed. It is not just about God. We usually start with some *'ayah* (Qur'anic verse) or *hadith*, and someone has a question about it, we try to resolve it. Also, we have general questions, or Dr. "Y" brings-up some questions, and he relates some of the knowledge to us. He tries to explain." She also spelled out how best to plan for Muslims: "I don't think the planning should be massive, like for the community to change its way, like you go for the big thing first. You have to start from the basics, and then things grow gradually. Any kind of hope or change should be very minimal, and when you conquer them, then things on top come naturally."

Discussion of Case 2. The findings in this case suggest that, in addition to the mother's ability to differentiate the Islamic basic principles from their historical and social practice, she was able to find for her offspring a well-rounded youth group. As an autonomous Muslim, this mother seems to have succeeded in guiding her daughter into realizing the place of God in her life. The young female's response that the dialogue group discussion was "not just about God" indicates a movement closer to Fazlur Rahman's description of the substantive teaching of the Prophet and the Qur'an as "undoubtedly for action in this world, since it provides guidance for man concerning his behavior on earth in relation to other men. God exists in the mind of a believer to regulate his behavior if he is religiomorally experienced." Rahman adds that it was the bane of later medieval Islam that was regulative, namely, God was made the exclusive object of experience and, hence, was negatively related to social morality (1982, 14).

Conclusions and Recommendations

I analyzed the historical transformation of the Muslim woman's role in order to find solutions in the dynamics of Islamic pedagogy that may modify the process. The past and current transformation of the Muslim woman's role from what is intended by the Qur'an is not effected by the West alone, but, knowingly or unknowingly, is also effected by Muslims, in particular, male elites and policymakers. I argue, therefore, that recent and present attempts to transform the educational systems in Muslim societies, whether in the form of "modern, secular, universal" schooling or recent "Islamization" of knowledge and education, are doomed to failure if Muslim educators do not examine the education of Muslim women from the perspective of gender justice and the Muslim woman's self-identification with Islam as a trusteeship. Similarly, any attempts to intervene by any external agency claiming to "defend" the rights of Muslim women—whether inside or outside the Muslim world—will create more problems than they will solve if in their course of action they continue to view woman as an instrument for hegemony instead of recognizing her as an agent of change, a trustee, within her own culture.

I propose a Muslim female perspective that relates and integrates Islam and education in service of social justice. This perspective is intended to replace the present idealistic, dichotomized, and polarized views of women and education with a view of woman as the perpetuator of social justice and not only as a passive preserver of Islamic culture. This perspective accepts the stability of the Islamic teachings in the Qur'an and takes into consideration, as suggested by Amina Wadud (1992), the social and cultural contexts in which the Prophetic practice has extrapolated these teachings. It differs from the Revivalist males' perspective, however, by recognizing females as active partners in the interpretation process and by realizing, as did Muhammad Iqbal (1962), the relevance of space and time to learning and to the reconstruction of Islamic thought.

In this "Islamic" feminine perspective of education and development, education becomes Islamic only when it fulfills the premise of producing an autonomous individual who intellectually and spiritually makes the choice to be *al-khalifah* and to follow the course of action toward achieving social justice described in the Qur'an and objectified by the Prophet Muhammad. This perspective will benefit not only Muslim women but the Islamic social organization and gender justice in general. Self-identification with Islam and gender justice in Islam are the primary organizing principles of this feminine perspective. This perspective takes into account Western and some Muslim approaches that tend to be linear, areligious, and rational, and the Islamic approach as well, which is spiral, religious, and rational. These principles signal some of the different ways in which Islamic feminists working from within the Islamic educational perspective are struggling to reconstruct the interpretation of Islamic concepts, not simply in favor of girls but ultimately also in favor of social justice for all. I explain this point when I argue that multicultural democratic education does not benefit minorities only but is intended mainly to keep the majority in tune with their ideals of a democratic pluralistic education and social structure (Barazangi 1993).

To construct an action plan that will capture the momentum of the interest in human rights for Muslim women, there is a need to reinstate woman as an educational agent, both at home and at the mosque in Muslim societies and communities, one who herself will outline her priorities as a trustee entrusted with changing history toward social justice.

PART TWO

Law

3

An Introduction to Muslim Women's Rights

AZIZAH Y. AL-HIBRI

‿ The topic of Muslim women's rights is vast; Muslim jurists have been writing about it for centuries. Because jurists are partly the product of their societies and these societies were and continue to be highly patriarchal, Islamic literature has been saturated with a patriarchal perspective on women's rights. This perspective has become so entrenched that it has been rendered invisible. For most Muslims it no longer represents the *ijtihad* of individuals. Instead, it has come to be viewed by them as an "objective" reading of Qur'anic text.

Because of the complexity of the topic of Muslim women's rights, I limit this introduction to a select number of issues usually raised in connection with Islamic family law. Some of these issues have been raised in local and regional women's conferences, but the answers have not always been satisfactory. Furthermore, there has been no systematic reexamination of traditional Islamic jurisprudence on these and other issues from a woman's perspective. This chapter provides a step in that direction.

Tawhid and the Concept of Equality

Family law, like other branches of Islamic law, derives from the concept of *tawhid*, or the belief in a single God. *Tawhid* is the core principle of Islamic jurisprudence.[1] From it flow many secondary principles, including the one that asserts that God is the supreme being and that all human

---

1. See Faruqi 1981.

beings are creatures of God.[2] Thus, the *tawhid* principle provides the basis for the fundamental metaphysical sameness of all humans as creatures of God.

The Qur'an then comments on further metaphysical similarities and empirical differences among humans. It states that human beings were all created from the same *nafs* (soul), thus reemphasizing their metaphysical sameness.[3] It also states that God created humans from a male and female and made them into nations and tribes, so that they would get to know (appreciate, befriend) each other.[4] The Qur'an then adds that the most honored humans in the sight of God are those who are the most pious.[5] Thus, at the same time that the Qur'an points out empirical differences among humans, such as those of gender, race, and ethnicity, it asserts their natural equality. It bases any ranking among them on their individual moral choices. Consequently, from the perspective of these Qur'anic passages, no man is superior to a woman by virtue of his gender alone.[6]

---

2. "Say: He is God, the One and Only; God the Eternal, Absolute; He begetteth not; nor is He begotten; and there is none like unto Him" (Qur'an 112:1–4). See also, "I [God] have only created Jinn and men, that they may serve Me" (Qur'an 51:56). All English translations of Qur'anic verses used herein are based primarily on the translation provided by Ali 1991. This author has modified that translation at times for the sake of greater accuracy or clarity.

3. See, for example, Qur'an 4:1; 6:98; 7:189, and 39:6.

4. "O humankind! We created you from a single (pair), a male and a female, and made you into nations and tribes, that you may know each other (not that you may despise each other). Verily, the most honored of you in the sight of God is the one who is most righteous. God has full knowledge and is well acquainted (with all things)" (Qur'an 49:13).

5. Qur'an 49:13

6. Qur'an 49:13. See, also, the various Qur'anic passages that emphasize the common origin of both genders and, hence, their similar nature and status. For example: "O Humankind! Reverence your God, who created you from a single soul, created from it its mate, and from them twain scattered (like seeds) countless men and women" (Qur'an 4:1). "It is God who has produced you from a single soul. Here is a place of sojourn and a place of departure. We detail Our signs for people who understand" (Qur'an 6:98). "Never will I suffer to be lost the work of any of you, be that person male or female. You are part of one another" (Qur'an 3:195). "Those who do righteous deeds, whether they are male or female, and have faith, shall enter heaven and not the least injustice will be done to them" (Qur'an 4:124). "Whoever works righteousness, whether male or female, and has faith, verily to them we give a new good and pure life, and we will bestow on them rewards in accordance with the best of their deeds" (Qur'an 16:97).

The Qur'an emphasizes this point through the story of the fall of Satan. Satan fell from God's grace because he refused to bow to Adam in direct contravention of a divine order. Satan's disobedience resulted from his arrogance, which was justified by a self-serving worldview. Satan believed that he was better than Adam because God created him from fire and Adam from clay.[7] This mode of arrogant reasoning shall be referred to herein as "Satanic logic."[8]

Underlying Satan's self-serving belief was a subjective hierarchical worldview that ranked fire higher than clay. In upholding this hierarchical worldview and its ramifications, even in the face of a direct divine order, Satan committed the cardinal sin of *shirk*. *Shirk* is the opposite of *tawhid*. It occurs when someone regards another will, in this case Satan's, as equal or superior to that of God. Satan fell into *shirk* because of his arrogance.

Islamic family law must be based on divine logic as revealed in the Qur'an and not on some hierarchical worldview foreign to it. The Qur'an states that God created humans, male and female, from the same *nafs* so that they may find tranquility, mercy, and affection with each other.[9] The Qur'an also states that male and female believers are each others' *walis* (protectors, guardians).[10] These themes permeate the Qur'an and make it very clear that there is no metaphysical, ontological, religious, or ethical primacy for the male over the female. The Qur'an also makes it crystal clear that divine will contemplates a relationship of harmony, consultation, and cooperation, as opposed to conflict and domination, between the two genders.[11]

Unaware that Satanic logic provided the underpinnings of a patriarchal world, most Muslim jurists (like their societies) uncritically upheld

7. "God said: What prevented thee from bowing down when I commanded thee? He said: I am better than he; thou did create me from fire, and him from clay" (Qur'an 7:12).

8. See, for example, al-Ghazali 1939, 3:338 (discussing the pitfalls of hierarchical logic).

9. "And among God's signs is this, that God created for you mates from among yourselves, that ye may dwell in tranquility with them, and God has put love and mercy between your (hearts): verily in that are signs for those who reflect" (Qur'an 30:21).

10. "The male believers and the female believers are each other's *walis*" (Qur'an 9:71).

11. Qur'an 30:21. In understanding male-female relations in Islam, it is significant to note that the Qur'an does not blame Eve for the "Fall of Adam" from God's grace. Rather, one is told, both participated equally in that decision (Qur'an 20:120−21). Muslims do not subscribe to the concept of "Original Sin" because God forgave Adam and tied the fate of each human being on earth to that individual's moral/spiritual choices (Qur'an 20:122ff.)

the central thesis of patriarchy, namely, that males were superior to females. This central patriarchal assumption distorted their understanding of Qur'anic text and led them to develop oppressive patriarchal jurisprudence. This patriarchal jurisprudence then became the basis of state laws that have oppressed women for centuries. Thus, oppression of women is the result of Satanic logic infiltrating Muslim laws and distorting Muslim beliefs. For this reason I find patriarchal interpretations (*ijtihads*) unacceptable to the extent they are based on Satanic logic and conflict with *tawhid*. I also recognize that these *ijtihads* were the product of their time and place (historical and cultural) and, hence, need to be reexamined in light of the change in human consciousness that has since occurred.

The Islamic Philosophy of Change

A proper understanding of Islam requires familiarity not only with its basic substantive principles but also with its philosophy of praxis. Central to the Islamic philosophy of praxis is the Islamic philosophy of change. With few important exceptions, the Islamic philosophy of change is one of gradualism.[12]

The Islamic philosophy of change does not stand alone. It is an integral part of the Islamic worldview. It is, therefore, no surprise that this philosophy is closely linked to another fundamental Islamic principle, namely, that a society must conduct its affairs on the basis of *shura* (consultation).[13] This latter principle is so basic that it has been viewed as the constitutional cornerstone of any Muslim state.[14] The Qur'anic philosophy of change is also linked to yet another important *Qur'anic* principle, namely, that there be no compulsion in matters of faith.[15] All these specific principles can be partly subsumed under the overarching principle of freedom of thought. Because abrupt change usually requires coercive action and coercion is the antithesis of freedom, it stands to reason that the Islamic philosophy of change is necessarily one of gradualism.

This divine philosophy of change remains the most suitable for the

12. See the discussion on this point in al-Hibri 1992, 9–10.
13. See, generally, al-Hibri 1992.
14. Ibid.
15. Qur'an 2:256.

improvement of the status of Muslim women around the world. Although gradual change is frustrating, it is, nevertheless, more stable and less destructive of society than a radical coercive change. Coercive change, which reflects a patriarchal preference for the use of force, lasts for only as long as the source of the coercion continues to exist. It also leaves a great deal of violence and pain in its aftermath. Furthermore, gradual change need not be agonizingly slow. If Muslim women (and men) join efforts to dismantle patriarchal society, the objective could be achieved within our lifetime. To achieve that end we need to develop a clear agenda of our strategic goals and a definite program of action that prioritizes these goals. Such a program must take into account the differing needs and wishes of Muslim women in each country. It must demand the proper and equitable implementation of Islamic laws. It must also stress the Qur'anic foundation for our demands and, simultaneously, actively encourage Muslims to re-engage in the process of *ijtihad*.

It is from this vantage point of the Qur'anic aversion to coercion and the need to develop an indigenous Muslim women's movement that I reject all attempts to exercise hegemony over the Muslim World by forcing upon it, whether through the introduction of international legal instruments or otherwise, a certain model of gender relationships suitable primarily for some other country, belief system, or culture. I also reject all attempts to use the suffering of Muslim women for the furthering of such schemes and the fragmentation of Muslim societies. I call for the establishment of an International Muslim Women's Human Rights Commission which reviews human rights violations in Muslim countries and takes effective steps for their cessation.

This recommended course of action is based on the fact that religious people will always strive to follow Divine Will regardless of existing social or political trends. Consequently, to implement real change, we need to show these people that the new laws do not defy Divine Will. Rather, they are thoughtful attempts to serve it better. This is especially important in Islamic law, which prides itself on being based on the twin requirements of rationality and *maslaha* (public interest). If one can show that neither is served by an existing law, then the door for change is thrust wide open and opposition melts away without heightened conflict.

For example, an Islamic law is usually based on an *'illah* (justification or reason).[16] By agreement of scholars, when the 'illah disappears, so must the law, unless there is another 'illah for it.[17] Much of our heritage of ijtihad, however, was formulated hundreds of years ago and has not been reexamined recently to determine whether the 'ilal (plural of 'illah) for the related laws are still in place. The latter observation is especially significant because systems of Islamic law have often incorporated customs of local communities within them, so long as such customs were not viewed as contradicting the Qur'an. This practice, incidentally, is part of the Qur'anic philosophy of celebrating, rather than obliterating or punishing, diversity. Yet, subsequent to that incorporation, many customs have disappeared in the Muslim world, but the laws that enshrine them have continued to exist.

Similarly, the concept of maslaha has played a major role in the development of Islamic law. The basic idea is that the Lawmaker's (God's) purpose in making divine laws is to advance public interest. Thus, jurisprudence based on maslaha analysis requires that in formulating our legal system, we must also ensure that this divine purpose is preserved. In other words, a system of Islamic laws must avoid harm and serve the public interest, which includes the interests of women.[18] This basic jurisprudential requirement is a formidable one in reclaiming Muslim women's rights. In using it, we need to specify in the case of each controversial law the harm (if any) it inflicts upon women and any negative impact it may have on public interest as a whole. This way, the whole society would welcome rather than resist change.

In this study I focus on select issues that have affected Muslim women's rights in the area of family relations. These issues have been severely impacted over the centuries by controversial patriarchal ijtihad that remains enshrined until this day in the laws of various Muslim countries. I reexamine the issues in light of Qur'anic text, traditional nonpatriarchal

16. Traditional jurists agreed that 'illah is basic to an interpretation. See Mahmassani 1962, 70–72.

17. See al-Zuhayli 1986, 1:662. For a detailed discussion of 'illah jurisprudence, see al-Razi 1992, 5: esp. 207–16.

18. The Qur'an says in verse 2:185: "God intends every facility for you. God does not want to put you to difficulties." Many other verses illustrate God's preservation of public interest through divine laws. A famous hadith says: "No harm [is permitted] and no harming each other [is permitted either]" (Ibn Majah n.d., 2:784).

ijtihad, and my present state of knowledge and consciousness as a Muslim woman preparing to live in the twenty-first century.[19]

Marriage Relations in Islam

Historically, marriage has been an institution that favored men over women. Through this institution basic women's rights such as the right to education, financial independence, and freedom of self-fulfillment were usually denied.[20] A fulfilled woman was, in fact, viewed as one who married, served her husband well, and bore him children. This view, although less common today, continues to exist both in the West and in Muslim countries. Yet it is in total contradiction to the Islamic view of women and marriage.

Islam guarantees for women, among other things, the right to an education similar to that of the male, the right to financial independence, and even the right to engage in *ijtihad.*[21] Islam also views marriage as an institution in which human beings find tranquility and affection with each other.[22] It is for this reason that some prominent traditional Muslim scholars have argued that a woman is not required to serve her husband, prepare his food, or clean his house.[23] In fact, the husband is obligated to bring his wife prepared food, for example.[24] This assertion is based on the recognition that the Muslim wife is a companion to her husband and not a maid.[25] Many jurists also defined the purpose of the marriage institution in terms of sexual enjoyment (as distinguished from reproduction). They clearly

19. In studying traditional *ijtihad* one must be discerning in one's approach. Generally, traditional as well as modern *ijtihad* is patriarchal, but passages in various works, for a variety of reasons, question or reject some basic patriarchal assumptions. Consequently, traditional *ijtihad* should not be rejected uncritically. Rather, it should be studied carefully to discern religious from sociopatriarchal assumptions. Muslims are bound by the first but not the second.

20. See al-Hibri 1997.

21. See Ridha 1984, 7–20. See also, al-Hibri 1997, 6–7; and al-Dakhil 1989, 4:291–97.

22. Qur'an 30:21.

23. See Abu Zahrah 1957, 166. See, also, the valuable discussion by Bennani 1993, 143–46. Zaidan 1994, 7:302–8.

24. See n. 23, above.

25. Some jurists have even suggested that the wife is entitled to a maid to serve her if she is not accustomed to serving herself. See al-Bardisi 1986, 306–7. See, also, n. 23, above.

stated that a Muslim woman has a right to sexual enjoyment within the marriage.[26] This view has important consequences in areas such as contraception and divorce.

It is these rights and views, which are derived from the Qur'an and classical *ijtihad*, that we must actively reclaim to realign the Muslim marriage institution along *tawhidi* principles. So long as patriarchal (hierarchal/authoritarian) logic prevails, Muslim women will be denied their God-given rights. Qur'anic concepts of family relations must be more adequately recognized and enforced in Muslim countries and communities to abolish the authoritarian structure of the marriage institution.

In striving for this result we must recognize the fact that patriarchal logic is deeply entrenched in all societies and is quite resistant to being uprooted. If we, however, follow the Qur'anic approach to change, we will receive the support of many Muslim men and achieve a great measure of success without sacrificing the social cohesion of Muslim communities.

In fostering change the Qur'an resorts to what has been known recently in the West as affirmative action. In a patriarchal society even a general declaration of equal rights is not sufficient to protect women. Consequently, divine wisdom gave women further protections.[27] Paramount among these protections is the ability of the Muslim woman to negotiate her marriage contract and place in it any conditions that do not contradict its purpose.[28] For example, she could place in her marriage contract a condition forbidding her husband from moving her away from her own city or town.[29] She could also insert a condition requiring him to support her in the pursuit of her education after marriage. She could also use the marriage contract to ensure that her marriage would foster, rather than destroy, her financial independence. This goal is usually achieved by requiring a substantial *mahr*.[30]

---

26. Al-Bardisi 1966, 39–40; Zaidan 1994, 7:239–40. See, also, al-'Asqalani 1986, 285–86.

27. Patriarchal jurisprudence managed to reinterpret these protections and transform them into limitations.

28. Maghniah 1960, 301–2. See, also, Abu Zahra 1957, 156–62.

29. Maghniah 1960, 301.

30. *Sadaq* is another term used interchangeably with *mahr* in the Arabic language. In the Middle East the term *mahr* is used more often than *sadaq*. *Sadaq*, however, is the Qur'anic term. "And give the women (upon marriage) their *sadaqat* freely as a gift; but if they, of their own good pleasure, remit any part of it to you, take it and enjoy it with good cheer" (Qur'an 4:4).

The *Mahr* Requirement

Despite many patriarchal and Orientalist interpretations that have distorted and even damaged the Muslim woman's rights in this area, the law of *mahr* was made clear quite early. The *mahr* is a requirement imposed by God upon men entering marriage as a sign of their serious commitment and a gesture of goodwill, a matter of great concern to women living in this patriarchal world.[31] In fact, the giving of *mahr* is not much different from the Western custom of giving an engagement ring to signal commitment. Islamic law, however, preserved for the prospective wife the right to specify to her prospective husband the type of *mahr* she prefers. One woman may prefer cash, another property, depending on her relative needs or even taste.[32] A third woman may choose something intangible (nonmaterial) as her *mahr*, such as education. That is acceptable also. A woman of meager means may prefer to ask for capital that she could immediately invest in a business. In fact, she could even use that capital to start her own business. Her husband would have no access to either the capital or income from that business even if he were in need because legally, her *mahr* belongs to her alone.[33]

It is for this reason that when the *khalifah* (caliph) ʿUmar attempted to cap the amount of *mahr* sought by women in his time, a Muslim woman vehemently objected. This old, unknown woman publicly challenged ʿUmar, telling him that he could not take from Muslim women their God-given right that was granted in the Qurʾan. The *khalifah* then withdrew his proposal immediately.[34]

31. Ibid. See, also, Abu Zahrah 1957, 169–70; Zaidan 1994, 7: 49–50, 52.

32. See, Abu Zahrah 1957, 173–81. See also, al-Bardisi 1966, 238–39; Zaidan 1994, 54–58. Jurists, however, have set a minimum amount acceptable for *mahr*. Many also argue that if the woman settles for a *mahr* that is below her station, her *wali* may interfere and ask for a proper amount. The reasoning underlying this view is that the woman's *mahr* reflects upon the status of her family (including her sisters who may be about to marry). It is also a protective measure for women who, it is argued, may be swept by emotion. These are clearly social and not religious considerations. For more on this and similar juristic views, see Abu Zahrah 1957, 172; al-Jaziri 1969, 4:49–50 (arguing the need for a *wali* because an emotional woman may marry beneath her, thus harming her family's status).

33. Mahmassani 1965, 494–95. For a discussion of the Muslim woman's financial rights and independence, see Zaidan 1994, 7:52; 10:333–38. See, also, Abu Zahrah 1957, 206–7.

34. See al-Jawzi 1985, 136–37. Ghandur 1972, 167–68. See, also, Zaidan 1994, 7:68, 71–77. Some Gulf states have recently passed laws capping the amount of *mahr*!

Sometimes women resort to the custom of dividing the *mahr* into two amounts: advanced and deferred. The advanced *mahr* is usually small and merely symbolic. It is due by the time of the marriage ceremony. The deferred *mahr* is usually a substantial lump-sum payment. Unless otherwise specified, it becomes due only in case of death or divorce. If the husband dies, the deferred *mahr* becomes an outstanding senior debt against his estate (not to be confused with the woman's share/inheritance in the estate of her husband).[35] If the couple divorce, the husband must pay the deferred *mahr* at the dissolution of the marriage. Thus, the concept of deferred *mahr* is somewhat analogous to that of lump-sum alimony in the United States. The only instances in which the woman is not entitled to her *mahr* upon divorce are instances in which she is primarily at fault in the dissolution of the marriage.[36] (See section on "divorce.") Consequently, whether payable because of death or divorce, deferred *mahr* provides the wife with a measure of financial security.

Mahr, therefore, is not a "bride price" as some have erroneously described it. It is not money the woman pays to obtain a husband nor money the husband pays to obtain a wife. It is part of a civil contract that specifies the conditions under which a woman is willing to abandon her status as a single woman and its related opportunities in order to marry a prospective husband and start a family. Consequently, as in Western prenuptial and nuptial agreements, the contract addresses matters of concern to the prospective wife and provides her with financial and other assurances. In short, it is a vehicle for ensuring the continued well-being of women entering matrimonial life in a world of patriarchal injustice and inequality.

Guardianship

As stated earlier, Islam rejects the view that humans are organized in a hierarchy, whether that hierarchy is based on gender, race or class. As the Qur'an clearly states, the most favored individuals in the eyes of God are those who are most pious.[37] This statement articulates the basic Qur'anic

---

35. Mahmassani 1965, 495. See, also, Abu Zahrah 1957, 174.
36. Abu Zahrah 1957, 204–6; see, also, Zaidan 1994, 7:112–13.
37. Qur'an 49:13.

criterion for ranking humans, and it is a criterion based on one's individual moral choices.[38] But Islam was revealed in a world awash with authoritarian patriarchal structures. Consequently, and in accordance with the principle of gradualism discussed earlier, the Islamic solution was to put in place certain mechanisms that would help women navigate the treacherous waters of the world in which they live. One of these mechanisms was put in place through the introduction of the concept of *wilayah*.

While recognizing the woman's right to manage her own affairs in all spheres of life, Islam provided the young and inexperienced woman with an additional safeguard, namely, an automatic consultative mechanism by which she could solicit advice from her father (or one who has a similar relation) about a prospective husband. This mechanism is referred to as *wilayah*.[39] It is understood that the father (a seasoned male) is in a good position to enlighten his daughter, who may be very young and naïve about prospective husbands (other males). But in the end, according to one major school of thought (the Hanafis), the daughter is free to disregard the advice and to make her own decision, for, the father's role is, after all, merely advisory.[40]

Yet even the Hanafis were swayed by the protective patriarchal winds of the time when they awarded the father the right to prevent his virgin (and, hence, innocent) daughter from marrying an ineligible prospective husband.[41] They also defined the notion of "eligibility" in terms that recognized class and racial biases. Other jurists defined this notion in line with the Qur'anic verse that based it on piety, but then they went on to award the father authoritarian rather than consultative powers.[42] In an Islamic society in which historically the Islamic process of political consultation

38. Individual choices are the prerequisite for personal responsibility. No such responsibility could justly exist if one's actions were not the result of one's free choice. The Qur'an emphasizes the doctrine of personal responsibility in various passages. For example, "Every soul draws the meed of its acts on none but itself: No bearer of burden can bear the burden of another" (Qur'an 6:164). This doctrine is also expressed in verses 17:15; 39:7; and 53:38, among others.

39. Abu Zahrah 1957, 132–34. See also, Maghniah 1960, 321; Zaidan 1994, 6:345.

40. Abu Zahrah 1957, 130; Zaidan 1994, 6:345.

41. Abu Zahrah 1957, 130, 136–46; Zaidan 1994, 6:345.

42. For an overview of the five Islamic schools of thought on this issue, see Maghniah 1960, 326.

and election was replaced by an authoritarian ruling process, it is not surprising that the family structure became infected with these same influences. Now, however, that citizens in the Muslim world are demanding the full measure of Islamic democracy to which they are entitled by divine revelation, women cannot be heard to demand less.

Family Planning

Another measure for guarding the interests of women in particular and the Muslim community in general is provided in the area of family planning. Islam values the family structure and, like Judaism and Christianity, encourages procreation. Islamic law, nevertheless, differs from both traditions in its liberal approach to family planning. It shares with some Judeo-Christian traditions the view that contraception is permissible. Coitus interruptus (al-ʿazl) was practiced by members of the Muslim community during the time of Prophet Muhammad. Indeed, the Prophet knew that some of his companions, including his cousin Ali, practiced it, yet he did not prohibit it.[43]

Al-Ghazali, a prominent fifteenth-century jurist, argues that contraception is always permitted. He makes an analogy between intercourse and a contract. A contract consists of an offer and acceptance. So long as the offer has not been accepted, he notes, it can be withdrawn.[44] He even suggests that a woman can engage in contraception to preserve her beauty but adds that it is disliked (makrouh) if used to avoid female offspring.[45] Jurists have, however, conditioned the practice of al-ʿazl upon the consent of the wife. Some even argue that if the husband practices al-ʿazl without the wife's permission, he has to pay her a fine because he has detracted from her sexual enjoyment, her established right.[46]

Until recently, the majority of traditional jurists have taken a relatively liberal view toward abortion that properly balances the rights of the mother and the rights of the child. They recognized a period of early pregnancy that could be terminated at will and a subsequent period in

43. Al-ʾAsqalani 1986, 285–86. For a detailed account on this matter, see al-Hibri 1993a.
44. See al-Ghazali 1939, 2:53. See also Mussallam 1983, 18.
45. Al-Ghazali 1939, 2:53–54. This position is based on such Qurʾanic verses as Qurʾan 16:58 and 81:8–9.
46. Omran 1992, 155–65. See also, Mussallam 1983, 32.

which the embryo became ensouled. The jurists argued that when the embryo became ensouled, increasingly stringent criteria should be used to justify abortion (such as the health of the mother). More recently, relying on medical data, jurists have adopted the view that the embryo is ensouled soon after conception. It is desirable that Muslim women physicians and jurists reexamine this recent conclusion to determine its validity.

Maintenance

Classical Islamic jurisprudence entitles the woman to maintenance by her husband. Even if fully financially independent, she is not required to spend any of her money except as she wishes.[47] Furthermore, the wife is under no duty to do any housework although she may engage in such work on a volunteer basis.[48] Some traditional jurists suggested that the wife was entitled to monetary compensation for her volunteer housework activity.[49]

The law of maintenance is based on the Qur'an, but unfortunately it has been used to assert the general superiority of men over women. The relevant Qur'anic verse simply states that men may gain *qiwamah* (advisory, caretaking status) vis-à-vis women if only they satisfy two preconditions.[50]

47. Al-Jaziri 1969, 4:563, 582, 584 (stating inter alia that if a husband is unable to maintain his wife, any amounts she spends from her own money for her maintainance becomes a debt of the husband, even if she is wealthy). See, also, Mahmassani 1965, 495. Zaidan 1994, 4:290–91, 297. Additionally, once the husband gives his wife her *nafaqah* (maintenance payments) for food or clothing, for example, she is free to spend the money as she likes and not necessarily on food or clothing, so long as she does not harm or weaken her health or detract from her appropriate dress (7:214–15).

48. See al-Bardisi 1966, 306–7; Bennani 1993, 143. See also Zaidan 1994, 7:302–8, for an overview of this matter.

49. See n. 48, above. See also, al-Sarkhasi 1986, 5:182–83; Bennani 1993, 165–66; Abu Zahrah 1957, 165–66. For contrary views see Bennani 1993, 144–45, Zaidan 1994, 7:302–8. In any case, the wife cannot be forced to cook (Zaidan 1994, 7:207).

50. The *ayah* states: "Men are *qawwamun* over women *bima* God has given the one more than the other and *bima* they spend of their own money (to support the other) (Qur'an 4:34). I have left the Arabic word in place where the translation was questionable. "*Qawwamun*" has usually been interpreted as "protectors," or even "bosses." See Zaidan 1994, 7:277 (*Qiwammah* of the man is one of disciplining and protecting the woman. He is *wali* of her affairs; he orders and enjoins, as *walis* do with their subjects. He is her boss, ruler and discipliner if she

First, the male must be the (financial) maintainer of the woman. In other words, if he is not carrying her financial responsibility, then he has no standing to interfere in her affairs by providing unsolicited advice. Second, the male must also possesses qualities (such as financial acumen, real estate expertise, etc.) that the advised woman needs to reach a particular decision but lacks (at that point). Without these two qualifications (which, incidentally, may change from time to time and from one decision to another), men may not even presume to provide advice or be caretakers (*qawwamun*).[51]

Because the Qur'an was revealed in a world that was and continues to be highly patriarchal, it engaged in affirmative action to protect women. The revelation about maintenance provided women against poverty. It also made clear that maintenance alone does not suffice for a man to claim *qiwamah* over a woman. The second Qur'anic condition specifying who may provide women with advice or care was thus a limitation on then current practices and not a creation of any new rights. Some jurists must have intuitively understood that difference and attempted to circumvent it.

They argued that the second condition for *qiwamah* is always satisfied because God has favored men as a group over women in matters of physical strength and intelligence.[52] Thus, men are always entitled to *qiwamah* over women. Furthermore, the jurists interpreted *qiwamah* in an authoritarian manner ("boss" or "head of the household"), in accordance with the spirit of their times.

---

strays). *Bima* has been interpreted as "because." Both these interpretations force a certain patriarchal meaning upon the verse. I have reexamined this verse in al-Hibri 1997 where I pointed out that the proper meaning of *bima*, as based on ancient Arabic language dictionaries, contains a sense of conditionality, temporal or otherwise. I pointed out, also, that the word *qawwamun* has a range of meanings, including that of a mere "adviser." I concluded that the role of a particular male as an adviser to a particular female is conditioned on (1) his having more than she does (in knowledge, money, power, or whatever is *relevant to the issue at hand at that time* so that he is in a better position to advise and help her) and on (2) his supporting her with his own funds. If any of these two conditions fail at any time, the man is not *qawwam* over that particular woman at that time. Indeed, as his *wali*, the woman may have an obligation to advise him. "The male believers and the female believers are each other's *wali*" (Qur'an 9:71).

51. Al-Hibri 1997, 26–34.

52. See Rida n.d., 2:380; 5:67–69. See, also, Zaidan 1994, 7:277–9.

I have argued so far that there is no basis in the Qur'an for the patriarchal assumption of superiority, or the authoritarian interpretation of *qiwamah*. My arguments, however, respond to the traditional assumptions about women and their role in the family. The neopatriarchal approach to this role is, unfortunately, even more disconcerting.

For example, the Draft Unified Arabic Personal Status Law (the "Draft Law") requires the prosperous wife to support her needy husband.[53] The new formulation goes outside the scope of what is advocated by most jurists insofar as it imposes upon women additional burdens. It also does not offer them any significant new benefits or guarantees in return. In a still highly patriarchal world, a woman legally required to share her wealth with her husband may wake up one day to find herself divorced or widowed with her personal wealth depleted. Under this scenario the woman would have no real possibility of either recouping or regenerating that spent wealth, especially in light of the legal and other obstacles facing women who seek jobs outside the home.

Despite all the rights and guarantees offered by Islam to women, most men still use women as uncompensated laborers in their households. Furthermore, they not only expect them to produce heirs but also to nurse these heirs. Witness, for example, the list of wifely duties provided in the Draft Law, which includes nursing her baby.[54] Yet most Muslim jurists do not require Muslim women to nurse their children except to save the life of the child.[55] Instead, the husband is required to hire a wet nurse (or buy milk formula) if the mother does not want to nurse. If the husband divorces the wife, and she nurses the child after the divorce, jurists agree that she is entitled to monetary compensation for that nursing.[56] Hence, while

---

53. "The Draft Unified Arabic Personal Status Law," Art. 52 (1985).

54. "The Draft Unified Arabic Personal Status Law," Art. 43 (1985).

55. See Abu Zahrah 1957, 403–5. See also, Zaidan 1994, 9:475–80, who details the various juristic views on this point. The Hanafi, Shafi'i, and Hanbali views state that the woman has a religious but no legal duty to nurse her child whether she is married to or divorced from his father. Her husband has no right to force her to nurse. The mother, however, is required to nurse if the child rejects all other substitutes or none are available. The Malikis require the mother to nurse *unless she is of a noble or educated family in which the likes of her do not nurse!*

56. See, Abu Zahrah 1957, 204–5. See, also, Zaidan 1994, 9:485–92. (This passage also states that, consistent with the Maliki position discussed in the previous note, Malikis argue

masquerading as Islamic family law, a significant amount of the present family law in Muslim countries is influenced by local custom and patri-archal tradition.

Polygyny

Western writers have treated polygyny as one of the most controver-sial Islamic practices. Thus, it may be surprising to discover that Qur'anic reasoning clearly favors monogamy. The major Qur'anic verses at issue are two. One *ayah* states: "If you fear that you shall not be able to deal justly with the orphans, marry women of your choice, two, or three, or four; But if you fear that you shall not be able to deal justly [with them], then only one, or that which your right hand possesses. That will be more suitable to prevent you from doing injustice."[57] The other *ayah* states that men cannot deal justly with their wives when they marry more than one woman.[58]

Some Muslim jurists have interpreted the first *ayah* to mean that a man has the right to marry up to four wives as long as he is equally just with each of them. In providing this interpretation, these jurists ignored the first part of the *ayah*, which conditions the permission upon a certain context that obtained at the time of its revelation, namely, one of justice and fairness concerning the treatment of orphaned wives.[59] Secondly, these jurists ignored the last part of the *ayah*, which states that (even in that context) justice considerations make it preferable to marry only one wife. Consequently, this highly conditional and fact-specific verse was inter-preted as if it articulated a general rule. Of the two conditions, the first was ignored altogether, whereas the second was reduced to the duty of exercising fairness in treatment and maintenance among the wives. These same jurists also ignored the second *ayah*, which flatly states that men are incapable of satisfying the condition precedent for engaging in polygyny, namely, justice and fairness.

Other traditional jurists, however, concluded that the Qur'an is clear

---

that a noble mother who nurses her child is entitled to compensation although still married to the father [9:486].)

57. Qur'an 4:3.

58. "Ye are never able to be fair and just as between women, even if it is your ardent desire" (Qur'an 4:129).

59. Al-Bukhari n.d., 3:117.

in advocating monogamy as the general rule. They also added that insofar as polygyny causes the first wife harm, it is forbidden altogether (*haram*).[60] Several traditional jurists also recognized the right of the woman to place in the marriage contract a condition barring the prospective husband from additional (polygynous) marriages.[61]

Yet practices of polygyny continue in some Muslim societies as a sign of economic or sexual power. As such, they are similar to the Western practice of having concubines or extramarital lovers. It is part of patriarchal custom and not religion. But religious scholars who attempt to criticize the practice or change the law are criticized for succumbing to Western influences. Witness the attack on the Tunisian Personal Status Code.[62]

Western neoorientalist critiques of Islam, thinly disguised as "feminist" critiques, have managed only to complicate the task of Muslim women. These critiques tend to be motivated more by a feeling of superiority and a desire for cultural hegemony than by a desire to help the female "Other" (in this case, the Muslim woman). The neoorientalist attitude is evidenced by the fact that only negative and distorted stereotypes of Muslim women are propagated in international fora. Furthermore, these Western "liberators" have taken it upon themselves to "explain" Islam, criticize the Qur'an, and redefine and prioritize the demands of Muslim women over these women's objections. This attack on Islam by unqualified biased commentators offends the religious sensibilities of all Muslims, male and female, regardless of their points of view.

Significantly, while Muslim women struggled repeatedly in international fora to raise basic issues of survival and development, such as hunger, water, war, and disease, patriarchal Western women have insisted on

60. See al-Bardisi 1966, 38. See also, Mahmassani 1965, 471 (arguing that the spirit of Islamic *shariʿah* is to limit the permissiveness of *jahiliyah* in the practice of polygyny and to warn against it. It placed conditions on the practice that are almost impossible to achieve. Consequently, Mahmassani notes, many jurists concluded that the better and safest [*al-ahwat*] course of action is to marry only one wife and that marrying more than one is *makrouh* [disliked].) See, also, Zaidan 1994, 6:287, 291–92, who discusses these views but argues in favor of polygyny.

61. See al-Jaziri 1969, 4:87–89. See, also, Zaidan 1994, 6:133, 292.

62. The Tunisian code derives its legitimacy from a modern interpretation of Islam. See Rahman 1980, 451.

making the veil, clitoridictomy, and polygyny their primary preoccupations instead. They have even selected and funded some secular "Muslim" women to act as spokeswomen for the rest of the Muslim women. Needless to say, this neoorientalist attack on Islam has adversely impacted the civil rights of Muslims in Western countries and has poisoned the well for Muslim women seeking to regain their God-given Islamic rights in their own societies. Unfortunately, this state of affairs has alienated many Muslim women from the Western feminist movement.

Marriage to Non-Muslims

In this ever-shrinking global village interfaith marriages have become a daily reality. Because Islam respects and recognizes the other two Abrahamic religions, Muslim interfaith marriages have not presented a problem except in cases where the Muslim party was a female.[63]

Muslim jurists agree that a Muslim woman cannot marry a non-Muslim man in a valid Islamic marriage contract.[64] The Qur'anic pronouncement that marriage to "People of the Book" is permissible was interpreted narrowly by jurists to cover only Muslim men.[65] Other verses were used to bolster this view. Still, some other jurists disagreed and rested the prohibition of the marriage of Muslim women to non-Muslims on cultural grounds that recognized the patriarchal nature of societies.[66] The marriage institution, they argued, was no exception.

Muslim jurists recognized the patriarchal nature of the marriage institution and the fact that other religions prohibited interfaith marriages. They feared that these combined factors, in an interfaith marriage where the wife was Muslim, would result in the effective denial of the Muslim wife's right to the free exercise of her religion. For this reason they focused

---

63. "God does not forbid you, with respect to those who do not fight you for (your) faith nor drive you out of your homes, from dealing kindly and justly with them: for God loves those who are just" (Qur'an 60:8).

64. Al-Hibri 1993b, 16:66.

65. "The food of the People of the Book is lawful unto you, and yours is lawful unto them. (Lawful unto you in marriage) are (not only) chaste women who are believers, but chaste women among the People of the Book, revealed before your time" (Qur'an 5:5).

66. For more information, see Rida n.d., 351.

their protective attention on the Muslim woman, barring her from marrying non-Muslim men.[67]

Under the minority view that this prohibition is not Qur'anic, The *'illahs* for it then lies in the combined circumstances mentioned above. As a result, the prohibition may change when its *'illah* ceases to exist.[68] In this case, the important question becomes: Has the *'illah* for this law ceased to exist? I think not.

Muslim women may, nevertheless, resent this "protective" attitude of the jurists. Some may feel, in fact, that their own marriage will be different and more egalitarian than those of society at large. If these women take that approach, then they need to face the same considerations a man faces in an interfaith marriage, namely, the religious upbringing of the children. In Islam a parent is responsible toward God for the religious guidance of his or her issue until their majority. Many Muslims in interfaith marriages have been unable to fulfill this particular duty, especially when they live in a predominantly non-Muslim community. This fact is, therefore, a major consideration against interfaith marriages in such circumstances.

Additionally, new circumstances warrant a reexamination of the traditional juristic permission for the Muslim male to enter into interfaith marriages. American custody laws favor women. Many Muslim men have divorced their non-Muslim wives only to lose custody of the children and, hence, the ability to provide their own spiritual direction to them. It thus appears that Muslim men in American society have significant intermarriage problems and now deserve the protective attention of Muslim jurists.

Divorce

Divorce in Islam is relatively simple and is a consequence of the Qur'anic view that spouses should live together on equitable terms or leave each other with kindness.[69] Present legal practices, however, can tie up a

---

67. Al-Hibri 1993b. See, also, Zaidan 1994, 7:6–10, arguing that Qur'anic verse 2:221 prohibits the Muslim woman from marrying a non-Muslim regardless of his religion.

68. Al-Hibri 1993b, 66–67. See, also, Mahmassani 1965, 479, stating the traditional juristic principle that a *shari'ah* rule based on an *'illah* follows the *'illah* in its existence or absence.

69. "The parties should either hold together in kindness or separate charitably" (Qur'an 2:229).

woman in family courts for a decade before she is granted a divorce. This state of affairs is especially offensive in light of the fact that some traditional jurists gave women the right to seek judicial divorce if they had no conjugal relations with their husbands for more than four months.[70]

There are many forms of divorce in Islam. The present standard marriage contract grants the male the right to an automatic divorce. Nevertheless, if properly informed, the prospective bride is entitled to negotiate with the prospective groom a marriage condition that gives her a similar right. Unfortunately, women have not been properly informed of this right. Furthermore, not every woman can successfully negotiate the marriage conditions she desires.

A woman who has not protected herself in the marriage contract can seek judicial divorce on a variety of grounds, including those of domestic violence and lack of support. As in the West, judges play a major role in determining the level of violent conduct by the husband that is deemed actionable. These levels vary from one country to another. In Yemen, for example, karahia (extreme dislike), without more, is one of the statutory grounds for judicial divorce or annulment (faskh).[71] In Jordan and Kuwait, verbal abuse is also one of the statutory grounds for judicial divorce.[72]

Additionally, a Muslim woman who has not retained for herself the right to divorce may do so using khul'. Under this form of divorce, the wife returns the mahr to her husband to end the marriage. This form is based

---

70. Abu Shaqqa 1990, 6:233, quoting Ibn Taymiyah as stating that some jurists view intercourse as the duty of the husband at least once every four months; others determine the period in accordance with the wife's need and the husband's capability. Ibn Taymiyah prefers the latter approach. The arguments usually used to impose such a duty on the husband derive from the fact that satisfying the wife's sexual needs facilitates her being chaste. This is why al-Ghazali recommends that the husband have intercourse with each wife once every four nights (assuming the husband has four wives) (2:52). Jurists also have given the wife the right for judicial divorce (tafriq) if her husband stops having intercourse with her for a time (Zaidan 1994 8:439).

71. Yemeni Presidential Order Promulgating Law no. 20 of the Year 1992 Pertaining to Personal Status Matters, bk. 2, chap. 1, ART. 54.

72. Jordanian Personal Status Code, Provisional Law no. 61 (1976), chap. 10, ART. 132. Kuwaiti Law no. 51 (1984) Regarding Personal Status, pt. 1, bk. 2, Title 3, ART. 126. Both codes further describe that harm as being of a kind "that makes it impossible for women of the wife's peers to continue the relationship."

on an incident that took place during the life of the Prophet.[73] Since then, however, most Muslim countries have required the husband's consent for the *khul* to take effect.[74] The requirement has made this form of divorce quite expensive because many husbands bargain for their consent.

In short, Islamic jurisprudence and court practices in this area are biased in favor of the male and deserve close scrutiny and urgent reform.

Conclusion

The Creator is also the Lawgiver. God knowingly created all humans, males and females, nations and tribes, from the same soul to enjoy each other's company. But God evaluates us only in terms of our piety. In conducting our human relations, we (whether male or female) must, therefore, be guided by an attitude of piety. Domination is contrary to piety. It is the consequence of Satanic logic, not divine wisdom. Consequently, all laws that attempt to dominate women by denying them equal rights must be revised to reflect the fundamental Qur'anic principle of human equality. In this chapter I have highlighted and critiqued some patriarchal elements of family law. Many other important matters remain, however, within and outside family law, that demand urgent attention. Clearly, we need to devote a great deal more time and effort to critiquing various elements of our traditional jurisprudence that are based on domination and suppression. We also need to contribute to the evolution of a better Islamic jurisprudence based on divine logic.

73. The wife of Thabit bin Qays came to the Prophet and said: "O Prophet of God, I do not fault my husband's manners or piety, but I want to leave him because I fear the loss of my faith if I remain with him." [In another version of the story, she wanted divorce because she simply could not stand her husband.] The Prophet then asked her, "Would you return to him his garden [which the husband had given her as *mahr*]?" She said, "Yes" and returned the garden. The Prophet then ordered the husband to leave her (al-Bukhari n.d., 3:273).

74. Pakistani case law presents a salient exception. See Hodkinson 1984, 271–96. Some countries, such as Yemen, permit judicial divorce or annulment (*faskh*) for reasons of dislike without the need for the woman to resort to *khul*. See n. 71 above.

4

Women's Self-Identity in the Qur'an and Islamic Law

MAYSAM J. AL-FARUQI

O Commander of the Believers! Why do you deny us a right
granted to us by God?
                                —Khalid and Nabda, *Our Beginning Wisdom*

The Problem of Self-Identity

❧ It is a fact that women in the Muslim world often face difficult situations and very real problems of social, economic, and political oppression.
Interest in this issue has heightened recently and women's groups and
scholars have addressed it, defining its scope and suggesting various solutions from their own perspectives. But for Muslim women, the relativity of
these perspectives is itself the problem, for by necessity, the adopted lens
will provide a particular reading of the problems at hand. More importantly, the proposed solutions themselves are going to be determined by
the way the problem is identified and defined.

One can readily categorize the different responses as from "within"
and from "without" the faith. The main response from within has been to
acknowledge some extreme forms of oppression, then reduce them to "external" abuses of the cultural and religious system of beliefs in Islam.
Otherwise, all differences in rights and obligations that arise in the religio-
cultural construct are justifiable religiously. They do not constitute, therefore, oppression and abuse. Any claim to the contrary is challenging the

72

faith itself and may lead to *kufr,* or heresy, and there is, therefore, no room for debate.

The responses from without are mainly of two kinds. The first kind considers the problem to be a universal one and ties the issue to gender rather than to socioeconomic or cultural circumstances. According to the "gender-feminist" (reference) approach, the problem is gender based. It is caused by the constant attempt by the male gender to oppress and dominate the female gender. This oppression is carried out also against "other" genders through the "claim" that there can be only two sexes—whatever this means. In any case, it is this domination that leads to the different definitions of the social roles of the sexes; these roles, like the definitions of sexual identity, are then social constructs that can and should be challenged and deconstructed. Any position to the contrary is usually taken to mean giving in to the system of oppression that arises from false social constructs.

The other response from without is not nearly as extreme. It does not ground the problem in gender but locates it in the surrounding culture and suggests, therefore, yet another solution—to amend the cultural and socioeconomic construct to rectify the abuses. There is no claim to launch a revolutionary war against the culture or religion involved. The cultural construct will be kept, but abusive structures rejected—either plainly in the name of "universal" human rights that would take precedence over any other ideology or by reformulating and reinterpreting, as a result of the marvelous flexibility of modern hermeneutics, the "true" universal essence of the culture or religion in question. The first version will be favored by non-Muslims (a good example is Mayer 1991, but this holds true for nearly all non-Muslim authors). The other, of course, will be the approach of Muslim apologists. In either case, however, the main reference for the advocated changes is the "modern" view of human rights, which provides the actual formulation of specific rights to be implemented by force of law or to be projected back in the old ideology as a "saving face" device. In other words, it is now an independent, "modern" ideology that provides the ultimate reference to values and women's rights, and it is expressed in the "universal" declaration of human rights. The latter, then, is the scale against which religious edicts are to be measured and either justified (apologetics) or amended (reformism). The problem, of course, is that in these responses, Muslim self-identity has been conveniently ignored and the Muslim woman's self-definition has been reformulated on a basis that has nothing to do with Islam. The claim of the reformists that some values of the Qur'an should be stressed over others (with the choice, of course, operating on the basis of Western ideals) follows the same principle and is equally out of the question. For as far as Muslim *believers* are concerned, everything that the Qur'an mandates is equal in ought. Hence, all of these approaches fail to interest the Muslim because they are clearly—and avowedly—from without the Islamic tradition (some might also claim that the gender-based approach is without any and all traditions).

Of course, women are concerned about their rights. It is not, however, only the existence of problems that matters but also, more importantly, the correct apprehension and definition. Western movements define them as relating to "womanhood," which is the same universally. But then, in the case of Muslims identifying themselves as such, what becomes of the self-identity of the Muslim woman, reduced here to a universal concept of womanhood, battered by a universal concept of manhood along universal lines of cultural patriarchal oppression that can be identified by a "universal" list of human rights and be fought by universal measures that can, at best, be tailored to their local culture as a dismissive gesture for those incapable of casting away their sentimental attachment to their religion? These approaches are unsatisfactory to the Muslim because they fail to identify her real problem, and they therefore fail to provide adequate solutions.

This is precisely the problem for self-declared Muslim women. They identify themselves as Muslim. But that dimension is not part of the reference of "universal" human rights. Yet Muslims take Islam to be the first source of identity, not an "additional" ideological superstructure. Indeed there is for a Muslim, man or woman, whatever the ethnicity or the race, only one source of definition and one reference—Islam. By contrast, in every approach from without, women are first defined by their sexual identity, which is directly contradicted by the content of the Islamic faith. All natural and biological identities are merely accidental and irrelevant to the very meaning of one's existence, according to the faith of Islam. Muslims then cannot but start from that Islamic source if they identify themselves as Muslim. No race (racism) or nation (nationalism) or gender (feminism) can constitute the starting point of the Muslim's source of identity. Rather the starting point is in—and only in—the system of beliefs about the world and about self that the individual willingly and rationally chooses. My reason, in other words, takes precedence over my sex. In that the ap-

proaches from without are asking women to do violence to their understanding of themselves and to seek answers outside their reason and beliefs, they become irrelevant except for the "token" Muslims—those who
are born in the religion but have no commitment to the faith and adopt
feminism as their ideology. Their choice is legitimate and valid and stems
(one hopes) from their rational understanding of themselves, but it applies
only to them. These "noncommitted" Muslims may identify with their
culture as they please, but it belongs to self-identified Muslims to define
their own understanding of their faith. And because the latter's starting
point is Islam, they will define and see the problems in a way necessarily
different from that of the gender and cultural approaches, which then
become irrelevant to the Muslim both procedurally and substantially. The
definition of the problem (and not just the solution) has to come from
within. That is not to say that the issues cannot be provoked and initiated
from without, as indeed they historically did stem from the "liberation"
movements that first arose in the West. But what does matter is that they
must be reformulated with Islam—specifically, the Qur'anic text—as the
starting point. Of course, the first approach delineated here, namely, that
of the "extreme conservative," is from within. And I have no problem with
this approach at an epistemological level. Nor do I intend to challenge its
proponents in the name of "gender," "Western rationalism," or anything
else that is external to Islam. It is true that I am examining issues that were
raised by Western movements that have called to question the validity of
many Muslim practices concerning women. Muslim women have come to
ask these questions as well and will continue to seek questions and knowledge even from China. Women ask these questions not as women but as
Muslims concerned whether the faith of Islam is indeed practiced the way
it defines itself. Women question the "extreme conservative" movement on
the basis of Islam itself, and Islam alone shall constitute the answer.
Hence, I do intend to challenge them not in form but in content and by
using the very principles they claim to follow.

The Source of Identity:
Laying the Common Ground

If I have gone into some detail on the validity of the various approaches, it is because it constitutes the crux of the matter. For I am

woman (or man) by accident but Muslim by choice, and any analysis that does not formulate the issue (let alone the solution) from the Islamic perspective is simply irrelevant to me in the decisions that, after all, affect my beliefs and my life. It is necessary, then, to identify the common ground that defines beyond custom, tradition, time, or place the faith and the methodology of interpretation of the faith to which most Muslims subscribe.

That common ground is relatively easy to define in the case of Islam. Muslims have consistently identified themselves through the Qur'an as the source of their faith. In other words, the religion is clearly textual, not based on an event (as with Christ's resurrection in Christianity) or any premise external to the text. It is the content of the text that defines all Islamic beliefs, including the divine authorship, God's nature, His unity and transcendence, and His relation to the world and to humankind. It is not because of the Prophet that Muslims accept the Qur'an but because of the Qur'an that they accept the authority of the Prophet. Of course, a religious text (or any text for that matter) implies an interpretation and, hence, the possibility of diverse readings. But whereas one accepts as a cliché the claim of open-ended nature of *any* text that can yield as much as the creative understanding of the reader can draw (although I suppose one will have, under the threat of being condemned to debate vacuous and mediocre writings, to limit that to "any great text"), one has to acknowledge, however, that the text does have an historical dimension, a particular *sitz im leben*, specific grammatical and lexicographic rules, and that these neither change nor can ever be nullified, regardless of the interpretation. New interpretations are always possible, but one that ignores or contradicts these basic and given rules is, however "creative" it may be, incorrect. There are several kinds of readings of the Qur'an—philosophical, "spiritual," historical, and so on—and corresponding definitions of the Islamic "self." But the primary definition of identity and the nexus of rights and obligations that accompany it belong to the domain of the law. In that it limits itself to explaining the *given* meaning of the legal verses of the Qur'an, it is legal criticism of the text that provides Muslims with objectified, tangible laws. One may consider oneself Muslim "at heart" and have a "spiritual" or a "mystical" or other definition of the true "Islamic" self, but if one takes the Qur'anic text as immediate reference, then its command to the believers to mind its injunctions and prohibitions is absolutely clear. Islamic law, in other words, derives its ought not from an institution (church or state or court) but from the Qur'anic text itself.

If, then, the Qur'an constitutes the source of self-identity of the Muslim, it is its legal verses that provide the Muslims' rights and obligations at the religious or the socioeconomic level. Whatever the philosophical or religious interpretations of the spiritual meaning of Islam, there is no room for disagreement over the definitive ought of the legal verses of the Qur'an (although, of course, there can be different interpretations of the actual legal meaning of the verses as evidenced by the endless argumentation among the various schools of law) and on the necessity of applying them as part of one's faith. A Muslim is Muslim if he or she accepts the absolute unity of God and the truth of the Qur'an as divine revelation. As such, a Muslim must uphold—and is subject to—the legal injunctions of the Qur'an. Beyond that, there can be as many levels of understanding as Muslim creativity can muster. But the legal and religious injunctions (such as to fast, to pray, to avoid incest, etc.) are the basic infrastructure, and it is because of these injunctions that there is universal acceptance of the absolute necessity of Islamic law among all schools of thought, philosophical or mystical, in all their varieties, as evidenced, for example, in the Sufi texts, which prescribe the shari'ah as the beginning of the mystical road.

Women in the Qur'an from the Legal Perspective

The Qur'an constitutes the one and only reference for anyone who wants to identify himself or herself as a Muslim.[1] Inasmuch as *fiqh* (the interpretation of the law) is a necessary reading of the Qur'an, it is part of this reference because the Qur'an must be "read" and interpreted. Islamic law will take care of the legal reading. In some cases, Muslims have very clear injunctions in the Qur'an. But in most domains of the law, it is the jurist (a person specifically trained in the science of Islamic law) who uses the various interpretation procedures identified in Islamic law to find what the most appropriate law is. It is not a derivation based on his or her "philosophy" but on specific rules that must be identified. The arguments

---

1. All translations of the Qur'an are either taken directly from or modified on the basis of Asad 1980.

for the derived law must be explicitly stated and the rules used in the process identified. *Fiqh* and the Qur'an are then intimately associated. But because some of the law is direct interpretation of explicitly stated *ahkam* (clear commands) in the Qur'an, whereas the larger part is derived on the basis of general principles, there can be and is a difference between the Qur'anic legal construct (as read by the law itself, of course) and the legally derived construct.

In all cases, the correct (legal) interpretation of the verses of the Qur'an is crucial to the issue of self-definition. The Qur'anic worldview is one in which creation is created with a single purpose—to worship (serve) God. The physical world and nature worship God naturally: "The seven heavens and the earth, and all that is in them, praise [obey] God. Nothing exists but it praises [obeys] God" (Qur'an 17:44). Humankind, however, has free will and although created to fulfill and carry out the vicegerency (*khilafah*) of God on earth, has the capacity, as the angels put it, to "spread corruption and shed blood" (Qur'an 2:30). The cosmic task of the *khilafah* is clearly that of all of humankind, regardless of their ethnic, racial, or sexual backgrounds: "O mankind, We created you all out of one pair, a male and a female; and We constituted you into peoples and tribes that you may know one another. Noblest among you is the most righteous" (Qur'an 49:13). The capacity to fulfill all of the divine requirements is clearly the same for all and so is the reward: "Whether male or female, whoever in faith does a good work for the sake of God will be granted good life and rewarded with greater reward" (Qur'an 16:97; also 4:32, 3:195, etc.). The self-worth of the individual is the same for all:

> Verily, for all men and women who have surrendered themselves unto God, and all the believing men and believing women, and all truly devout men and truly devout women, and all men and women who are true to their word, and all men and women who humble themselves [before God], and all men and women who give in charity, and all self-denying men and self-denying women, and all men and women who are mindful of their chastity , and all men and women who remember God unceasingly: for [all of] them has God readied forgiveness of sins and a mighty reward. (Qur'an 33:35)

The task to live according to the religious precepts is to be carried out by each individual regardless of gender. The absence of gender in referring to the foundations of humanity is remarkable. When God creates human-kind, the word used is *khalifah,* which applies to both men and women. When God offers His vicegerency to the universe, it is humankind (*al-insan*) that accepts it (Qur'an 33:72). When the Qur'an speaks of the origin of humankind, it refers to "the male and female from whom you sprang out" and has Adam and Eve created from a single soul. When the first sin is committed, it is both Adam and Eve who are at fault. They both repent and are both forgiven. The rights to own property, to get education, to work, to marry, to divorce are all granted equally in the Qur'an and clearly practiced as such during the life of the Prophet. Nowhere does the Qur'an affirm a difference based on race or gender in the endowment of intel-ligence, ethics, talents, or anything needed to carry out the vice-gerency, and that is consistent with the absolute transcendence and the absolute justice of God that are maintained throughout its text.

In the socio-economic order, however, in the realm of family and property, the Qur'an clearly differentiates between the rights and obliga-tions of the two sexes. For instance, the Qur'anic system of inheritance provides the brother twice the inheritance of the sister, and from a feminist view, that would appear to be a discrimination against women and their right to equality. There is certainly no notion in the Qur'an of blind equal-ity. Indeed, there is an egalitarian socioeconomic order that takes the fam-ily as its starting point rather than the individual and assigns different obligations depending on age or gender. It is because it starts from a given family cell that it adjusts conditions precisely in order not to slight the individual and to maintain equal justice for all.

The differentiation between male and female obligations is established with a view to create a system of interdependence and partnership in the family. The latter is the primary cell of the social fabric and the founda-tion of the social order. That is why most of the laws of the Qur'an deal with it, and it is partly because of the instinctive popular understanding of this fact that family remains the last bastion in secularized Muslim soci-eties of Islamic law despite all secular governmental efforts to shift it to the secular legal systems that were imposed on the Muslim world by colonial powers.

Taking this primary cell as the starting point, Islamic law provides different obligations to the various members. The child is helpless, and its rights must be met and protected, which creates a series of obligations toward it that must be fulfilled. The child, of course, is the product of a couple, and as such, these obligations will be shouldered by both the father and the mother. In that process, the mother finds herself having to carry the child, nurse it, and provide it with its immediate needs as an infant; that is recognized as effort and toil by the Qur'an: "[man's] mother bore him by bearing strain upon strain and his utter dependence on her lasted two years" (31:14). And "in pain did his mother bear him and in pain did she give him birth; and her bearing him and his utter dependence on her took thirty months" (45:15). The mother, then, already contributes a substantial share at the physiological level. In the egalitarian system of the Qur'an, the father must, therefore, face an equal obligation because the mother already faces obligations set by biological laws. He will then be responsible for the financial upkeep of both the mother and the child, hence allowing his wife to discharge her natural obligation. At any time in her life, a woman may find herself pregnant and caring for another life whose needs must be provided. She should never in this condition shoulder alone that responsibility. She should never have to devote her time to finding a means for survival when another helpless life is utterly dependent on her and may be, therefore, made to suffer. Because of the already existing biological demands on the woman, she never has to shoulder *also* the financial responsibility of a family, and Islamic law never makes her liable to providing for her family. Her partner, who is equally responsible for the welfare of the child—whose rights are absolute—must provide for its needs by contributing to its main provider, namely, the mother.

If the husband himself cannot discharge his duty for any reason (death or incapacitation), it is still the duty of the extended family and behind it, of society, to help provide the woman with her basic needs because society has a vested interest in the new generation and must provide help if the woman's guardians are unavailable or incapable. Because the time for such need cannot be foretold, it becomes a necessary and general law for men to always provide for women whether these are in immediate need or not. For behind the woman is the possibility of a child whose rights are absolute and must be met without question. Hence, never does a woman in the Islamic socioeconomic order have to provide for her basic needs. Her father and her brother are obliged to provide for her, and when she marrys, it is her husband's turn. Within the family cell, the brother is the closest to his sister. He is the one, therefore, who will be her financial guardian in case she needs help (in addition to supporting his own wife and children). That is why the law in the Qur'an is not generalized to all males receiving twice the inheritance of all females (as is evidenced for instance in the inheritance shares of the grandparents).

The inheritance system follows the distribution of responsibilities within the family cell. It is a clear indication of one's duties toward the extended family because the family cell is not the nuclear family but the extended one. And by providing for the extended family, the law intends—in addition to spreading wealth as much as possible in society—to strengthen its ties and the system of interdependence that is the ultimate safety net for a society based, in the Islamic worldview, on community self-help and immutable moral responsibility rather than state agencies and relative state laws. Contrary to what non-Muslims (and a few Muslims) think, this is a system that is fair and well expounded in the Qur'an. There is no question in the linguistic and legal understanding of the Qur'an that the system of interdependence and the financial responsibility of the male are firmly indicated in the Qur'anic construct, and the jurists correctly understood it as such. Critics of this system fail to follow the rules of linguistic understanding and the rules of legal interpretation, hence disqualifying their arguments from consideration by Islamic law. For these rules must be followed in arguing the legal meaning of Qur'anic verses, and, indeed, one finds that the latter do provide a clear understanding of the financial responsibility of the male, an understanding confirmed by the rest of the Qur'anic construct and the practice of the Prophet as well. The critics miss fundamentally the point of the system of interdependence and financial responsibility: it is not a system of abuse as far as Muslim women are concerned. On the contrary, it is a system in which the inequitable division of biological tasks have been straightened out. It would have been an abusive system if it had denied women their right to property and to ownership as Western law did until the twentieth century. That, indeed, is the true means to control an individual. This however, is never the case in the Qur'an or in Islamic law. Women did have a right to inheritance and to property, and court records throughout history show them managing their property on their own. That, of course, constitutes the ultimate form of independence. But the fact that the legal system was simultaneously fostering interdependence is, of course, the reason why women were still fully taken care of by their male relatives. There is clearly no intention in the Qur'anic view to subject the women to male "ownership": the dowry that the husband is to offer his bride is hers alone (another safety net) to deal with as she wishes. Not only is she not prohibited from deriving income from inheritance or work and keeping it to herself, the law protects that income by refusing to allow the male—or the family—have any claim to it. She can do with her property as she pleases, and she may refuse any help from her financial guardian if she so wishes. His obligation, however,—in case she ever is in need—never ceases and remains firmly set by virtue of the law. In the Qur'an and in the time of the Prophet, this guardianship does not preclude women from being full members of society and from participating in all its realms, business, politics (Qur'an 60:12) and even war (Qur'an 3:195). It was Khadijah, the Prophet's first and most beloved wife, who proudly and independently ran her own business; indeed, the Prophet worked for her and it was because of her that his free time could be devoted to the contemplation that readied him for the call to prophecy.

Women in the Commentaries:
The Issue of Verses 4:24 and 2:228

Women did not fare as well in the commentaries on the Qur'an, all written by male writers. The commentaries are very important, for they are part of the jurist's reference in explaining the legal aspects of the verses of the Qur'an. Certainly, the commentators did clearly understand, explain, and maintain unambiguously the Qur'anic provisions concerning women's rights. The verses that seemed open to interpretation, however, were often given a decidedly misogynistic explanation. Those were the verses that contrasted (rather than compared) men's and women's rights only in the family realm. There are not many of those; in fact, two verses become the crux of the incorrect understanding on which most of the negative extrapolations of the law will later be based. The Qur'an, as was shown, established the same principles of religious identification and worth for both men and women. Without quite saying so, there is a subtle shift in the commentaries to imply that this may not be the case.

It is in reference to verses 4:34 and 2:228 that commentators started implying a biological difference in intelligence, capacity, and piety between men and women. This is an interpretation that is extrapolated and read into the verses, and I show that not only does it contradict all other provisions of the Qur'an in which no such "natural" difference is ever mentioned and in which the emphasis on equality in front of God is manifest; it also actually misinterprets the verses in terms of linguistic analysis.

Verse 4:34. Verse 4:34 is usually translated as "Men are responsible for women because God has made the ones excel the others and because they support them from their means." Different commentators and interpreters ascribe different meanings to this "excellence", be it intelligence, capacity, or physical strength. As it stands, this interpretation makes the verse linguistically awkward. The second clause in the sentence is quite clear in explaining the substantiation of the responsibility conferred upon the male: it does not say "because" but "with what (*bima*) they spend from their means"; because there is a conjunctive "and" between the first clause and the second clause and because the first clause starts also with "with what" (*bima*), the verse should read: "men are responsible for women with what God has made men 'excel' over women." But whatever it is that God made men excel, it cannot be "with it" that they are responsible for women. If it were a general state of excellence, some general form of superiority, the verse should have read *"because* God made men excel over women *and with what* they spend from their means on them." But that is not at all the linguistic construction of the verse. The element in which men "excel" is to be used in the same way as their means are used—if the Qur'an is to be linguistically accurate. "Excellence," however, cannot be substantiated and used the same way monetary means are; it is meaningless to say that men are responsible for women "with" their excellence; they should be responsible *because* of it.

This ascribed meaning makes the sentence incoherent, and the premise of Qur'anic interpretation is the linguistic coherence of the text. The problem of the construction arises because the words of the Qur'an are not interpreted here literally but allegorically. The key word in the sentence is *faddala*, which means "to favor." The literal rendition of the verse is "Men are responsible for women with what God favored the ones over the others." It is a totally unwarranted extrapolation (happily made by many male commentators but clearly a matter of wishful thinking) to maintain that the favor is their state of excellence. If the verse meant plain favor (as in favoring someone over the others as used, say, in verse 2:47), it would not have used the expression *bima* (with which) that substantiates this favor. But the verse clearly is not dealing with a general state of favoritism; even if it had, to presume that this favoring comes from men's excellence is totally unwarranted. God could have, for the sake of the argument, favored them on the basis of their endearing childish rush to believe that they are excellent—or their "virile," unquestioning self-confidence. Favoritism is not necessarily linked to excellence.

Plain, unjustified favoritism is, however, linked to plain immorality. It would be truly unfair for God to favor any of His creatures above the others, and, of course, the Qur'an flatly denies that He ever does. God has no chosen people, or a fortiori, a chosen gender. All creatures are equal and derive equally from a single pair; for all their biological differences, the ones who find favor with God are the ones who are righteous, a task that all can equally fulfill. The issue is so important to the Qur'an that all those who believe otherwise (i.e., Jews and Christians who think they might be chosen and granted paradise over and above everyone else) elicit the strongest verses of rebuke (e.g., 2:111, 5:18, 2:94, etc.). God, in other words, is portrayed as an equal opportunity salvation provider. For Muslim men to interpret this verse the way some members of the Jewish and Christian faiths interpreted their religion warrants the same rebuke. To transpose favoritism from religion or ethnicity to gender is not any less reprehensible. It is, therefore, the true meaning of this word *faddala*, to favor, that one must find out to explain the verse accurately.

The word *favor* when applied to God in the Qur'an is never used in the sense of arbitrary preference. In the Qur'an, its meaning is "to provide," and when God provides sustenance or, in fact, anything to human beings, He is said to favor them. Indeed, anything that God provides is a favor. He does not "provide" excellence, however, although all of humankind is created in a state of excellence (Qur'an 85:4), which is their potential. Excellence, in other words, has to be achieved, for it comes only from living up to the moral law, which is equally provided to all. Hence, not only are there no verses whatsoever substantiating any presumed state of excellence in any of God's creatures, but such a claim contradicts every other verse in the Qur'an. Because the Qur'an itself maintains that it always explicates its own meanings, one must look for the Qur'anic meanings associated (and not just presumed) with the word.

In the Qur'an, God "favors" or provides humankind with reason over all of creation; some prophets with a "Book" over others; David and So-lomon with the capacity to hear the secret language of nature; the Hebrews with security and sustenance. But these do not offer a ground for "favoritism." They are provisions that are earned: by humankind for ac-cepting the responsibility of the vicegerency; by the prophets for their moral excellence; by the Hebrews for having kept their belief in God; by anyone who believes and is "favored" with guidance for having faith, and so on. Sometimes, the favor is a test, as when God provides more goods to some than to others (17:20, 21). Whenever humankind is provided suste-nance (that is, all the time), that constitutes a favor from God. This last usage of *faddala*, namely, "to provide sustenance," is found throughout the Qur'an. It is so common is used every day every time an Arabic speaker gives thanks to God for sustenance or otherwise. That one's sustenance is *fadl* from God is on the lips and, in a calligraphic form, in the homes of most Muslims.

Now the verse is saying that God did "provide" the ones (men) some-thing over what He provided the others (women). To assume that this provision is a natural and biological superiority is nothing but an assump-tion that is not corroborated by the Qur'anic text and runs counter to it. *What,* then, according to the Qur'an *itself,* did God provide men that He did not provide women? The obvious and only answer, found a few verses earlier, is, of course, the double share of inheritance that is sustenance and, hence, "favor"—double the "favor" or sustenance that women get. In this sense, God does, indeed, and in obvious terms, provide men with more means than He provides women. Any other interpretation of what is provided to men has absolutely no confirmation from the Qur'an, whereas this one is based on its very words (4:11); the expression is used within an entire section that starts from the beginning of the same *surah* (chapter) with the issue of possessions in conjunction with marriage and inheritance. The reason for providing men with more than women is very clear, and, as detailed above, it is part of the test (living up to the responsibilities) of the masculine side of society. All schools of law are unanimous that verse 4:34 obligates the man to always be *financially* responsible for his female rela-tives.[2]

2. The claim that this may be a hypothetical situation cannot be sustained on the basis of grammatical and linguistic analysis. The verse is not framed as a suggestion but as a clear

Now, then, the verse becomes harmonious linguistically and makes perfect sense: "Men are responsible for women using that which [lit., "with what"] God has provided some [men] over [what He has provided] others [women] and that which ["with what"] they spend from their own means." The second clause is there, of course, to remind men that even if there is no inheritance, men are still responsible for giving from what they actually earn; responsibility does not stem from the inheritance per se but from their obligation to be equal partners in the family. The use of *bima* (with which) becomes fully warranted, and the two clauses can be harmoniously linked by the conjunctive and.

If one returns to the passage of the Qur'an that includes this verse, one finds that it also fits with the verses that immediately precede it. In the two verses before to this one, the Qur'an had precisely discussed the issue of coveting shares that God provides to some more than to others. "And do not covet what God has provided (*faddala*) some of you over others." Not only does one have here the same context as in verse 4:34 relating to financial means and inheritance shares but one can also see the exact construction used in the latter: *"la tatamannu ma faddala Allah bihi ba'dakum 'ala ba'd."* Literally, the verse is saying, "Do not covet that with which (*bi ma*) God favored some of you over the others." All jurists and commentators universally agree that *faddala* here refers not to a state of excellence but to providing sustenance, in fact, specifically, to the inheritance shares going to men over those accorded to women. Yet, just two verses later and although still dealing with the same financial context, the commentators conveniently forget this context and the obvious similar linguistic structure and offer a tangential interpretation of *faddala* that has no basis in the text and is contradictory to the other verses of the Qur'an.

Verse 4:32 continues as follows: "For men shall have a benefit from what they earn and women shall have a benefit from what they earn. Ask

---

command, and there are no hypothetical prepositions used, but rather a substantiating causal preposition. Similarly, the claim that "providing some over the others" could refer to "providing some of the men over some of the women" cannot be maintained. The referents in the sentence are clearly the "men" and the "women" of the first part of the verse. Besides, it would make the Qur'an incoherent, since the double share in inheritance is clearly provided to men and not to women. Nor could one see what it is that some men would have over the other men. Of course women may always refuse financial assistance, but this will not nullify men's responsibility both morally and in the eye of the law.

therefore God to provide from His favor (*fadl*) for you; behold, God has indeed full knowledge of everything." Men's and women's rewards, in other words, depend on their deeds and are nothing but what they earn from their own actions, something the Qur'an repeats several times. They do not depend on any "endowed excellence," which, were it to exist in the first place, would not be subject to claim anyway. Having clarified that women will benefit like men from what they earn, the Qur'an goes on, confirming that, however, each has been provided a certain share of inheritance by divine decree: "And unto everyone have We appointed heirs to what he may leave behind: parents and near kinsfolk, and those to whom you have pledged your troth; give them, therefore, their share. Behold, God is indeed a witness unto everything." But then, it explains the reason for this difference in shares, which is dissassociated from the rewards in the hereafter and is not justified grounds for envy: "Men are responsible for women with [by using] what God has provided the ones over the others and with [by using] what they spend out of their possessions." And what God has provided the ones over the others is a larger share of inheritance. Contrary to the second clause, which has men spending "something" out of their possessions, the first clause unambiguously requires that *all* that God provides men over and above the shares of women will be used to satisfy the requirement of responsibility. Hence, building on the former verse that affirmed that men and women have different shares in inheritance by divine decree, verse 4:34 explains why the larger share provided men should not be coveted and envied because it is to be used solely to help them carry out their responsibility in the family and the community.

One still must consider the circumstances that led to the revelations of the above verses. These circumstances can be taken by the jurists to explain further the content of the verses. Of course, the Qur'an remains by definition its own best and most authoritative explanation: "God bestows from on high the best of all teachings in the shape of a divine writ fully consistent within itself, repeating each statement [of the truth] in manifold forms" (Qur'an 39:23), and that is the primary principle behind interpreting the verses, which is commonly accepted and must be admitted by any commentator—unless the commentator would like to contradict the verse just quoted. That is precisely the principle followed here in finding out the meaning of God's favor to men (namely, the double share in inheritance). Any other interpretation (such as men's intelligence or piety) should be able equally to take the Qur'an itself as evidence and fit the context in the same way as this interpretation does. Failing that, any such interpretation is merely extrapolation, at best, and false, at worst.

According to the commentaries and hadith collections, verse 4:32 (advising one not to covet another's God-given share) was revealed to answer the question of a woman, possibly one of the wives of the Prophet. She had worried that women might not get the same return on the Day of Judgment as men would, if the latter were to get already in this world a larger share of sustenance. The Qur'an reassured the women and cautioned against unwarranted envy that some might feel because of inheritance distribution. Verse 4:34, however, detailing men's responsibility, is said to have been revealed on another occasion in which a woman complained to the Prophet about being hit by her husband. This verse then was revealed with its continuation: "And as for those women whose illwill (nushuz) you have reason to fear, admonish them [first]; then leave them alone in bed; then beat them; and if thereupon they pay you heed, do not seek to harm them. Behold, God is indeed most high, great."

Let me consider first whether the fact that the two verses were revealed on different occasions would invalidate in any way the explanation that I just gave of verse 4:34. According to the rules of interpretation followed by the jurisprudential reading of the Qur'an (and that is what is of interest here), the occasions of the verses are to be taken into account. By definition, the legal interpretation of the Qur'an is based on the whole text and must take all of its content into account. As such, an interpretation corroborated by the verses of the Qur'an is stronger than an interpretation corroborated only by a source external to the Qur'an, for an external source may naturally be inaccurate or incomplete, whereas the verses of the Qur'an are absolute references. Therefore, any interpretation derived from a source external to the Qur'an (as the reports on the circumstances surrounding specific verses are) and contradictory to the Qur'an must be discarded. Taking all of these rules into account, one can conclude that the interpretation of verse 4:34 rests on firm grounds. Hence, even if I were to assume that the verse was indeed revealed in its entirety on the occasion of the violence committed against a woman, one still must understand the linguistic meaning of the verse so that however one looks at it, one ends up having to say that a verse was revealed of which only the second half was relevant to the occasion. That does not in any way invalidate the interpretation provided above. It simply invalidates the assumption that the "beating" is occasioned by the former part in which economic responsibility is discussed and that it must be used to understand the latter. The Qur'an is full of instances in which the different parts of verses are not directly linked, so the subject matter is the first and most important reference in connecting them to each other for legal understanding.

Clearly, I have here two different subjects within the same verse. The first half deals with financial responsibility, which falls on the shoulders of all men in relation to all of their female relatives. It constitutes a logical continuation, indeed a logical conclusion to, as I just showed, the subject matter of the verses that preceded it. The second half, however, shifts to a new topic, that of *nushuz* and its implications. Here, the disciplining is expressly linked to *nushuz* but not at all to the economic responsibilities of men. Otherwise, if the ground were economics, one would have to say that regardless of what women do, men would be entitled to discipline them, something that, clearly, no jurist or commentator is willing to say. Whereas the first half of the verse had to do with the legal responsibility of men toward all women, the second half discusses matters restricted to husbands and wives, that is, a breach of marital relations and not a possible breach between, say, a father and his daughter. Clearly, a section of the Qur'an ended in the middle of verse 3:34; the second half starts a new section.

Despite this obvious fact some commentators will specifically use the second half (the permission to discipline one's wife) to reinterpret in reverse the provision of larger shares of inheritance as a provision of a state of excellence of all men. That their disciplining of their wives becomes the sad (and only) substantiation of their state of excellence is indeed an irony that would make one smile if it were not for the fact that such a simple-minded view is then attributed to God Himself.

But I still have to analyse the context of the second half of the verse. Even if I accept the stories related in that respect, it is quite likely that only the second half of the verse was revealed on that occasion. It is quite possible that the *hadith* reporters referred later to the whole verse (rather than only to the second half) because by then the Qur'an had been compiled in a way that placed these different parts together. (The order of the Qur'an was established by the Prophet on divine inspiration according to aesthetic rules and not thematic or chronological rules). Hence, the situation that brought about the revelation of the second half of the verse is probably not related in any way to the first half (as is the case, according to the commentaries, with the "men shall have a benefit" part of verse 4:32). But there still are some crucial problems with the *hadith* statements about a woman complaining to the Prophet. It is suspiciously incomplete (al-Tabari 1992, vols. 3–4)). A woman complains about violence and does not explain the reason for it? But the Qur'an—and the Prophet—had banned wanton violence, and to give a blanket approval of it without first checking whether the husband actually intended to harm his wife does not make any sense. She must have been asked (if the *hadith* is true) about the reason for her husband's acts, or it must have been already known. She must have provided an answer that prompted such a verse. For one must remember that in another *hadith* (al-Bukhari 1994, vol. 7: 150 and Shawkani A.H. 1344, 7:34ff), a woman simply declared to the Prophet that she could not abide her husband and wanted separation on that ground, which he granted. A *fortiori*, a woman who complains about violence would no doubt receive similar treatment. The Prophet admonished his followers against using violence toward women. The Qur'an, in addition to the injunctions of proper and gentle behavior for all, allowed divorce for both men and women (Qur'an 2:229). Clearly, it could not now tell the men to just go ahead and "beat their wives" if the latter showed them dislike and disobedience (which is how the commentators understand the word *nushuz*) and expect the women to put up with such behavior and not seek a divorce. A woman who already dislikes her husband is not going to mend her ways and start liking him when he also starts beating her (psychology 101). Hence, unless the Qur'an were to prohibit her from getting a divorce, (which it does not), to simply tell men that they may beat their wives is absurd and sanctions breaking up marriages. The verse must relate to a much more serious issue than the *bon plaisir* of the male sanctioned by his economic responsibilities that would then become a cover for unjustified privileges.

There must be, then, a much different and restricted meaning to the word *nushuz* if the whole of the Qur'an is to be consistent with itself. And, indeed, there is. The word *nushuz* (which occasions the disciplining) cannot mean simple disobedience, for, after all, the Qur'an explicitly expects women and all individuals to follow the divine law over and above the will of their spouses or their parents (9:24). Nor could it apply to trivial matters and contradict the rest of the injunctions of the Qur'an. Nor would it even relate to serious problems of "irreconcilable differences," which are grounds for divorce in the Qur'an. If, according to the Qur'an, a woman has the right to work, to ownership, and to divorce, what then could possibly be the husband's right that she might be disobeying and that could justify punishment?

The field of possibilities is then quite narrow. Many commentators and jurists will, therefore, turn to the one obvious right that spouses have in marriage: sexual access. For most commentators, the wife who refuses herself to her husband is committing *nushuz,* and he may discipline her. But this explanation is very problematic. If the woman refuses herself, she presumably dislikes her husband, and if he tries to fix things by beating her, then the marriage is decidedly headed in the wrong direction. The Qur'an, which, it should always be borne in mind, granted her the right to divorce, could not possibly give such a simplistic solution so clearly against basic logic and common sense. Besides, it could scarcely make sense in this case to counsel in the same breath that the men "punish" their wives by abandoning their beds! Clearly, this is an explanation that could only make sense to a male ego although, of course, not to male reason.

The fact that most commentators and jurists resort to the subject of sexual access is not altogether wrong, for the verses that deal with *nushuz* in the Qur'an refer always to husband and wife and not to men and women. Obviously, it has something to do with marital relations, and the crux of marital relations is sexual access. Some form of sexual misconduct must be involved. The best way to find out what *nushuz* is exactly, of course, is to use the rest of the Qur'an (as it asks the reader to do) and to consider all the verses that deal with this issue, including the *nushuz* of the husband.

Usually ignored in the discussion is the fact that the man may also be guilty of *nushuz:* "and if a woman has reason to fear *nushuz* from her husband or that he might turn away from her, it shall not be wrong for the two to settle things peacefully between themselves" (Qur'an 4:128). Quite inconsistently, the commentators will not explain here the husband's *nushuz* as disobedience to his wife although the same word is used and in the same context, namely, that of marital relations. Instead, they take it to mean bad behavior on the part of the husband that may justify a divorce (as in beating!). But for the Qur'an to use precisely the same word in exactly the same context does not allow such a fanciful shift of interpretation. Clearly, there is something that both men and women may do that can be bad enough to warrant discipline, in the verse referring to women, and divorce, in the verse referring to men.

Instead of focusing on "sexual access," the commentators should have focused on the legal dimension that intervenes with respect to the marital bond, namely, *exclusive* sexual access. There is only one form of sexual misconduct that would, in accordance with common sense, warrant disciplining, and that is sexual misconduct outside of marriage. The actual act of adultery (*zina*) is addressed elsewhere in the Qur'an and is not called *nushuz*. Besides, it calls for much heavier punishment for both parties. Therefore, one can safely assume that *nushuz* is a stage before adultery and refers to unwarranted behavior in which a wife or a husband are making some sexual advances to another party but without carrying out an illegal act. *Nushuz*, then, would be reprehensible enough to justify action, but not the punishment of adultery. Indeed, this interpretation can be corroborated directly from the verses of the Qur'an (4:34–35):

> Men shall be responsibile for women, using that which God has provided to them over what He has provided to women and that which they spend from their own means. And the righteous women are the truly devout ones, *who guard the intimacy* [*al ghayb*, secrecy, privacy] which God has [ordained to be] guarded. And as for those women whose *nushuz* you have reason to fear, admonish them [first]; then leave them alone in bed; then beat them; and if thereupon they pay you heed, *do not seek to harm them*. Behold, God is indeed most high, great (35). And if you have reason to fear that a breach might occur between a married couple, appoint an arbiter from among his people and an arbiter from among her people; if they both want to set things aright, God may bring about their reconciliation. Behold, God is indeed all-knowing, aware. (Emphasis mine)

Al ghayb, the secrecy or privacy in question, means the intimate relations that must remain exclusive to the married couple. The word *nushuz*, which literally means to stand up to fight or to rebel, is not used in a vague and indiscriminate way. It refers specifically to the sentence that immediately precedes it: "the righteous women are the truly devout ones, who guard the intimacy which God has ordained." *As to those who do not do so*, they become guilty of *nushuz* and should be reprimanded. It is obvious that *nushuz* is not left to the fanciful interpretation of the reader but used explicitly in reference to the previous sentence. There is a clear command that the intimacy of marriage be guarded exclusively. The text then addresses the case of those who disobey this divine command and become guilty of *nushuz*. There is consistent and self-containing meaning in the passage as to what *nushuz* refers to, and any extrapolation (such as disobeying the wishes of the husband) is only an extrapolation that is not backed by the text.

The righteous women are those who guard the intimacy that is the hallmark of marriage. If they do not however, and instead act provocatively with other men, showing undue interest, the Qur'an counsels a number of steps. Admonishing them and reminding them of the proper rules of behavior comes first. Then, men may show displeasure by refusing sexual contact, which makes sense in this context. Finally, that is, only if she persists, they may resort to discipline, one of the steps by which the Qur'an effectively eliminated the practice of "crime of honor" that was carried out in Arabia and, indeed, crept back into Islamic law under the loose category of "tradition and custom." Because provocative behavior to someone other than the husband is clearly illegal and frowned upon, it does warrant punishment (contrary to the simple act of disobeying the husband's whims and desires), and the reason why the Qur'an will allow physical punishment is that it is clearly for a reprehensible act that actually was met with violence in pre-Islamic Arabia.

This situation was probably the reason behind the husband's acts in the story that brought about the verse, which might not have been explicitly stated by the wife but must have been known to the Prophet. The aim of the verse, then, would not be to give men blanket disciplinary authority over women but to prohibit licentious behavior while restricting male overreaction and prohibiting the usual pre-Islamic punishment. The crime was very serious in the eyes of pre-Islamic society and remains serious in the framework of Islamic morality (and most traditional societies). The Qur'an admits that this kind of behavior is immoral and infuriating to the husband but is sending the message that violence is not accepted and should only be a token gesture, certainly not in the form of harm or murder. Hence, it is ruled that no harm may be involved in the act of disciplining, according to the unanimous view of all jurists and all commentators. That is why the Qur'an adds insistently: "And do not seek to harm them." In other words, forego masculine pride and the notion of an irreparable in-

sult. The purport of the verse is, then, to limit the use of customary violence; the wife who acts in such a way would know she is wrong, so it is
not inconsistent for the Qur'an to condemn such behavior and to expect
her to agree with the disciplining. If, however, the issue becomes really
serious or the husband is extremely angry, then the Qur'an demands outside intervention, which further limits the use of violence.

The same meaning of *nushuz* can be found in the verses dealing with
men (Qur'an 4:127–130):

> (127) And they will ask thee to enlighten them about the laws concerning
> women. Say: "God Himself enlightens you about the laws concerning
> them"—for [His will is shown] in what is being conveyed unto you through
> this divine writ—about orphan women [in your charge], to whom—because
> you yourselves may be desirous of marrying them—you do not give that
> which has been ordained for them; and about helpless children; and about
> your duty to treat orphans with equity. And whatever good you may do,
> behold, God has indeed full knowledge thereof (128). And if a woman has
> reason to fear *nushuz* from her husband or that he might turn away from her
> [i'rad], it shall not be wrong for the two to set things peacefully to rights
> between themselves; for peace is best, and selfishness is ever-present in
> human souls. But if you do good and are conscious of Him, behold, God is
> indeed aware of all that you do (129). And it will not be within your power
> to treat your wives with equal fairness, however much you may desire it;
> and so do not allow yourselves to incline toward one to the exclusion of the
> other, leaving her in a state, as it were, of having and not having a husband.
> But if you put things to rights and are conscious of Him, behold, God is
> indeed much-forgiving, a dispenser of grace (130). And if husband and wife
> do separate, God shall provide for each of them out of His abundance; for
> God is indeed infinite, wise.

The whole section deals with multiple marriages, which were allowed by
the Qur'an earlier also in reference to orphans (4:2,3). Certainly, in the socioeconomic construct of the Qur'an, marrying orphans and providing sustenance to them was one of the main reasons for allowing multiple marriages.
But marrying more than one wife leads a man to treat one differently from the
other(s). Hence, a wife or one of these married orphans (who was the justification for the second marriage) may fear *nushuz* or sexual interest in someone else
from her husband or even that he may turn away completely from her (i'rad).

Of course, in this case, the *nushuz* is not illegal as it may be with the wife (who cannot have two husbands) and, hence, is not punishable. But it is equally reprehensible, and the rights of the wife remain. Therefore, the husband is advised not to practice *nushuz* or *i'rad* (showing more sexual interest in another partner in the former case or altogether ignoring the former wife in the latter), although to discourage multiple marriages, he is told in no uncertain terms that this is almost impossible. *Nushuz*, then, for men, is showing more sexual interest in one wife than in the other. If the wife remains upset, the parties are advised to work out first a settlement (one should keep in mind the priority in the Qur'an not to resort to divorce and to make sure that the husband continues to provide for his wife because maintenance and security of life come first) and, failing that, a divorce.

Nushuz then can be deduced from the verses as referring to not guarding the intimacy associated with marriage and showing attraction to a person other than one's spouse. That it always has to do with another partner is clear from the fact that the Qur'an specifically refers to multiple marriages in the case of the *nushuz* of men. Quite consistently, the Qur'an uses the same word for the same meaning in both cases. For women, however, the act is more reprehensible because there can be no proper justification for it, whereas for the men, the case considered is the one taking place within the framework of (multiple) marriages, so it is not illegal but reprehensible and grounds for divorce. But since *nushuz* deals with misconduct rather than adultery (a form of sexual harassment, really) the word "beating" is not a correct translation (especially since Islamic law interprets the discipline as a clearly symbolic act, and prohibits any act that is actually violent or that leaves so much as a physical mark on a person's body, as is the case with "beating".) The *nushuz* of the male outside of marriage brings automatically the same punishment from the judges as the one advocated by the Qur'an for women: a reprimand or a good measure of disciplining at the hands of the judge.

Verse 2:228. The other verse that is misinterpreted also falls in the category of the socioeconomic order and the rights of divorce. Verse 2:228 states that "the divorced women shall undergo, without remarrying, a waiting period of three monthly courses; for it is not lawful for them to conceal what God may have created in their wombs, if they believe in God and the Last Day. And during this period, their husbands are fully entitled to take them back, if they desire reconciliation; but in accordance with justice, the rights of the wives [with regard their husbands] are equal to the [husbands'] rights with regard to them, although men have precedence over them. And God is almighty, wise."

Here too, the difference between men and women is set in the middle of a discussion of socioeconomic rights and responsibilities and *not* in a general discussion of the natural differences between men and women. This last provision at the end of the verse was not used as an interpolation in, say, verse 33:35 quoted above, which so clearly maintains the full equality of men and women. It comes after a reminder to all that husbands and wives have equal rights, but then it mentions a certain degree in this context: men *in this case* have a certain right above those of women, even as the rights of men and women had been clearly enunciated earlier.

The rights that I am discussing are not the rights to education or welfare. They are specifically the rights associated with divorce. And, as usual, another verse from the Qur'an—the next one, as a matter of fact—will clarify this matter of precedence. The next verse makes clear that, as the Qur'an had ruled earlier, divorced women are entitled to keep their dowry; that is their fundamental right. But now, adds the Qur'an, if the woman, too, wants the divorce or initiates it because she (alone or along with her husband) cannot keep within the bounds prescribed by God for proper marital behavior, then it is only fair that she should return the dowry to the husband because the divorce was not (or not entirely) his fault. Hence, in this case, a woman may not keep her dowry, which the Qur'an had given her as an absolute right. Indeed, it is so absolute that this verse does not *force* the woman to return the dowry but merely suggests that she ought to do so. For even though the rights of men and women have been set and will not be changed, in all fairness, in this particular case, men do have a right and the woman should return the property that her husband provided her in good faith. "If you have cause to fear that the two may not be able to keep within the bounds set by God, there shall be no sin upon either of them for what the wife may give up [to her husband] in order to free herself." It will not be a sin; although it would run counter to the blanket rule that women always keep their dowry.[3] The verse neither restricts the woman's right to divorce nor even forces her to

3. Even in the case where a husband accuses his wife of adultery but she does not admit to the latter, he is granted a divorce but he is expressly not allowed to take back the dowry, as reported by Bukhari 1994.

give up her property. It simply advises that in this case that would be the proper thing to do. Again I explain here the terms of the Qur'an with the Qur'an itself. The context—divorce rights—and the next verse are all that I need to bring forth the meaning of this difference in "precedence" or "degree." As to extrapolations to other things that this "degree" might involve, they are only extrapolations with no basis in the text of the Qur'an, be they the fanciful wishes of men that they are a degree more handsome than women or the fanciful wishes of women that men will also get an additional degree of punishment in the hereafter.

In both the case of verse 4:34 and that of 2:228, there is, indeed, a differentiation between some rights and responsibilities of men and women. In both cases the context is that of family rights and responsibilities in marriage and divorce. Never is there a spelling out of any biological difference making men and women anything other than partners. By contrast, verses abound maintaining that they are indeed complementary partners with equal rights. The difference between males and females is rooted in the socioeconomic distribution of communal responsibility rather than gender. There is no talk in the Qur'an of the fragile, ignorant woman who must be protected; rather she is given all the rights the male has and is expected to fulfill her duty in society in the same way as he does. The ultimate aim of the socioeconomic construct of the Qur'an is to create a system of interdependence in which the extended family unit is the norm and in which, therefore, the community is set to take full care of its members on both legal and moral grounds so that whatever happens on the wider social and political scale, the individual is still protected. It adjusts the imbalance of biological tasks by countering them with economic responsibilities. It guarantees the possibility of individual independence through private property, but it avoids falling into the traps of individualism and selfishness (which ultimately destroy and break up society) by making members legally and morally responsible for each other.

Women in Islamic Law

As a rule, Islamic law followed closely the injunctions of the Qur'an, and the tremendous creativity and intelligence of the juristic system, one of the crowning achievements of Islamic civilization, testify to this fact. The jurists understood well that they were dealing with divine law and that it was to God Himself that they had to report. This led to care and humility that can be seen throughout their work. They were human beings, however, and the exercise of the law depends on human reason. And human reason depends on its cultural milieu and the relative understanding of a time and place. Hence, it is not surprising that this dependence becomes apparent once the jurists were not encouraged anymore to develop new laws to fit new situations but had to turn to previous rulings, which, moreover, had been in some cases taken from custom and tradition, something the law had allowed for specific cases or to solve immediate issues. This change, however, coupled with the fact that once a juristic opinion is rendered, it is allowed to remain in force even if, by consensus of the jurists, it is found to be wrong or contradictory to the Qur'an, when combined with the wrong interpretation of two verses from the Qur'an led eventually to a reified system in which society managed to curtail severely the rights of women.

Certainly, most of the problems of women arise from custom rather than Islamic law. There still are some problems, however, whether stemming from tradition or from the understanding of the jurists, that can be found in Islamic law in contradiction with the actual rulings of the Qur'an. An obvious example is that of divorce. A man is allowed to get a divorce without waiting for the period mandated by the Qur'an. The jurists disapprove of it, but, as a matter of fact, allow it. By contrast, they limit the access by women to divorce by having them go through a court although the Qur'an does not have any such provision. The jurists resort to justifications based on the instability, ignorance, and fickleness of women. The Qur'an believes she is intelligent and stable enough to handle her own property and her own buisness, but jurists seem to think she cannot handle her own married life. Meanwhile, the speedy divorce they accord to men over and against the objections of the Qur'an can, of course, serve only an unstable and fickle husband. Hence, the law, in actuality, helped provide unwarranted privileges to men and restrict the rights granted to women by the Qur'an itself.

One must say, however, that these limitations are all a matter of juristic opinion rather than central tenets of the law. As a whole, the jurists never attempted to cancel or annul the rights provided by the Qur'an. Nor do Muslim women have any problem with the Qur'anic law and its socioeconomic construct, which is, in the view of Muslims, a system of great wisdom and stability, fostering a healthy community while protecting the individual. Nor is there a problem with most parts of Islamic law—except those interpretations that clearly contradict the rights granted absolutely by the Qur'an itself.

As far as Muslims are concerned, the Qur'an is paramount and must be accepted as the only reference. Islamic law is equally paramount and what is derived based on the science of jurisprudence must be followed. The limitations that ended up in Islamic law around women did not come from the Qur'anic text. They are usually derived for the protection of cloistered women who have no knowledge of the world around them. But the reasons because of which the law allowed society to erect these "protective" walls in matters of marriage, divorce, freedom of movement, and so on, are either based on (doubtful) psychological explanations of the female psyche, which cannot constitute legal ground, or on the interpretation of the verses dealing with the so-called masculine "excellence" or "degree," in other words, Qur'anic text, which *is* legal ground. One can see how the tendentious interpretation of these verses could then bring about a number of explanations that are deemed grounds for legal limitations on women that ultimately result in negating her God-given rights. One can also see the absolute necessity for a correct linguistic and legal reading of the verses of the Qur'an.

Of course, one should be careful about passing value judgments on a previous time-period without taking into account its specific circumstances. There is no question that the kind of economic possibilities that opened to both men and women after the industrial revolution were simply not available at the time many of the juristic laws were elaborated. It was much more important to guarantee to everyone a basic livelihood and security and, in the process, that meant a greater measure of protection for women. And the jurists were certainly dealing with a situation on the ground and had in mind guaranteeing the best conditions possible for the women of their society. To be true to facts, one must admit that they turned a deaf ear to the mysogynistic interpretations of most commentators and preserved firmly women's basic rights at a time when no other law system in the world accorded them any rights. Nearly all the contentions that women today can make concerning the proper rules of marriage and divorce have actually been made by one jurist or another who had managed to free himself from his cultural surroundings. Nonetheless, because centuries of reading have been dominated by a particular male perspective, a certain interpretation of the verses, not always complete and correct—as just seen in this case study—came to predominate.

All this does not invalidate the fact that women's rights were curtailed and that in today's circumstances Muslim women (and men) should demand the review of these juristic rulings in the light of the Qur'an—this time a Qur'an read accurately. The jurists, who never claimed a special link to divinity, knew that their knowledge was relative. They could and they did agree on wrong rulings, such as allowing the practice of a hasty divorce, even as they condemned it. Even the great 'Umar ibn al Khattab, known for the accuracy of his judgment, made a mistake in interpretation that caused him to be corrected by a woman in his assembly: "Commander of the believers! Why do you deny us a right granted to us by God?" He had tried to set certain limitations on one of these rights, which is exactly what some jurists later did, hence effectively negating them. But 'Umar immediately withdrew his contention, and this is what one expects from Muslim jurists today. It is essential today that women bring back this kind of questioning and that they strive to re-read the Qur'an from a feminine perspective of their own rights. That is not because there is a feminine versus a masculine reason but simply because there are things that a woman from her social perspective can perceive which may escape a man from his social perspective. The same is true of the other side. Both men and women share, however, the same reason, and if their arguments are valid and follow the principles of interpretation of the Qur'an, they can effectively convince each other on the grounds of this God-given reason.

Our goal as Muslims, then, is to make sure that we all properly understand the divine guidance lest it becomes a way to perdition. The incorrect understanding of the Qur'an that has influenced part of Islamic law must be redressed. Muslims who believe that they must live by Islamic law properly explained and justified in accordance with the principles of Islamic jurisprudence must see that all incorrect rulings be redressed, else they will be following other than the divine law. This call to review all unjustifiable practices in society and in the law should be maintained and pursued by a distinctly Muslim movement. It is not a "feminine" movement, for it concerns Islamic laws that belong to all Muslims equally. It is not a "feminist" movement either because its basis is Islam and not gender: the injunctions of the Qur'an still take precedence over anything and everything even if, to the Western feminist, they do not provide blind equality. This movement should, therefore, concern itself solely with the issues of *Muslims* under Islamic law although, of course, we wish that all societies would undertake the same questioning within their own systems of beliefs. This movement should have the participation of every Muslim in applying the correct Islamic laws in their daily lives and in seeking the correct understanding of the Qur'an and the weeding out from the law of unIslamic practices and rulings. It should try to change the reified social consciousness of Muslims, burdened by years of social customs and traditions, for, clearly, it is not the law by itself that can bring about a change. Islamic law provided women with numerous rights that were simply ignored in society. Education—and instilling the lesson of moral responsibility in people—is what brings about a change in practice.

If we insist on the necessity of reviewing these issues and changing Muslim practice, it is because of the absolute claim in the Qur'an that we will face our Maker one day and we will be called to account on whether we followed His will or the misunderstandings (however well-meaning) of an earlier age. It is a moral responsibility for both Muslim men and women who will be called to account equally on the Day of Judgment. And we do know that, although they were not given "superior" intelligence or piety, our men have—in addition to undeniable charm—reason, integrity, and faith. And it is with that reason, in the name of that integrity, and for the sake of that faith that we must make sure that all members of our society are never denied the rights granted to them by God.[4]

4. The author thanks Laila Latib for all her help and suggestions.

5

Her Honor

An Islamic Critique of the Rape Laws of Pakistan from a Woman-Sensitive Perspective

ASIFA QURAISHI

❧ I remember as a child having to describe Pakistan as that small country next to India. I have not used that description in a long time. By now, Americans have heard of Pakistan, and the reference is no longer exotic. Instead, the name conjures up confused images of women and non-Muslims in a third world country struggling to battle Islamic fundamentalism. Recent reports of the unjust application of Pakistan's rape laws, enacted as part of the "Islamization" of Pakistani law, further cement the impression that Islam is bad for women. The reports, unfortunately, are true. The impression is not.

In this chapter I critique the rape laws of Pakistan from an Islamic point of view, which is careful to include women's perspectives in the analysis. Unlike much of what is popularly presented as traditional Islamic law, this woman-affirming Islamic approach reveals the inherent gender-egalitarian nature of Islam, which is too often ignored by its academics, courts, and legislatures. I demonstrate here how cultural patriarchy has

This chapter first appeared as an article in the *Michigan Journal of International Law* (1997, 18: 287). In this effort I am indebted to many people for their assistance, guidance, and support. I humbly thank Laila al-Marayati, Azizah al-Hibri, Mohammad Fadel, Yaser Haddara, Hassan Hathout, Justice Javed Iqbal, Mohja Kahf, Fathi Osman, Akmal Salimi, my unique family, and my dear husband.

instead colored the application of certain Islamic laws in places such as Pakistan, resulting in the very injustice that the Qur'an so forcefully condemns.

Critique of the *Zina* Ordinance

Power of Law: The *Zina* Ordinance
and Its Application in Pakistan

In 1977, under President Zia-ul-Haq, Pakistan enacted a set of *Hudud*[1] Ordinances, ostensibly to bring the laws of Pakistan into "conformity with the injunctions of Islam" (PLD 1979, 51; Bokhary 1979, 162; Major Acts 1992, 10). These ordinances, setting forth crimes such as theft, adultery, slander, and alcohol consumption, became effective in February 1979 (PLD 1979, 51; Bokhary 1979, 164; Major Acts 1992, 10). The "Offence of *Zina* (Enforcement of *Hudud*) Ordinance, VII of 1979" (*Zina* Ordinance) criminalizes *zina*, or extramarital sexual relations (also a crime under Islamic law).[2] The *Zina* Ordinance states:

> A man and a woman are said to commit *zina* if they wilfully have sexual intercourse without being validly married to each other. *Zina* is liable to *hadd* [punishment] if
>
> (a) it is committed by a man who is an adult and is not insane with a woman to whom he is not, and does not suspect himself to be married; or
>
> (b) it is committed by a woman who is an adult and is not insane with a man to whom she is not, and does not suspect herself to be married. (PLD 1979, 52; Bokhary 1979, 176; Major Acts 1992, 11)

Under its heading of *zina*, the *Zina* Ordinance includes the category *zina-bil-jabr* (*zina* by force), which lays out the definition and punishment for sex-

---

1. The word *hudud* (pronounced and sometimes transliterated *hudood*) is the plural of *hadd*, a term denoting the Islamic legal categorization of crimes for which the definition and punishment is set by God (Doi 1984, 221).

2. In this chapter I do not address the rationale or propriety of criminalizing consensual sexual relations whether under Islamic law or under the many other penal codes of the world that criminalize such behavior. Rather, the focus of the present study is the law of *nonconsensual* sexual relations laid out in the *Zina* Ordinance in Pakistan and as addressed in Islamic jurisprudence.

ual intercourse against the will or without the consent of one of the parties. The section articulating the crime of rape, as *zina-bil-jabr,* states:

> A person is said to commit *zina-bil-jabr* if he or she has sexual intercourse with a woman or man, as the case may be, to whom he or she is not validly married, in any of the following circumstances, namely:
>
> (a) against the will of the victim,
>
> (b) without the consent of the victim,
>
> (c) with the consent of the victim, when the consent has been obtained by putting the victim in fear of death or of hurt, or
>
> (d) with the consent of the victim, when the offender knows that the offender is not validly married to the victim and that the consent is given because the victim believes that the offender is another person to whom the victim is or believes herself or himself to be validly married.
>
> *Explanation.*—Penetration is sufficient to constitute the sexual intercourse necessary to the offence of *zina-bil-jabr.*
>
> *Zina-bil-jabr* is *zina-bil-jabr* liable to *hadd* if it is committed in the circumstances specified [above]. (PLD 1979, 52; Bokhary 1979, 182; Major Acts 1992, 11–12)

Finally, the *Zina* Ordinance then specifies the evidence required to prove both *zina* and *zina-bil-jabr:*

> Proof of *zina* or *zina-bil-jabr* liable to *hadd* shall be in one of the following forms, namely:
>
> (a) the accused makes before a Court of competent jurisdiction a confession of the commission of the offence; or
>
> (b) at least four Muslim adult male witnesses, about whom the Court is satisfied, having regard to the requirements of *tazkiyah al-shuhud* [credibility of witnesses], that they are truthful persons and abstain from major sins (*kaba'ir*), give evidence as eyewitnesses of the act of penetration necessary to the offence. (PLD 1979, 53; Bokhary 1979, 182; Major Acts 1992, 12)[3]

3. I have not included the punishments specified for each crime as that is not within the focus of this chapter. Here, I am primarily concerned with the definition and categorization of each of these offenses. Briefly, however, the *hadd* punishment prescribed in the ordinance for a *zina* offense is either public stoning or whipping. For a *zina-bil-jabr* conviction, it

When this law was enacted in 1977, proponents argued that it enacted the Islamic law of illegal sexual relations. The accuracy of that claim is addressed in detail later.[4] First, it is important to first note that the application of the *Zina* Ordinance in Pakistan has placed a new twist and a renewed urgency on the question of its validity. The twist is this: when a *zina-bil-jabr* case fails for lack of four witnesses, the Pakistani legal system has more than once concluded that the intercourse was therefore consensual and, consequently, has charged rape victims with *zina*.

A few cases will disturbingly illustrate the concern. In 1982, fifteen-year-old Jehan Mina became pregnant as a result of a reported rape. Lacking the testimony of four eyewitnesses that the intercourse was in fact rape, Jehan was convicted of *zina* on the evidence of her illegitimate pregnancy (*Mina vs. State*, 1983 PLD Fed. Shariat Ct. 183). Her child was born in prison (Mehdi 1990, 25). Later, a similar case caused public outcry and drew public attention to the new law. In 1985, Safia Bibi, a sixteen-year-old, nearly blind domestic servant reported that she was repeatedly raped by her landlord/employer and his son and became pregnant as a result. When she charged the men with rape, the case was dismissed for lack of evidence because she was the only witness against them. Safia, however, being unmarried and pregnant, was charged with *zina* and convicted on this evidence (*Bibi vs. State*, 1985 PLD Fed. Shariat Ct. 120).[5]

Short of conviction, women have also been held for extended lengths of time on charges of *zina* when they allege rape (Asia Watch 1992, 41–60). For example, in July 1992, Shamim, a twenty-one-year-old mother of two charged that she was kidnaped and raped by three men in Karachi. When a rape complaint was lodged against the perpetrators, the police instead arrested Shamim, and charged her with *zina* when her family could not post the fee set for her release. The police held her in custody for six days, during which she reports that she was repeatedly raped by two police officers and a third unnamed person (Amnesty International

---

prescribes imprisonment and/or fine and/or public whipping (PLD 1979, 51 [*Zina* Ordinance] 6). See n. 25, below, for citations to discussions of punishments for *zina* in Islamic law.

4. See, below, pts. 1, B, pt. 2.

5. She was sentenced to fifteen lashes, three years imprisonment, and a fine. Public outrage eventually led the appellate court to set aside the punishment (Patel 1991, 25–26); Jalal 1991, 102; Mehdi 1990, 24–26; Khan 1986, 27).

1993, 11-12). There have been numerous reports of such custodial rapes in Pakistan.[6]

Police action and inaction in rape cases in Pakistan have, in fact, been widely reported as an instrumental element to the injustice. There is evidence that police have deliberately failed to file charges against men accused of rape, often using the threat of converting the rape charge into a *zina* prosecution against the female complainant to discourage women from reporting.[7] And when the perpetrator is a police officer himself, the chances of pursuing a case against him are nearly nonexistent. Shahida Parveen faced this very situation when she reported that in July 1994 two police officers broke into her house and locked her children in a room while they raped her at gunpoint. A medical examination confirmed that she was raped by more than one person, but the police refused to register her complaint (Amnesty International 1995, 14).

Political rivals have further exploited women by using rape as a weapon against each other. In November, 1992, Khursheed Begum, the wife of an arrested member of the Pakistan People's Party was abducted on her way home from attending her husband's court hearing. She states that she was blindfolded, driven to a police station, and repeatedly raped there by police officers, who asserted political motives for the attack (Amnesty International 1992, 207; Scroggins 1992, A10; Rashid 1991, 14). Later the same month, forty-year-old Veena Hyat, of one of Pakistan's elite families and the daughter of a prominent politician, stated that she was gang raped for twelve hours in every room of her house by five armed men. Despite her father taking the unusual social risk of publicly reporting the attack, a judicial investigation concluded that there was insufficient evidence to

6. See Asia Watch 1992, 41–60; Patel 1991, 36; Mehdi, 1990, 27, citing a report by attorney Asma Jahangir of fifteen incidents of police rape of women in detention in 1988–89; Seminar 1982, 286–87, convenor Tahir Mahmoud noting cases of rape . . . in private (including those committed by policemen) are alarmingly on an increase in the [Indo-Pakistani] subcontinent.

7. Amnesty International 1995b, 35, reporting the Jan. 17, 1994, gang rape of five women, stating that police pressured women to report only robbery and to conceal rape; Amnesty International 1993, 11–12, citing the Shamim case, and the similar Imamat Khatoon case. In 1992 more than two thousand women were in jail awaiting trial for *zina* (Asia Watch 1992, 69). Many women are eventually acquitted after enduring long trials (Patel 1991, 28).

convict the alleged perpetrators (Zia 1994, 55–57; Economist 1991, 43; Rashid 1991, 14; Robinson 1992, 11).

Cases such as these resulting from the unfortunate application of the *Zina* Ordinance are widely reported in the Western media.[8] The issue is now a primary topic in women's and human rights discussions globally[9] and stirs up an expected share of frustration, anger, defensiveness, and arrogance from all sides. The debate, however, begs the question: What *is* the Islamic law of rape? Any real substantive analysis of the *zina-bil-jabr* law and its application must first approach it from this framework, the same framework upon which the law purports to base itself. I, therefore, ask the critical question: *Does* Pakistan's *Zina* Ordinance accurately articulate the Islamic law of rape?

Law of God: The Qur'an on *Zina*

The Pakistani *Zina* Ordinance subsumes rape—as *zina-bil-jabr*—under the general *zina* law of unlawful sexual relations. To analyze the appropriateness of this categorization, one must first analyze the Islamic law of *zina* itself. The preamble of the Pakistani *Zina* Ordinance states that it is enacted "to modify the existing law relating to *zina* so as to bring it in conformity with the Injunctions of the Holy Qur'an and *Sunnah*" (Major Acts 1992, 10).[10] Indeed, the term *zina* itself appears in the Qur'an. In warning generally against the dangers of adultery, the Qur'an states:

> And do not go near fornication [*zina*] as it is immoral and an evil way. (*Qur'an* 17:32).[11]

8. See Branion 1992, 276; Curtius 1994, 2; Fineman 1988, pt. 1, 5; Heise 1991, C1; Khan 1985, 791; Khan 1986, 27; O. J. Simpson, *Business Wire* 1995; Rashid 1991, 14; Robinson 1992, 11; Scroggins 1992, A10; Whitehorn 1994, 23.

9. See, for example, United States Department of State 1994, 1370, 1382; Amnesty International 1994, 232–33; Amnesty International 1995c; Asia Watch 1992, 53–60; Amnesty International 1992, 207–8; Patel 1991, 15, 19, 26–28, citing activities of the All Pakistan Women's Association, Pakistan Women Lawyers' Association, Pakistan Women's Rights Committee; Amnesty International 1995b, 14, 35; Amnesty International 1993, 10–13; Jalal 1991, 103–9, describing activities of the Women's Action Forum in Karachi; Hodson 1994, 16, quoting Prime Minister Bhutto urging a change of the *zina* laws; Iqbal 1995; Jabbar 1991, 7–8; Sarwar 1995.

10. *Sunnah* is a term used to describe the traditions of Muhammad (Kamali 1991, 44).

11. Another verse generally urging against fornication states: "Devotees of Ar-Rahman

Later, the Qur'an more specifically sets out actual legal prescriptions criminalizing illegal sexual relations:

> The adulteress and adulterer should be flogged a hundred lashes each, and no pity for them should deter you from the law of God, if you believe in God and the last day; and the punishment should be witnessed by a body of believers. (Qur'an 24:2);

Following this definition of the offense are extremely strict evidentiary rules for the proof of such a crime:

> Those who defame chaste women and do not bring four witnesses should be punished with eighty lashes, and their testimony should not be accepted afterwards, for they are profligates. (Qur'an at 24:4)[12]

Thus, after criminalizing extramarital sexual relations,[13] the Qur'an simultaneously attaches to the prosecution of this crime nearly insurmountable

---

[The Merciful] are those . . . who do not invoke any god apart from God; who do not take a life, which God has forbidden except for a cause that is just, and do not fornicate [*zina*] and any one who does so will be punished for the crime" (Qur'an 25:63, 68). Note that all English renditions of the Qur'anic verses cited in this chapter come from the Ahmed Ali translation, published as *Al-Qur'an* (Ali 1984).

12. The verse goes on to specify a relaxed evidentiary standard between spouses, understandable given the personal nature such an accusation would have on the marital relationship: "Those who accuse their wives and do not have any witnesses except themselves, should swear four times in the name of God, the testimony of each such person being that he is speaking the truth. And (swear) a fifth time that if he tell a lie, the curse of God be on him. The woman's punishment can be averted if she swears four times by God as testimony that her husband is a liar. Her fifth oath being that the curse of God be on her if her husband should be speaking the truth" (Qur'an 24:6–9). For further discussion of this spousal *zina* situation, see Doi 1989, 126–28; Kamali 1991, 156; al-Shafi'i 1987, 146–47. Here, there is no discrepancy in weight of testimony based on the gender of the party because in a charge of adultery between spouses, a woman's word is equal to that of a man.

13. As noted earlier, in this chapter I do not address the punishments prescribed for the crime of *zina.* See pt. 1, A. Interestingly, the answer is not as concrete as these verses might imply. Traditions of the Prophet Muhammad involving the stoning of adulterers have created much debate among Islamic jurists regarding the role of the death penalty and corporal punishment in *zina* sentencing. See, for example, Amin 1985, 27–28, citing 1981 Pakistan *shari'ah* (Islamic law) Court ruling that stoning for adultery is not correct Islamic practice; Bokhary 1979, 181, citing legal debate in Pakistan over the propriety of stoning as punish-

evidentiary restrictions: four eyewitnesses are required to prove a charge of sexual misconduct.[14]

Islamic jurisprudence further interprets the Qur'anic *zina* evidentiary rule of quadruple testimony to require the actual witnessing of penetration during sexual intercourse, and nothing less.[15] This interpretation is based on the reported *hadith* (tradition) of Muhammad in which, after a man persisted in confessing to adultery (the Prophet having turned away to avoid hearing the information several times prior), Muhammad asked several specific questions to confirm that the act was indeed sexual penetration (al-Bukhari 1985, 8:528–35 [bk. 82, nos. 806, 810, 812–14]; Abu Daud 1990, 3: nos. 4413–14).[16] Moreover, Islamic evidence law requires the witnesses to be mature, sane, and of upright character (Salama 1982, 109; El-Awa 1982, 126–27; Siddiqi 1985, 43–49). Furthermore, if any eyewitness testimony was obtained by violating a defendant's privacy, it is inadmissible.[17] And lastly, the *Hedaya*, a key reference of Hanafi jurisprudence[18]

---

ment for adultery. The focus of this study, however, is limited to the definition of the crime itself and the categorization of rape as *zina*. The topic of what punishment the state should inflict upon those convicted of such a crime must wait for another day.

14. See Doi 1984, 236–40, summarizing the crime of *zina*; Doi 1989, 117–28, summarizing the crime of *zina*; El-Awa 1982, 13–15, a general discussion of *zina* law as laid down in Qur'anic verses. The proof of *zina* section of the *Zina* Ordinance, which also requires four witnesses, comes to mind. Thus, in setting *zina* as a crime in Pakistani law and requiring four witnesses as necessary proof of such a crime, the ordinance does, in fact, appear to be based, at least in structure, on Islamic law. As discussed in the following sections, however, the details of the *Zina* Ordinance and especially its subcategorization of rape as a type of *zina* is *not* Islamic law.

15. Coulson 1994, 127; Doi 1989, 122; Siddiqi 1985, 69; Bassiouni 1982, 5, citing the rule of thumb that a hypothetical thread must not have been able to pass through the two bodies; Seminar 1982, 271.

16. It is interesting to note that although the man was punished based on his confession, the woman was apparently never prosecuted or even investigated. The significance of this point will be apparent later in the discussion of the context of the Qur'anic verses on *zina* and their impact on women's privacy (pt. 1, B).

17. Al-Saleh 1982, 69–70, citing an incident where Caliph 'Umar ibn al Khattab and a companion passed a party in which, behind locked doors, individuals were drinking alcohol; because of Islamic injunctions against spying, the two disregarded the private party and returned home; Siddiqi 1985, 19–19–20, citing the requirement to knock before entering a residence, even of family. But see Hedaya 1982, 194 (bk. 7, chap. 3, allowing evidence unlawfully obtained).

18. See n. 53, below, for an explanation of the Islamic schools of law.

prominent codification of Muslim law in India,[19] even sets a statute of limitations for charging *zina*.[20]

Why are so many evidentiary restrictions prescribed by God for a criminal offense? Islamic scholars posit that it is precisely to *prevent* carrying out punishment for this offense. By limiting conviction to only those cases where four individuals actually saw sexual penetration take place, the crime will realistically only be punishable if the two parties are committing the act in public, in the nude. The crime is, therefore, really one of public indecency rather than private sexual conduct.[21] That is, even if four witnesses saw a couple having sex, but under a coverlet, for example, this testimony would not only fail to support a *zina* charge, but these witnesses would also be liable for slander.[22] Thus, while the Qur'an condemns extramarital sex as an evil, it authorizes the Muslim legal system to prosecute someone for committing this crime *only* when it is performed so openly that four people see them without invading their privacy. As Cherif Bassiouni puts it, "The requirement of proof and its exigencies lead to the conclusion that the policy of the harsh penalty is to deter public aspects of this form of sexual practice" (Bassiouni 1982, 6).[23]

This analysis is consistent with the tone of the Qur'anic verses that immediately follow the above verses regarding *zina*. After the verses establishing the crime and the attendant standard of proof, the Qur'an states:

19. See Mahmassani 1987, 23, 49, for the history and significance of the Hedaya.

20. This statute of limitations, significantly, does not apply to a charge of slander (Hedaya 1982, 188 [bk. 7]). In addition to the above restrictions, where a *zina* conviction is a result of confession rather than testimony, the confession may be retracted at any time (including during execution of the sentence) (Salama 1982, 120).

21. Salama 1982, 118, "the nature of such rigorous proof makes it a crime of public indecency rather than adultery."

22. Qur'an 24:4, stating that those who charge women with *zina* and do not have four witnesses should be given eighty lashes and their testimony should not be accepted thereafter. See, also, al-Tabari 1989, 13:110–14, describing an incident where Caliph 'Umar punished witnesses supporting a *zina* charge against al-Mughirah b. Shu'bah, governor of Basra, because of conflicting details in their testimony about an eye-witnessed act.

23. See, also, El-Awa 1982, 17, "The desire to protect public morality and to safeguard it against corruption by publicizing the offense is the reason for limiting the methods of proof"; and 29, "This punishment is prescribed in fact for those who committed the crime openly . . . with no consideration for the law or for the feeling of the community" (quoting Shalabi 1960, 201).

Those who spread lies were a clique among you. Do not think it was bad for you: In fact it has been good for you. Each of them will pay for the sin he has committed, and he who had greater share (of guilt) will suffer grievous punishment.

Why did the faithful men and women not think well of their people when they heard this, and [say] "This is a clear lie?"

Why did they not bring four witnesses (in support of their charge)? And since they did not bring the four witnesses, they are themselves liars in the sight of God. Were it not for the grace of God and His mercy upon you in this world and the next, you would have suffered a great affliction for the false accusation.

When you talked about it and said what you did not know, and took it lightly—though in the sight of God it was serious—Why did you not say when you heard it: "It is not for us to speak of it? God preserve us, it is a great calumny!" God counsels you not to do a thing like this, if you are believers. (*Qur'an* 24:11–17).

The Qur'an's call to respond to charges of sexual misconduct with "it is not for us to speak of it" echoes the *hadith* in which Muhammad was reluctant to take even a man's confession of adultery.[24] The Qur'an contemplates a society in which one does not engage in publicizing others' sexual indiscretions. Qur'anic principles honor privacy and dignity over the violation of law except when a violation becomes a matter of public obscenity.

Placing these Qur'anic verses into context will further emphasize the importance of this concept in Islamic law and, in particular, its close connection to the dignity of women. The verses setting forth the crime of *zina* and the accompanying verses denouncing public discussion of the matter were revealed just after the famous "Affair of the Necklace" in which Muhammad's wife, ʿAʾisha, was mistakenly left behind by a caravan in the desert when she went looking for a lost necklace (al-Tabari 1910, 18:86–101; al-ʿUmari 1991, 2:82–84).[25] She returned home with a young single man who had happened upon her and had given her a ride home. Rumors of

24. See the text accompanying n. 16, above.

25. This is a primarily Sunni account of the context of these verses. Many Shiʿi scholars do not attribute these verses to the "Affair of the Necklace" incident. Spellberg 1994, 81–82, citing Shiʿi author al-Qummi, but also noting Shiʿi author al-Tabarsi, who took the Sunni position.

'A'isha's time alone with this man spread quickly throughout the small town of Medina until the above verses finally ended the gossip. Thus, the very revelation of these verses was prompted by an incident involving attacks on a woman's dignity, 'A'isha's honor. Indeed, the verse setting forth severe punishment for slander is directed specifically against charges impugning a *woman's* chastity: "Those who defame chaste *women*, and do not bring four witnesses, should be punished with eighty lashes, and their testimony should not be accepted afterward" (Qur'an 24:4; emphasis added). Men do not seem to be of particular concern here.

Why is the focus on women? Looking at the issue from a cultural perspective, this focus is not surprising. In nearly every culture of the world, women's sexual morality appears to be a particularly favorite subject for slander, gossip, and insult.[26] The tendency of patriarchal societies, in fact, is to view a woman's chastity as central to the honor of her family, especially of the men in her family. For example, under the British common law (the law in Pakistan before the *Hudud* Ordinance), rape was a crime punishable against men, to be lodged by the husband of the woman raped against the man who violated her (Hale 1778, 637–39).[27] The woman's place was apparently on the sidelines of a prosecution by her husband against her rapist.

This cultural phenomenon—that a family's honor lies in the virtue of its women—exists in many countries today; Pakistan is one of them. Studies indicate that in Pakistan, when women are jailed for long periods of time on charges of *zina*, their families and friends are reluctant to help or even visit them "as accusation of *zina* is a serious dishonor" (Patel 1991,

26. See, for example, Spender (1980) discussing the asymmetry of language and insults that tend to be based on women's sexuality.

27. See, also, Mehdi 1994, 116, sec. 3.3.1, stating that before the *Hudud* Ordinances, the penal law of Pakistan included adultery as an offense but defined it as intercourse by a man with the wife of another without his permission; women were not punished even as abettors; Zia 1994, 25–26, stating that under the pre-*Hudud* criminal legal system inherited from the British, a complaint of adultery could only be lodged by the husband; Dripps 1992, 1782, "Until the twentieth century, . . . female sexual autonomy had little to do with the law of rape. The law instead struck a balance between the interests of males-in-possession and their predatory counterparts." The Pakistani Penal Code before 1979 borrowed from this English common law of rape (Pakistan Penal Code 1860, ' 375), legislating and elaborating on rape defined as "the ravishment of a woman without her consent, by force, fear, or fraud," citing English common law precedent.

27). Even more disturbing, suicide is perceived as the honorable solution to the humiliation, especially if sexual violation is involved. For example, when Khursheed Begum was raped in 1992,[28] her husband and son "wish[ed] she had committed suicide" even after human rights activists explained to them that the rape was not her fault (Scroggins 1992, A10). This attitude lends itself easily to manipulation and the development of a tribal attitude wherein women's bodies become tools for revenge by men against men. Indeed, increasingly in Pakistan, "[i]n cases of revenge against the male members of [a] family, instances have come to light where their women are violated" (Patel 1991, 36).[29] Even within a family, physically harming (even killing) women for alleged infidelity or some other embarrassment to the family—often by some sort of burning—is an unfortunate tradition in the Indo-Pakistani subcontinent.[30] And, as world human rights organizations have documented, "honor killings" of women suspected of sexual indiscretion, carried out by a male family member, are, unfortunately, not limited to this part of the world.[31]

The Qur'an, however, has harsh words for the exploitation of women's dignity in this way. As if anticipating the misogynistic tendency of society, the Qur'an first establishes that there is to be no speculation about a woman's sexual conduct. No one may cast any doubt upon the character of a woman except by formal charges with very specific, secure evidence (four eyewitnesses to actual intercourse) that the woman is disrupting *public* decency with her behavior.[32] If such direct proof does not materialize, then anyone engaging in such a charge is subject to physical punishment

28. See pt. 1, A, above.

29. See also Zia 1994, 30, "The motivation of feudal enmity, revenge for honour via the sexuality of the woman, collusion of male authorities in attributing all blame on the woman, and State sanctioning of control over women even in the extreme form of murder, are all feeding impulses in most sex crimes [in Pakistan]." Haeri 1995, 161, arguing that "political rape" is a modern version of "'feudal' 'honor rape.'"; Sarwar 1995, "Women are also considered property, and the repositories of male honor. If a man wants revenge from someone, the surest way is to strike at him through his 'honor'—his wife or daughter."

30. Amnesty International 1995c, 3, reporting burnings; Sarwar, 1995, "In addition, Pakistani society tacitly condones 'honor killings'—the murder of a female relative on suspicion of 'illicit relations.'"

31. See, for example, Amnesty International 1995a, 92, discussing honor killings in Egypt and Iraq.

32. See pt. 1, B, above.

for slander. (For even if the information is true, any witness who is not accompanied by another three will be punished for slander [Qur'an 24:11–17]. As for the public at large, they must leave her alone, regardless of the outcome. Where the public refuses to perpetuate rumors, responding instead that "it is not for us to speak of" (Qur'an 24: 16–17), the patriarchal tendency to invest the honor of society in women's sexuality loses force. In the face of any hint of a woman's sexual impropriety, the Qur'anic response is, walk away. Leave her alone. Leave her dignity intact. The honor of a woman is not a tool; it is her fundamental right.

Pregnancy as Proof of Zina? Given the Qur'an's strict standard of proof for a *zina* case, one might now wonder whether the conviction of women such as Jehan Mina and Safia Bibi for *zina* on the evidence of their pregnancy alone[33] could be justified by Islamic law. In traditional Islamic jurisprudence the majority opinion[34] is that pregnancy is *not* sufficient evidence alone to prove *zina* because the Qur'an specifies nothing less than four eyewitnesses, and a fundamental principle of Islamic criminal procedure is that the benefit of the doubt lies with the accused.[35] Other Muslim scholars, however, have held that pregnancy does amount to proof of illegal sexual relations where the woman is unmarried and has not claimed rape. Imam Malik and, reportedly, Ahmad ibn Hanbal, for example, considered unmarried pregnancy prima facie evidence of *zina*.[36] This opinion is based

33. See pt. 1, A, above.

34. Islamic jurisprudence was developed by jurists whose approaches to and interpretations of the Qur'an and *Sunnah* became various schools of Islamic law (Mahmassani 1987, 15–17). Today, five schools are commonly discussed: the four *Sunni* schools (Hanafi, Maliki, Shafi'i, and Hanbali) and the *Shi'i* school (Ja'fari). For more information and background see Mahmassani 1987, 15–39.

35. See al-Maqdisi 1994, 8:129, 145, stating Hanafi and Shafi'i schools of thought hold that pregnancy alone does not constitute sufficient evidence for punishment of *zina* but noting that the Maliki school of thought presumes punishment unless there are signs of coercion; Siddiqi 1985, 71, but citing 'Umar's reported position that pregnancy furnishes sufficient proof of *zina* against unmarried woman; Seminar 1982, 271, stating that majority of jurists hold that pregnancy is not *prima facie* evidence of *zina*.

36. See Malik 1982, 392 sec. 41.4, stating that an unmarried pregnant woman who claims that she was forced to have sex is liable for punishment unless she can prove her claim; Salama 1982, 121. See, also, Coulson 1994, 174–75, stating Malikis held pregnancy is prima facie evidence of *zina*; El-Awa 1982, 130–31, "[T]he offence of *zina* may be proved

in large part upon the reported positions of the three famous caliphs, 'Umar ibn al-Khattab, Uthman ibn 'Affan, and 'Ali ibn Abi Talib, that "[a]dultery is public when pregnancy appears or confession is made" (Salama 1982, 121).[37] The difference of opinion is also the result of differing interpretations of the role of circumstantial evidence in *hudud* cases.[38]

The rationale that "adultery is public with pregnancy" is clearly problematic. Although the rationale does incorporate the concept that the real criminality in *zina* is the public display of adultery, it fails to contemplate the potential discrimination against and harming of women. As a practical evidentiary matter, this perspective does not take into account modern medical advances such as artificial insemination, which might be alternative explanations for the pregnancy, not to mention pure force. More substantively, though, it unfairly shifts the burden of proof against women. Forced to prove that the intercourse was nonconsensual to avoid a *zina* prosecution, a woman is automatically put in the position of defending her honor against accusations that do not meet the Qur'anic four-witness requirement. This unfairness is not supported by the spirit of the Qur'anic verses, which discourage presumptions about a woman's sexual activity by insisting that no presumptions be made about women's sexual activity without four witnesses to the actual act.[39] The shift in burden of proof is even more patently unfair when the pregnant woman is a victim of rape. In that instance, an unmarried pregnant woman must overcome the burden of a prima facie case against her simply because the attack has resulted in pregnancy.

Moreover, the Qur'anic insistence on four witnesses, as noted earlier, establishes that the *act* of intercourse must be public, not its consequences.[40] It is public sex that is deterred, not public pregnancy. A pregnant woman

---

against an unmarried woman if she is pregnant," citing Maliki jurists who considered circumstantial evidence important and admissible as proof.

37. See, also, Abu Daud 1990, 3:no. 4404, quoting 'Umar ibn Khattab's statement that fornication exists "when proof is established or if there is pregnancy, or a confession"; al-Bukhari 1985, 8:536–37, bk. 82, no. 816.

38. Salama 1982, 120–21, summarizing the role of *qara'in* (presumptions, or circumstantial evidence) in *hadd* jurisprudence.

39. See pt. 1, B, above.

40. Ibid.

looks the same in public whether the pregnancy occurred from rape, *zina,* or legal marital intercourse, and in modern societies of large populations, it is generally not obvious which of these three applies to a pregnant woman on the street. Nor, indeed, should the public (or courts) speculate about it without solid eyewitness proof of the actual act of penetration, according to Islamic law. Furthermore, pregnancy is something that only applies to women. If pregnancy alone constitutes sufficient evidence of *zina,* the result seems to forget that the very purpose of the *zina* verses is to protect women's honor. Women, again, tend to be more susceptible to accusation, and the Qur'an addresses this susceptibility directly by enjoining any charges against women without solid proof.[41] If pregnancy is allowed as sufficient proof of *zina,* a pregnant adulteress will be convicted without any testimonial proof while her adulterous partner escapes punishment with *his* reputation intact. The woman-affirming spirit of the *zina* verses is lost.

Drafting Problems in the Zina Ordinance

The Same Brush: Why Rape as a Form of Zina? As noted, the Qur'anic verses regarding *zina* do not address the concept of *non*consensual sex. This omission is a logical one. The *zina* verses establish a crime of public sexual indecency. Rape, by contrast, is a very different crime. Rape is a reprehensible act that society has an interest in preventing, whether or not it is committed in public. Therefore, rape does not logically belong as a subset of the public indecency crime of *zina.* Unfortunately, however, the *Zina* Ordinance is written exactly counter to this Qur'anic omission and it includes *zina-bil-jabr* (*zina* by force) as a subcategory of the crime of *zina.*[42]

Where did the *zina-bil-jabr* section in the ordinance come from then, if it is not part of the Qur'anic law of *zina*? In Islamic jurisprudence addressing *zina,* there is significant discussion of whether there is liability for *zina* under duress.[43] But the language of the *zina-bil-jabr* section in the Pakistani Ordinance does not appear to be drawn from these discussions. (That is, it is not presented as an exception to *zina* in the case of duress.) Rather, the

41. Ibid.
42. See pt. 1, A, above.
43. See pt. 2, A, below.

zina-bil-jabr language is nearly identical to the old common law of rape in Pakistan, the borrowed British criminal law in force in Pakistan before the *Hudud* Ordinances. The old common law Pakistani rape statute read:

> A man is said to commit "rape" who, except in the cases hereinafter excepted, has sexual intercourse with a woman under circumstances falling under any of the following descriptions:
>
> *Firstly.* Against her will.
>
> *Secondly.* Without her consent.
>
> *Thirdly.* With her consent, when her consent has been obtained by putting her in fear of death, or of hurt.
>
> *Fourthly.* With her consent when the man knows that he is not her husband, and that her consent is given because she believes that he is another man to whom she is or believes herself to be lawfully married.
>
> *Fifthly.* With or without her consent, when she is under [fourteen] years of age.
>
> *Explanation.* Penetration is sufficient to constitute the sexual intercourse necessary to the offence of rape.
>
> *Exception.* Sexual intercourse by a man with his own wife, the wife not being under [thirteen] years of age is not rape (Pakistan Penal Code 1860, sec. 375).[44]

With the exception of the statutory rape section (under "Fifthly"), the language specifying what constitutes rape is almost identical to the *zina-bil-jabr* language under the *Hudud* Ordinance. Even the explanation that penetration is sufficient to constitute the intercourse necessary is the same. Did the Pakistani legislators, in writing the *zina-bil-jabr* law, simply relabel the old secular law of rape under the Muslim heading of *zina* (as *zina* by force,

---

44. For comparison, the *zina-bil-jabr* section reads: "A person is said to commit *zina-bil-jabr* if he or she has sexual intercourse with a woman or man, as the case may be, to whom he or she is not validly married, in any of the following circumstances, namely: (a) against the will of the victim, (b) without the consent of the victim, (c) with the consent of the victim, when the consent has been obtained by putting the victim in fear of death or of hurt, or (d) with the consent of the victim, when the offender knows that the offender is not validly married to the victim and that the consent is given because the victim believes that the offender is another person to whom the victim is or believes herself or himself to be validly married." *Explanation.* Penetration is sufficient to constitute the sexual intercourse necessary for the offence of *zina-bil-jabr*. Bokhary 1979, 182 (with comment and annotation); Major Acts 1992, 11–12.

or *jabr*) and reenact it as part of the *Hudud* Islamization of Pakistan's laws-right along with the four-witness evidentiary rule unique to *zina*? If so, this cut-and-paste job, albeit, a well-intentioned effort to retain rape as a crime in Pakistan's new *Hudud* criminal code, reveals a limited view of Islamic criminal law, which, as illustrated, ultimately harms women.

Sexuality and Suspicion. Rape law in the United States has long reflected cultural patriarchal assumptions about female sexuality and consent. A frequent casualty in rape trials is the rape victim's reputation as the court attempts to sort out the issue of consent (Dripps 1992, 1782). This problem is exacerbated in Pakistan because the convoluted placement of rape as part of the *Zina* Ordinance encourages the use of a woman's unsuccessful claim of rape as some sort of default evidence of *zina*. Thus, there is a strong tendency to suspect any charge of rape to be a "loose woman's" attempt to escape punishment for *zina*. Female sexual stereotypes danger-ously fuel these cases. For example, on appeal of one rape conviction, the Pakistani Federal Shariat Court stated:

> [W]herever resort to courts is unavoidable for any reason, a general pos-sibility that even though the girl was a willing party to the occurrence, it would hardly be admitted or conceded. In fact it is not uncommon that a woman, who was a willing party, acts as a ravished woman, if she is surprised when in amorous courtship, love-making or in the embrace of a man she has not repulsed.[45]

Such biased and derogatory observations against women by the Islamic court in Pakistan reveal a basic cultural male bias in the perception of women and female sexuality.

This bias also manifests itself in conclusions that a given sexual en-counter must have been consensual if there is no physical evidence of resistance by the woman (another issue familiar to rape law reformers in the West). Many Pakistani judgments of rape have been converted into *zina* cases because of the absence of evidence of such resistance (Jilani 1992, 72). This stereotypical concept of women supposes that if a woman does

---

45. Zia 1994, 29, quoting Federal Shari'at Court; Ahmad 1995, 8, citing a case of alleged rape of a fifteen-year-old girl wherein the defendant was acquitted and the court described the victim as a girl of "loose character" who "has a habitual case of enjoying sexual inter-course," reported at PLD 1982, Federal Shari'at Court 241 (Ahmad 1995).

not struggle against a sexual assault, then she must be a sexually loose woman, justifying a conversion of the charge to *zina*. This attitude unfairly generalizes human reaction to force and the threat of violence. And this generalization works to the detriment of women who have been subjected to a rapist's attack and survived only by submitting without physical resistance.

Ironically, this is exactly the type of speculation regarding women's sexual activity that the Qur'an explicitly condemns in the very verses establishing the crime of *zina*.[46] Judicial and societal speculation about women's sexual looseness clearly does not correspond with the Qur'anic admonition that "it is not for us to speak of." The intertwining of rape with *zina* in the Pakistani Ordinance, however, encourages such speculation. Rather than constituting a separate violent crime against women, rape—under the title *zina-bil-jabr*—is perceived more as a woman's expected defense to a *zina* charge and, thus, becomes subject to judicial speculation.[47]

Bearing Witness: Exclusively Male Testimony. I have reviewed the strict Qur'anic quadruple testimony standard of proof for *zina* cases and Islamic evidence law regarding the nature of the testimony requiring upright, sane witnesses and testimony obtained without violation of privacy.[48] The *Zina* Ordinance of Pakistan, however, adds a limitation on the admissibility of evidence that I have not yet addressed: the witnesses must all be men.[49] That is, the standard of proof in the *Zina* Ordinance for *zina* or *zina-bil-jabr* is either confession or testimony by "at least four Muslim adult male witnesses" (PLD 1979, 183; Bokhary 1979, 182; Major Acts 1992, 12).

The Qur'anic *zina* verse setting forth the original four-witness requirement, however, does not stipulate only men.[50] This verse refers to these four witnesses with the Arabic masculine plural, *shuhada* (witnesses), which

---

46. See pt. 1, B, above.

47. Jilani 1992, 71, "The offense of rape (*zina-bil-jabr*) is also dealt with by the same law [of *zina*]. The effect of this is that rape has become more of a defense against prosecution for adultery or fornication, rather than being considered as an independent crime."

48. See pt. 1, B, above.

49. Apparently, the exclusion of female evidence was challenged through a petition in the Federal Shari'at Court, but the male only witness requirement still exists in the ordinance (Mehdi 1994, 118).

50. Qur'an 24:4, "Those who defame chaste women and do not bring four witnesses [*shuhada*] should be punished."

grammatically includes both men and women, unless otherwise indicated.[51] The inclusion of the word *male* in the *Zina* Ordinance thus prompts the question, Was this interpretation taken from Islamic law, or is it a Pakistani cultural gloss on the rule?

Despite the Qur'anic use of the plural noun inclusive of both men and women, many Islamic jurists and scholars have traditionally limited the four witnesses in a *zina* case to men.[52] In fact, all major schools of thought have adopted restrictive interpretations of women's ability to testify as witnesses in general although some (significantly including the famous jurists, al-Tabari, Ibn Taymiyya, and Ibn al-Qayyim) have disagreed.[53] The rationales accompanying this rule are interesting, however. For example, the *Hedaya* states:

> Evidence is of several kinds, that of four men, as has been ordained in the Qur'an; and the testimony of a woman in such case is not admitted; because . . . "in the time of the Prophet and his two immediate successors it was an invariable rule to exclude the evidence of women in all cases inducing punishment or retaliation"; and also because the testimony of women involves a degree of doubt, as it is merely a substitute for evidence, being accepted only where the testimony of men cannot be had; and therefore it is not admitted in any matter liable to drop from the existence of doubt. (Hedaya 1982, 353–54 bk. 21, chap. 1)

Although the principle that reasonable doubt should negate convictions of violent crimes is a laudable one, the reasoning leading to it appears to stem from a condescending patriarchal view of women.[54] This attitude continues even in more modern texts on Islamic law:

51. Wadud-Muhsin 1992, chap. 1, discussing Qur'anic grammar and its emphasis on the duality of men and women.

52. Ajijola 1981, 134; El-Awa 1982, 17, 124–26, defining *zina* witnesses as four adult men.

53. Fadel 1997, discussing Islamic jurisprudence on women as witnesses, addressing sociological influences on the restrictions on women's testimony; noting alternative interpretations among jurists; Salama 1982, 118, "All jurists reject the testimony of women," but citing some scholars who accept testimony of women in *zina* cases if there are two women for each man; Coulson 1994, 127; El-Awa 1982, 17, 1124–26, defining *zina* witnesses as four adult men.

54. Traditional Muslim jurists have used similar biased reasoning to justify the requirement of two women witnesses for one man in general non-*zina* evidence law. These include: aiding male pride, because the losing party's resentment will be greater if losing to a woman,

In the case of [*zina*] the testimony of four male witnesses is required as a female is weak in character (Ajijola 1981, 134). The concern of Islamic law for complete truthfulness of evidence and certainty of proof is abundantly clear from its rules of evidence. Avoiding conviction only on a single witness testimony and reluctance to act upon the evidence of women only are indications of the fool-proof system of guilt-determination prescribed by the Qur'an and *Sunnah* (Menon 1981, 237). It is to be observed that the evidence of women against men is not admissible in wine drinking [prosecutions] because the evidence of females is liable to variation, and they may also be suspected of absence of mind, or forgetfulness (Siddiqi 1985, 119). Regarding property cases, where two witnesses are required,[55] the Imam al-Shafi'i has said that the evidence of one man and two women cannot be admitted, excepting in cases such as hire, bail, and so forth, because the evidence of (a) woman is originally inadmissible on account of their weakness of understanding, their want of memory and incapacity of governing, whence it is that their evidence is not admitted in criminal cases (Siddiqi 1985, 45). In property cases, where two witnesses are required and the evidence of two women is admissible in place of two men, the evidence of four women alone, however, is not accepted, contrary to what analogy would suggest, because if it were, there would be frequent occasions for their appearance in public, in order to give evidence; whereas their privacy is the most laudable. (*Hedaya* 1982, 354, bk. 21, chap. 1).[56]

Assumptions such as these of the lack of memory, incompetence, and general weak character of all women obviously stem from a patriarchal per-

---

and protection of society, because the practice of women leaving the home will lead to social disorder and corruption (Fadel 1997).

55. See Wadud-Muhsin 1992, 87, for alternative analysis of the Qur'anic requirement of two women witnesses for one man in two-witness-minimum cases.

56. Similar patriarchal attitudes toward women manifest themselves even outside discussions of competent witnesses. One modern commentator rationalizes the disparity between husband and wife in ease of obtaining a divorce by saying that, because of emotional instability resultiing from the menstrual cycle, "If women were given the power of unilateral divorce, it is probable that millions of them would divorce their husbands and it is probable that millions of divorces would have ensued and there would be chaos in society" (Doi 1989, 95). See also Wadud-Muhsin 1992, 35, citing Zamakhshari's statement that men are preferred by God over women in terms of "intelligence, physical constitution, determination and physical strength."

spective in a male-dominated intellectual community. The Qur'an, how-ever, does not bear this attitude, because it establishes the equality of men and women before God and the responsibility of both equally as vice-gerents of God on earth.[57] But where cultures are male-dominated, the absence of the active and intelligent participation of women in the public sphere naturally might breed such attitudes, and these have apparently made their way into the analysis and application of Islamic law in such societies and places in history.

Educated Muslims today, however, would quickly dismiss as simple igno-rance any claims that women are inferior in intellectual capacity, memory, or character. As for the societal harmony arguments that women do not venture out into public space, Muslim women today do not necessarily fit into the mold described in these quotes. Nor, indeed, did all women of Muslim history.[58] To reason that women should not be witnesses to a *zina* or *zina-bil-jabr* case because this would encourage their going out in public is pointless in a society where, for example, the medical evidence in a *zina* prosecution might easily be submitted by a woman doctor, the prosecuting or defense attorney could be a female litigator, and the presiding judge a woman jurist. The caution against women entering public space has long been dropped in most parts of Pakistan and other countries of the modern world.

The limitation of testimony exclusively to men appears to be an incor-poration into Islamic law of an antiquated custom that has now changed, and in Islamic law, "all rules in the *shari'ah* [Islamic law] that are based upon customs change when custom changes" (Mahmassani 1987, 116).[59] Modern Islamist writings, in fact, have been instrumental in establishing

57. Wadud-Muhsin 1992, 34–38, 64–66, describing the equality of women and men laid out in the Qur'an; distinctions between humans are only on the basis of character, women not defined by biology alone.

58. See al-'Asqalani 1907, 341–42, discussing Laila al-Shifa bint 'Abdullah, who was appointed by Caliph 'Umar to oversee the Medina marketplace; Kahhala 1991, 2:300–301, also discussing al-Shifa bint 'Abdullah, 5:67–70, summarizing biographies of prominent Muslim women, including the story of the Baghdadi ruler Umm al-Muqtadir billah, who set up a female courtier as a judge to hear disputes in the public square, citing al-Tabari, Ibn Athir, Ibn al-Jawzi, Ibn Miskawih; Qadri 1982, 57, describing cases involving women litigants before a male judge; Walther 1995 describing prominent women throughout Muslim history, including Umm al-Muqtadir billah.

59. See, also, Kamali 1991, 285, summarizing changeability of rules where *'urf* [custom] has changed, citing al-Shafi'i's different rules in Iraq versus Egypt.

that such exclusion of women from public space is an unfair cultural practice that is not an inherent part of Islam:

> In the 1970s, some Islamists began a serious reexamination of the dominant conservative position. They concluded that the inclusion of women in all facets of the political process was entirely consistent with Islam, that Islam does not require strict segregation of the sexes, and that much of the conservative position was based on custom rather than on the absolute principles of Islam. (Ghadbian 1995, 27)

Among the many respected leaders of the modern Islamist movement who follow this attitude are Hasan al-Turabi of Sudan, Rachid al-Ghanouchi of Tunisia, and Muhammad al-Ghazali and Yusuf al-Qaradawi of Egypt.[60]

The exclusivity of male testimony as an application of cultural male bias to the Islamic law of *zina* is unfair. But the exclusion of female testimony becomes appalling when expanded to apply to *zina-bil-jabr* as well. It is a clear travesty of justice to deny a victim of rape the right to testify to this violent attack merely because she is a woman. In applying the exclusively male evidence rule of traditional *zina* law to the crime of *zina-bil-jabr,* Pakistan has transformed what was merely an unfair antiquated male bias into a direct violation of the human rights of women. The direct contradiction to the Qur'anic injunctions to stand up firmly for justice is obvious.

Moreover, depriving women as an entire gender of the right to testify

60. Ghadbian 1995, 27, citing Hasan al-Turabi's paper, "Women in Islam and Muslim Society," which "laid down the theoretical basis of the reformist approach to gender relations, endorsed unequivocally a fully participatory role for women in politics and in every other sphere of society and declared that traditional restrictions on women's freedoms had nothing to do with Islam"; quoting al-Ghanouchi's statement: "We began to ask ourselves sheepishly, to what extent does our movement express Islam's approach to women, and to what extent have we freed ourselves from the residue of the era of decline and from our reactions against the Bourgibian degeneracy?" Citing also Muhammad al-Ghazali's book *Al Sunnah al Nabawiyah bayn Ahl al fiqh wa Ahl al Hadith* (cited in Ghadbian 1995), which focuses on verses and *hadith,* which conservatives interpret as excluding women from positions of authority, and asserting that "some authentic juristic interpretations of Islamic law allow women to serve in any public capacity—as judges, ambassadors, cabinet members, and rulers"; citing the 1990 *fatwa* (ruling) of al-Qaradawi that women can seek parliamentary and judicial positions and issue *fatwas* with the same authority as men.

in a *zina* or *zina-bil-jabr* case—where a woman's honor is generally at issue—has serious societal ramifications. First, it prevents women from fulfilling the Islamic duty to bear witness to the truth repeatedly emphasized in the Qur'an.[61] But even more significant is the fact that the permanent rejection of testimony is itself a Qur'anic *hadd* penalty. That is, in its verse prohibiting slander the Qur'an establishes that deprivation of the right to testify is a severe punishment, one of the two consequences of falsely accusing a woman: "Those who defame chaste women, and do not bring four witnesses, should be punished with eighty lashes, and *their testimony should not be accepted afterward,* for they are profligates" (Qur'an 24:4, emphasis added). A law that disallows women's testimony in *zina* cases, then, is tantamount to sentencing all women to one of the Qur'anic punishments for slander. This is ironic given the fact that the slander verse is specifically addressed to the preservation of women's honor—something that is stripped when one's testimony is not accepted. As one commentator puts it, "In a Muslim society the rejection of an individual's testimony is tantamount to outlawing him, [and, thus] the rejection of the testimony of one who has committed a *hadd* offence is a deterrent measure" (El-Awa 1982, 34). Elimination of all female testimony in *zina* cases thus subjects women to part of the same punishment as if they had committed a *hadd* crime, the most serious type of offense in Islamic law. Quite different from honoring women, as the Qur'an dictates, this practice dishonors all women by insinuating incompetence and weakness of character—the same qualities attributed to a slanderous witness.

Finally, there is a practical problem. If the rationale for rejecting a slanderer's testimony is deterrence, then why not also apply this deterrence to stop women from slandering each other? That is, if women's testimony is automatically inadmissible, then a woman will naturally not be deterred by the injunction that a slanderer's testimony will no longer be admitted. Hence, part of the Qur'anic *hadd* punishment for the offense of slander (that the slanderer's testimony is rejected ever after) becomes meaningless to women. Certainly, the punishment of flogging may yet be a deterrent, but why, then, is there the additional punishment of rejecting future testi-

---

61. See, for example, Qur'an 4:135: "O you who believe, be custodians of justice (and) witnesses for God, even though against yourselves, or your parents or your relatives . . . and if you prevaricate or avoid (giving evidence), God is cognizant of all that you do."

mony? And why would it apply only to men? The Qur'an gives no indication that it means to deter women any less than men in its injunctions against slander.[62] To simply nullify part of the Qur'anic punishment for slander, then, seems quite a radical result to be based merely on outdated cultural attitudes regarding women's competence and societal place.

Problems with Zina as Ta'zir. Islamic criminal law acknowledges two categories of crime and punishment. The first, known as *hudud,* encompasses crimes specifically articulated by God in the Qur'an and through the *hadith.* Islamic jurisprudence acknowleges, however, that society may legislate additional crimes and punishments as needed. These societally legislated crimes and punishments are called *ta'zir. Ta'zir* crimes can sometimes carry much lighter evidentiary or sentencing schemes than Qur'anic *hudud* crimes.[63] In Pakistan, when the strict quadruple witness standard of proof is difficult to meet, it has become increasingly common for *zina* cases to be prosecuted as *ta'zir* crimes, as opposed to *hudud* crimes.[64] The *Zina* Ordinance includes a clause providing for *ta'zir* prosecutions of *zina* where there is less evidence:

> *Zina* or *zina-bil-jabr* liable to *ta'zir.*
> Whoever commits *zina* or *zina-bil-jabr* that is not liable to *hadd,* or for which proof in either of the forms mentioned [confession or four witnesses] . . . is not available and the punishment of *qazf* (slander) liable to *hadd* has not been awarded to the complainant, or for which *hadd* may not be enforced under this Ordinance, shall be liable to *ta'zir.* (PLD 1979, 53; Major Acts 1992, 13).[65]

62. See pt. 1, B, above.

63. For further explanation and distinction between *hadd* and *ta'zir* crimes in Islamic law, see Coulson 1994, 124; El-Awa 1982, 1–2; Siddiqi 1985, 158; El-Awa 1976, 41.

64. See United States Department of State 1994, 1372, "In contrast to past years, women are now frequently granted bail for *Hudud* offenses, and convictions have been markedly reduced"; Asia Watch 1992, 50–52; Mehdi 1990, 23, stating that under the working law of rape, almost all cases are tried under *ta'zir;* Rahman 1994, 999–1000, "Because of the difficulty of obtaining four male Muslim witnesses, men accused of *zina-bil-jabr* have in reality become exempted from the maximum punishment. Although maximum *hadd* punishments have been imposed, none have ever been carried out. The majority of *zina* or *zina-bil-jabr* cases are thus heard at the lesser *ta'zir* punishment level").

65. The section goes on to prescribe the punishment for *zina* of imprisonment for ten years, thirty lashes, and a fine and for *zina-bil-jabr,* twenty-five years imprisonment and thirty lashes.

One seemingly positive aspect of *ta'zir* rape prosecutions in Pakistan is that the relaxed evidentiary rules allow women's testimony besides various forms of circumstantial evidence not allowed in a *hadd* prosecution. The actual impact upon women in *zina* cases, however, has not been positive. One writer states:

> Even though this level of punishment permits the testimony of women, observers of Pakistan's legal system have noted the bias against women victims and defendants. Courts appear to extend the benefit of doubt to men accused of rape. However, they set rigorous standards of proof to female rape victims who allege that the intercourse was forced. This gender bias has resulted in: (1) women who find it so difficult to prove *zina-bil-jabr* [under the *hudud* requirement of four male witnesses] that they find themselves open to the possibility of prosecution for *zina* [under the relaxed *ta'zir* evidentiary rules]; (2) men accused of *zina-bil-jabr* being subject to diminished charges [because the *hudud* evidence is not proved]; and (3) women who are wrongfully prosecuted and who are afforded restricted protection against such prosecution. (Rahman 1994, 1000)

Thus, the relaxed evidentiary rules of *ta'zir* (corresponding to its lesser punishment) open the *zina* law to further manipulation by authorities, who may threaten a woman with prosecution for *zina* under *ta'zir* evidence if there is not enough proof to convict under *hudud*. If the woman is charging rape, this exacerbates the potential injustice of the situation. A woman might watch her rapist be acquitted for lack of four witnesses but herself be subject to prosecution for *zina* under the looser evidentiary rules of *ta'zir*.

This phenomenon should sound familiar: "Those who defame chaste women, and do not bring four witnesses, should be punished with eighty lashes, and their testimony should not be accepted afterwards, for they are profligates" (Qur'an 24:4). This is the Qur'anic verse that started this *zina* discussion. It contemplates the possibility of adultery charges being brought against women upon less evidence than four witnesses and condemns it as a grievous slander. By allowing prosecution for *zina* as a *ta'zir* punishment, and thereby loosening the evidentiary rules, the Pakistani *Zina* Ordinance has succeeded in contravening the very Qur'anic verse upon which it is based.[66] In fact, *zina* is the only *hadd* crime for which the Qur'an

66. See, also, Patel 1991, 30–31, making the same argument that there can be no *ta'zir*

sets out a specific punishment for not meeting its strict evidentiary rules.[67] The Qur'an thus indicates that, unlike other *hadd* crimes, there can be no *ta'zir* punishment for *zina*. That is, for this one crime, if four eyewitnesses are not produced, the state and society must walk away and not speak of it again.[68]

But the *Zina* Ordinance goes even further in ignoring the Qur'anic injunction of all-or-nothing proof of *zina*. It includes a provision for "attempt" of *zina*, setting forth punishment of imprisonment, whipping, and a fine (PLD 1979, 55; Major Acts 1992, 14–15). Again, this directly contradicts the spirit of the Islamic law of *zina*. Both the Qur'anic verses quoted above and the *hadith* of Muhammad establish that unless the act was actual penetration, it is not punishable by the state.[69]

There is a compelling Qur'anic spirit against either a *ta'zir* or an attempt version of *zina*. Unfortunately, the Pakistani *Zina* Ordinance has lost sight of the unique status of *zina* as a *hadd* crime of public indecency and expanded it to areas that inevitably result in injustice and discrimination against women—the focus of the Qur'anic verses on the subject in the first place.

Rape in Islamic Jurisprudence

In this critique of the Pakistani *Zina* Ordinance, I have demonstrated that the crime of *zina* set forth in the Qur'an is primarily a societal crime of public indecency, and for that reason strict evidentiary standards of proof are attached to its prosecution. As noted, some of the application of the Qur'anic evidentiary standard for *zina* has been skewed by patriarchal culture to the detriment of women's rights. The inadmissibility of women's testimony in *zina* cases, including rape prosecutions, is one such example. The creation of a *ta'zir* version of *zina* and the subcategorization of rape

---

punishment for *zina*). This argument, in fact, was the basis of a challenge to the *ta'zir* punishment implemented in *zina* cases in Pakistan. Patel 1991, 30–31, citing a 1983 petition challenging 9(a) and 10 of the *Zina* Ordinance on this ground.

67. Al-Shafi'i 1987, 247 "Only the witnesses in the case of adultery should be scourged."

68. See pt. 1, B, above.

69. See pt. 1, B, above.

under *zina* in the first place are other examples of aspects of Pakistan's *zina* law, which unfairly dishonors its women.

So far, the rationale for the strict evidentiary requirements for *zina* is an affirmance and protection of both female and male honor: unlawful sexual intercourse will be prosecuted by the state only when it is publicly indecent. Within the privacy of one's home the immorality of the act is something left between the individual and God. The same rationale would not, however, apply to the crime of rape. In rape, public display is not the crucial element to the criminality of the act. Rather, the attack itself is a crime of violence whether committed in public or in private. Rape is not consensual sexual intercourse, but a violent assault against a victim, man or woman, boy or girl, during which the perpetrator uses sex as a weapon. Consistent with the analysis thus far, the Qur'an does not include any direct mention of rape under the general crime of *zina*. How, then, has Islamic law addressed the crime of rape?

Duress: Rape as a Negation of Intent for *Zina*

In their chapters on *zina* Islamic legal scholars have acknowledged that when one or more parties engaged in *zina* under duress, they are not liable for *zina*.[70] A *hadith* of the Prophet Muhammad establishes this principle: upon a woman's reporting to the him that she was forced to commit adultery, he did not punish her, and he did punish the perpetrator.[71] Similar rulings by Caliph 'Umar ibn al-Khattab[72] and Imam Malik (Malik 1982, 392) further cement this principle in Islamic law. Islamic jurisprudence, in fact, devotes much attention to the concept of duress as a negation of intent, thus eliminating liability for an offense.[73] The application of this

70. See *Hedaya* 1982, 187, defining compulsion generally; al-Maqdisi 1994, 8:129, 145, including the discussion of exemption from *zina* liability for a male forced to commit *zina*; Seminar 1982, 269, "[It] is an agreed position that females subjected to rape against their consent and without their will would be exonerated from any liability under Islamic law."

71. Al-Bukhari 1985, 8:chap. 7; *Mishkat al-Masabih* 1990, 1:762, citing *hadith* in Tirmidhi and Abu Dawud.

72. See Malik 1982, 392, citing a case in which Caliph 'Umar prosecuted the rapist of a slave girl and did not prosecute her); al-Maqdisi 1994, 8:129, citing a case in which Caliph 'Umar released a woman who asserted rape.

73. See, generally, Abou El Fadl 1991, 305.

field of law to zina results in a thorough analysis of liability in possible permutations of forced zina. Thus, the Hedaya devotes several paragraphs to resolving conflicting stories regarding a sexual encounter where one party claims it was consensual and the other claims it was not (Hedaya 1982, 353–54). Matters become more complicated where the witnesses to the encounter are of different genders (Hedaya 1982, 353–54). There is also discussion and difference of opinion about whether a man can be forced to commit zina and, thus, not be liable for hadd punishment (Hedaya 1982, 187; al-Maqdisi 1994, 8:129).

Thus, the discussions of forced sex in jurisprudential writings on zina exhaustively discuss nonconsensual sex as a negation of the requisite mental state for zina, but does Islamic law address rape as an independent crime? As it turns out, contrary to what the Pakistani legislation would suggest, Islamic jurisprudence has not only categorized rape as a separate criminal offense (under hiraba) but has also allowed civil compensation to rape survivors (under jirah). I address these two remedies in turn.

Hiraba: Rape as a Violent Taking

Hiraba is another hadd crime defined in the Qur'an. It is variously translated as "forcible taking," "highway robbery," "terrorism," or "waging war against the state." The crime of hiraba is based on the following Qur'anic verse: "The punishment for those who wage war [yuharibuna] against God and His Prophet, and perpetrate disorders in the land is: kill or hang them or have a hand on one side and a foot on the other cut off or banish them from the land" (Qur'an 5:33).

Islamic legal scholars have interpreted this crime to be any type of forcible assault upon the people involving some sort of taking of property.[74] It differs from ordinary theft in that the Qur'anic crime of theft (sariqa) is a taking by stealth, whereas hiraba is a taking by force (Doi 1984, 250, 254; El-Awa 1982, 7) (thus, the popular translation as "armed robbery"). Although

74. El-Awa 1982, 7–10; al-Hariri 1986, 5:409–11; Sabiq 1993, 2:446, chapter on hudud, describing hiraba; Siddiqi 1985, 139–44. See also Doi 1984, 250, explaining the context of the verse revelation: some people came to Muhammad under the auspices of new converts and complained that the weather in Medina was disagreeable to them, and Muhammad sent them to live outside the city with cattle belonging to the state; they subsequently killed the cattle keeper and stole the cattle and this verse was revealed shortly thereafter.

it is generally assumed to be violent public harassment, many scholars have held that it is not limited to acts committed in public places (Sabiq 1993, 2:447).

It is in the discussions of the crime of *hiraba* where the crime of rape appears. A brief review of the traditional descriptions of *hiraba* reveals that rape is specifically included among its various forms. For example, in *Fiqh-us-Sunnah*, a modern summary of the primary traditional schools of thought on Islamic law, *hiraba* is described as: a single person or group of people causing public disruption, killing, forcibly taking property or money, attacking or raping women (*hatk al-ʿarad*), killing cattle, or disrupting agriculture (Sabiq 1993, 450). Reports of individual scholars on the subject further confirm the *hiraba* classification of rape.[75] Al-Dasuqi, for example, a Maliki jurist, held that if a person forced a woman to have sex, his actions would be deemed committing *hiraba* (Doi 1984, 253). In addition, the Maliki judge Ibn ʿArabi, relates a story in which a group was attacked and a woman in their party raped. Responding to the argument that the crime did not constitute *hiraba* because no money was taken and no weapons used, Ibn ʿArabi replied indignantly that "*hiraba* with the private parts" is much worse than a *hiraba* involving the taking of money, and that anyone would rather be subjected to the latter than the former (Sabiq 1993, 2:450). The famous Spanish Muslim jurist, Ibn Hazm, a follower of the Zahiri school, reportedly had the widest definition of *hiraba*, defining a *hiraba* offender as:

> One who puts people in fear on the road, whether or not with a weapon, at night or day, in urban areas or in open spaces, in the palace of a caliph or a mosque, with or without accomplices, in the desert or in the village, in a large or small city, with one or more people . . . making people fear that they'll be killed, or have money taken, or be raped (*hatk al-ʿarad*) . . . whether the attackers are one or many. (Sabiq 1993, 2:450)

Thus, even this cursory review of traditional Islamic jurisprudence shows that the crime of rape is classified not as a subcategory of *zina* but as a separate crime of violence under *hiraba*. This classification is logical as is the "taking" of the victim's property (the rape victim's sexual autonomy)

75. Al-Hariri 1986, 410–11, summarizing the Maliki school definition of an *hiraba* offender as someone who "obstructs the road, even without intending to take money, intending to harm someone, or intending to rape a woman (*hatk-il-harim*)."

by force. In Islam, sexual autonomy and pleasure is a fundamental right for both women and men;[76] taking by force someone's right to control the sexual activity of one's body is, thus, logically classified as a form of *hiraba*. Note that this principle could also be applied to expand the Islamic law of rape to include the rape of men as another instance of the violent taking of an individual's sexual autonomy.[77]

Moreover, classification of rape under *hiraba* promotes the principle of honoring women's sexual dignity established in the Qur'anic verses on *zina*. Rape as *hiraba* is a separate violent crime during which sexual intercourse is used as a weapon. The focus in a *hiraba* prosecution would be the accused rapist and his intent and physical actions, rather than second-guessing the consent of the rape victim as is likely to happen in a *zina-bil-jabr* case.[78]

Finally, *hiraba* does not require four witnesses to prove the offense, unlike *zina*. Circumstantial evidence and expert testimony, then, presumably form the evidence used to prosecute such crimes. In addition to eye-witness testimony, medical data, and expert testimony, a modern *hiraba* prosecution of rape would likely take advantage of modern technological advances such as forensic and DNA testing.

Jirah: Rape as Bodily Harm

Islamic legal responses to rape are not limited to a criminal prosecution for *hiraba*. Islamic jurisprudence also creates an avenue for civil redress for a rape survivor in its law of *jirah* (wounds). Islamic law designates ownership rights to each part of one's body and a right to corresponding

76. See al-Bukhari 1985, 7:nos. 135–36; al-Ghazzali 1984, 2:106–7, a book on the etiquette of marriage, citing *hadith* regarding the rights of a wife for sexual pleasure; Mussallam 1983, 28–38, including *hadith* and a discussion of contraception if it interferes with a wife's sexual satisfaction; al-Hibri 1982, 213, citing *hadith* about foreplay; al-Hibri 1993b, citing schools of thought on the role of woman's sexual pleasure in the legality of a marriage contract.

77. It is interesting to note that the concept of a woman's sexuality as her property is, in fact, not a new one to the crime of rape. The Western crime of rape evolved from the early Roman law of "raptus," which was defined as "a form of violent theft that could apply to both property and person" (Alexander 1995, 211). See, also, Dripps 1992, 1781.

78. See pt. 1, C, 2, above.

compensation for any harm done unlawfully to any of those parts.[79] Islamic law calls this the law of *jirah* (wounds). Harm to a sexual organ, therefore, entitles the person harmed to appropriate financial compensation under classical Islamic *jirah* jurisprudence (al-Maqdisi 1994, 36).[80] Thus, each school of Islamic law has held that where a woman is harmed through sexual intercourse (some include marital intercourse), she is entitled to financial compensation for the harm. Further, when this intercourse was *without the consent* of the woman, the perpetrator must pay the woman both the basic compensation for the harm and an additional amount based on the *diyya* (financial compensation for murder, akin to a wrongful death payment).[81]

Because rape could occur even without a clear threat of *physical* force (thus, perhaps, not constituting *hiraba* but, nonetheless, constituting sex without consent), the categorization of rape under the Islamic law of *jirah* also makes logical sense. This categorization would provide financial compensation to every victim of rape for any harm done to his or her body as a result of the attack. Taking the analysis further, because the right to control one's own sexual activity is a fundamental Islamic and human right, it could be argued that foreign invasion of one's sexual organs against one's will constitutes harm, even when there is no physical bruising or tearing. Modern Islamic jurisprudence and legislation could, therefore, choose to provide that either instead of, or in addition to *hiraba* punishment against the rapist, a woman might also claim compensation for her ordeal under the principle of *jirah*. Again, this analysis would also provide for male rape victims.

Interestingly, Western legal discourse has just recently begun to reevaluate the crime of rape and is still struggling to overcome its male-oriented articulation of the crime. If Islamic jurisprudence were to continue its development in the direction outlined above, *jirah* principles

79. Al-Maqdisi 1994, 3, introduction; describing law of *jirah*, classification of injuries, and so on.

80. Note that the law of *jirah* (in addition to other principles of Islamic law) providing for compensation for physical harm even between spouses would support modern Islamic legislation against domestic abuse.

81. Al-Maqdisi 1994, 36, discussing varying applications of *jirah* under four Sunni schools of thought; Bokhary 1979, 219, stating where someone is forced to commit *zina*, she is not punished for *zina* but entitled to compensation.

would provide an interesting alternative remedy. Islamic law has the unique resource of a *jirah* system of established bodily compensation law to apply as one response to the crime of nonconsensual intercourse, if it were recognized in modern Islamic legislation. In Western history, ancient Roman law also recognized compensation as a means of resolving a rape dispute, but it took a more patriarchal approach: it found that the *father* (or other male authority) of the rape victim was owed damages because rape implied his inability to protect the woman (Dripps 1992, 1780–81). Islamic law, with its radical introduction of a woman's right to own property as a fundamental right, already employs a gender-egalitarian attitude in this area of jurisprudence. In fact, there is a *hadith* specifically directed to converting the early Muslim population from this patriarchal attitude of male financial compensation for female sexual activity. During the time of Prophet Muhammad, a young man committed *zina* with his employer's wife. The father of the young man gave one hundred goats and a maid as compensation to the employer, who accepted it. When the case was reported to the Prophet, he ordered the return of the goats and the maid to the young man's father and prosecuted the adulterer for *zina* (Abu Daud 1990, 3: bk. 33, no. 4430; al-Bukhari 1985, 8:bk. 81, nos. 815, 821, 826). Early Islam thus established that there should be no tolerance of the attitude that a woman's sexual activity is something to be bartered, pawned, gossiped about, or owned by the men in her life. Personal responsibility of every human being for his or her own actions is a fundamental principle in Islamic thought.

Recent discussions of marital rape among Western scholars[82] can also be compared to the debate among Islamic legal scholars regarding whether a husband is obligated to pay his wife when she is physically harmed from sexual intercourse, which brings up an interesting question: Is there a recognition of marital rape in Islam?[83] In the context of *jirah* it would appear so: where there is any physical harm caused to a spouse, there may be a claim for *jirah* compensation.[84] Even in these discussions of appropriate *jirah*

82. See, for example, De La Mothe 1996, 857.

83. Notably, the Pakistani *Zina* Ordinance categorically eliminates this possibility by defining *zina-bil-jabr* as unconsensual intercourse with someone "to whom he or she is not validly married" (pt. 1, A, above), a description also popular in old common-law definitions of rape).

84. See pt. 2, C, above.

compensation, the question of the injured party's consent plays a central role. Some Islamic jurists consider consent to be presumed by virtue of the marital relationship, whereas others maintain that where harm occurs, it is an assault, regardless of the consent, and, therefore, compensation is due (al-Maqdisi 1994, 8:36).[85] In this modern era, one might take these precedents and their premium focus on consent and apply the Islamic principle of sexual autonomy to conclude that any sex without consent is harmful as a dishonoring of the unwilling party's sexual autonomy. Thus, modern Islamic jurists and legislators, taking a gender-egalitarian perspective, might conclude that Islamic law does recognize marital rape and assign the appropriate injunctions and compensation for this personally devastating harm.

Conclusion: A Modern Islamic Gender-Egalitarian Law of Rape?

And so I return to the initial question: *Do* Pakistan's criminal laws articulate the Islamic law of rape? As discussed here, they do not. But they could have. Islamic jurisprudence includes a law of rape with two very appropriate avenues to respond justly to the crime, its seriousness, and its effect on women, in particular. Unfortunately, the drafters of Pakistan's *Hudud* Ordinance and the shari'ah court that implemented it took no notice of this precedent in creating Pakistan's *zina* law. The result has been injustice to the women of Pakistan and a disservice to Islamic law. This brief investigation into some of the traditional Islamic jurisprudence on rape shows that it is more than feasible for modern Muslim legislators to take the tools offered in Islamic jurisprudence on *hiraba* and *jirah* to form a comprehensive gender-egalitarian law of rape that does not counteract the positive honoring of women that is inherent in the Qur'anic verses on *zina.* Rape should be specified as a form of *hiraba* in the *hiraba* section of modern *hudud* statutes, thus identifying it as a violent crime for which the perpetrator is subject to serious punishment. In fact, Pakistan already has a *hiraba* chapter in its *Hudud* Ordinance (Major Acts 1992, 7). Modern Islamic legis-

---

85. See also Jilani 1992, citing a case in which medical evidence revealed marks of violence on woman's body but found no rape because of the existence of a marriage certificate: "At best, it can be said to be misuse of the wife," said the court.

lation might also designate rape as a harm under *jirah*, thus creating grounds for rape victims to receive some compensation for the harm caused to their bodies and sexual autonomy.

Modern Islamic jurists, legislators, and members of the judiciary and the bar must work out the logical details of these laws and what combination of *hiraba* and *jirah* should apply in a given situation and society. A greater challenge, perhaps, is changing the cultural attitudes toward women that helped to create the existing laws in the first place. That ongoing effort must be undertaken simultaneously with any official legislative changes in order to give real effect to such legislation and to give life to the Qur'anic verses honoring women.

6

The Scholar and the *Fatwa*

Legal Issues Facing African American and Immigrant Muslim Communities in the United States

AMINAH BEVERLY MCCLOUD

Scholarship and authority in Islam have always been the prerogative of an elite group of men who have been invested in traditional methods and interpretations. When Muslims and, recently, non-Muslims think of legality in Islam, all thoughts are directed to the *fatwa* (legal opinion), and all eyes look to the East for the source of tradition and authority. Here in the United States, predominately American-trained Islamicists are negotiating the terrain that is normally the domain of the ʿalim (one learned in religious knowledge), *mufti* (jurisconsult), and *qadi* (the Islamic "judge") in the Muslim world. There certainly will be new, dynamic entries to the body of Islamic law as time goes on, and there will be further reforming of the categories of *qiyas* (analogical reasoning), *istihsan* (juristic preference), and *istislah* (consideration of the public interest) to make new tradition.

Legal issues facing Muslim Americans span several categories, including family law, civil rights law, and criminal law. Differences in culture and religion, intertwined and inseparable, provide the foundation for almost all the disputes. As with most religious communities in America, a period of time passes while the community establishes itself in the (traditional) system before it ventures out to try to engage the larger community.

For the moment, scholars of Islam, and sometimes informed *imams,* are providing the majority of the answers to questions about Islam—its philosophies, history, beliefs and practices. Active as the "new authorities," they are called upon to give expert testimony, thereby shaping a legal view and public understanding of Islam and Muslims in this country. I often find myself in this precarious situation. For better or worse, these testimonies set legal precedents but remain generally unknown in the Muslim community.

Muslims often look differently, act differently, and certainly worship differently than the larger American community. The immediate consequences of this difference have been various discrimination and civil rights violations. In many cities animosities toward Islam and Muslims have been initiated or nurtured by the local media. Job discrimination and other civil rights violations usually follow. The most prominent Muslim organization tracking violent and nonviolent discriminations against Muslims is the Council on American-Islamic Relations (CAIR). Through its efforts, many incidents of employment and public discrimination against Islam and Muslims are no longer isolated events, but are responded to nationally. As Muslims enter politics and law and are able to balance understanding of Islam with U.S. law, the incidents of discrimination, one hopes, will significantly decline.

Furthermore, the struggle for rights among America's most prolific and notorious litigants—prisoners—has been the source of much case law that defines religion. Muslim prisoners have sued, for example, for the right to have their given names changed to Arabic names, for the right to study Islam, and for the right to practice the fast of Ramadan and have it recognized as Islamic. Here enters the scholar in the role of expert witness, stating under oath what Islam is and what it is not, who is "Muslim" and who is not. These questions are at least fourteen hundred years old in Muslim circles and have over the centuries been given various answers. What the court, the district attorney, or the warden's office wants, however, is an immediate, definitive answer that can withstand appeals and/or further litigation (Moore 1991, 136–56).

The scholar of Islam trained in an American university will ostensibly give the broadest view possible, taking in all of the twists and turns of history and its testimony to the perennial relationship of power and knowledge. Scholars of Islam know what a *fatwa* (legal opinion) is and who is qualified to give one. They also know that the class of "learned men" has often suffered from corruption and that their *fatawa* (pl. *fatwa*) have sometimes reflected a concern for patronage. U.S. court officers, guidance counselors, lawyers, and mediators seek information that they can use and that has been reasoned with an understanding of U.S. law. The scholar, knowingly or unknowingly, becomes the agent who gives legal advice that, one hopes, is grounded in Islamic knowledge.

The implications of this situation are far-reaching for the Muslim world's self-understanding. In the Muslim world "learnedness" on issues of the law has always been first and foremost male. Moreover, it is the accumulated line of men, with each stage certified along the way. Its maleness notwithstanding, the study of the law in Islam is analogous to the study of law anywhere. In the United States, however, there is no long-standing inquiry of Islamic law, and the history of Islam in this country is still relatively young. The lack of knowledge of Islamic law in this country has often meant that "Islam" and "Muslims" can be almost anything that anyone chooses. Because various Islamic communities have arrived with various cultural manifestations of Islam and disparate understandings of what it means to be a Muslim, all claims are taken to be valid until proven invalid. Muslim scholars of every possible variant of Islamic law arrive in the United States with each ethnic community, often speaking very little English and having little if any knowledge of U.S. law and culture.

The Muslim community in America is divided in several ways, with ethnicity heading the list. Internal frictions in the Muslim world reveal themselves in the U.S. context in the form of racism and in various forms of nationalism, often following patterns of European and American race and class distinction. American communities self-segregate despite claims of egalitarianism and Muslim "brotherhood" (McCloud 1995). Legal matters, however, admit only class and "Americanness." The result is that a Muslim is a Muslim is a Muslim unless he or she is wealthy or has diplomatic immunity, both of which tend to transcend the law. As previously stated, for the majority of Muslims, there are increasing experiences of discrimination and other injustices (including inside the Muslim community), thus increasing the contact of Muslims with U.S. law, whose officiators, in my experience, often attempt fairness in understanding. These attempts often lead them to seek out the academic scholars in Islam. These scholars may be Muslim or not, female or male, objective or not. Whoever they are, they are expressing opinions that are recorded as fact. Why, one may ask, do the scholars not consult with the communities and their leaders? One answer is that there is a refusal on the part of those within Muslim communities who are trained in Islamic law. Another answer is simply that it has never been done. Muslims, even inside their ethnic enclaves, generally follow "what has always been." When faceed with a new game with different players, there is no available reasoning for a new strategy, so there tends to be no strategy. The game continues, however, and its results will certainly add to the annals of Islamic law.

As a budding Islamicist and an African American *Muslimah* (Muslim woman), my position in academia is at best tenuous while in the Muslim community it is generally invisible. Islamic Studies is still relatively new. The study of Islam has been a subcategory in orientalist university departments of Arabic, Near East Studies, Middle Eastern Studies, and/or Arab History. As a result, scholars in these fields do not understand the worldview of Islam, and their perspectives on the religion are often rigid and narrow. My voice, however, is increasingly heard in legal documents, articles, and consultations on issues involving Muslims that reach the stage of litigation. Rendering an opinion on legalities in Islam is a position of privilege extended only to non-Muslim Islamicists and Muslim males, so my position is destined to be controversial.

I have been asked to look at and render an "Islamically based" opinion on a number of types of situations from who is a Muslim to how to distinguish *sawm* (the Islamic fast) from other religious feasts to issues around women's rights and Islamic marriages. For this brief overview, I briefly explore the issues surrounding Muslim women, particularly marriage and divorce.

American Muslim women, on one level, are the "free-est" Muslim women on the planet, that is, on the level of access to public participation in whatever public arena they choose. There is mandatory public education, guaranteeing that women have basic education. If women want to and can work, jobs are available. For physically abused women, there are shelters with skills training components. Women can drive cars and live on their own without neighborhood retaliation. This list is long. Muslim women are also exposed to a society where everyone is almost free to do anything one can think of—good or evil—and assert it as a right.

Their actual lived-out freedom, however, closely conforms to their level of acceptance of the historical patriarchy of the Muslim world. As a result, many Muslim women find themselves in situations of legal import both within the Islamic and U.S. legal systems, yet without the knowledge of how to benefit from the rights accorded by either.

In Islam the marriage contract is, if executed properly, a document of protection and security. In various Muslim countries marriages are registered according to particular custom and are very public. When Muslims have immigrated to the United States, their marriages have generally received the protection of the courts. Marriage contracts are understood as prenuptial or nuptial agreements.

"Islamic" marriages (marriages without a civil license) are considered common-law marriages in those states that have common-law statutes; U.S. family law generally recognizes "common-law" marriages. There are still about a dozen states that demand a civil contract registered with the state. Common-law statutes are used by the U.S. courts in establishing paternity, inheritance, alimony, child custody, and property rights in disputes and litigations. Nevertheless, marriages that have been contracted in other countries are sacrosanct, whereas marriages undertaken in the States run a risk in absence of the civil contract. American Muslims often espouse the view that the only marriage of significance is the "Islamic marriage," but this marriage often takes place without a contract, bringing into serious question the intentions of the parties involved. This is ironic, not to mention illegal, from an Islamic juridical perspective because traditionally there is no valid marriage without a marriage contract.

Furthermore, there is no valid Islamic marriage without a contract that specifies the *mahr* (dowry). No matter what else is included, the dowry must be specified and its agreement witnessed. The entire dowry or an agreed-upon portion of it, in some cases even symbolic, must be given at the time of the marriage. The rest, if necessary, can be deferred, but, this, too must be specified and witnessed. There are several possible extenuating circumstances that should compel American Muslim women to consider their marriage contracts with great care. For example, some women enter new marriages with children from previous ones. This should require a careful delineation of the care and training to be provided in the new marriage. In the event of the death of the parental spouse, the contract is one place (in addition to a will) wherein arrangements are agreed upon. When the wife is a student, a professional, or simply wealthy, the contract can and should include agreed-upon stipulations regarding these issues.

Marriage in Islam is, furthermore, intimately bound to the issue of inheritance, one of the traditional mainstays of the Muslim community. The Islamic laws of inheritance cannot apply for "unmarried" people. In spite of guidance and protection offered by the Qur'an, Muslim women in America continue to fail themselves in consultations and litigation because they do not fulfill their obligations and/or exercise their rights. They still "marry" and have children without marriage contracts. From the Islamic perspective, the *niyyah* (intention) of any Muslim who would marry without a contract could not be good. If there is no dowry, there is no marriage, and, therefore, no rights accrue.

Although U.S. family law recognizes "religious marriages" as; "common-law marriages" in many states, it does not recognize religious divorce in most states. Thus, if there has never been a (U.S. legal) marriage and there is discussion of divorce "Islamically," one must get a civil divorce in addition to a religious divorce really to be divorced and for the rights of divorce to accrue (e.g., maintenance, child support, and even the right to remarry). I suspect that quite a few women besides men qualify as bigamists. Lawyers and judges regularly consult academicians about the religious legalities of the community "goings on."

A frequent example is a woman who petitions the court for child support. The court needs divorce papers to ascertain what was agreed upon at the time of the divorce. It is ascertained that there was a religious divorce from an "Islamically" nonvalid marriage. What is the court to decide? Most judges and lawyers do not feel that they have the freedom to speak on the peculiarities of individual religious interpretation, thereby going beyond their legal bounds. Unfortunately, this sometimes has disastrous results, including the complete removal of the child from either custodial parent. Clearly, agreements that are witnessed and, therefore, are binding in U.S. (and Islamic) law work to the benefit of Muslim women who are mindful. The absence of the written contract results in everything being left up to a dispassionate judge. Women's rights to alimony and child support depend on their income unless there has been a prior agreement which states things differently.

Related to the subject of marriage and divorce is the issue of polygyny, both in sequential marriage (where one has never obtained a real divorce) and in simultaneous marriages. Remembering the Qur'anic affirmation of the right to marry up to four women (and forgetting the historical context and stipulations of that affirmation), Muslim men have sought polygyny with haste. As leaders of various communities set the example, marriages of years of devotion fall into chaos. Muslim women often find themselves in a religious dilemma: Who can go against what Allah permits? Some Muslim women have found themselves in court, ironically, not pursuing charges of bigamy, but like other American women, filing charges over some sort of fraud. All of the potential legal consequences of the practice of polygyny in the American Muslim context have not yet appeared, but they are bound to find their way into the courts as more and more women seek alimony and child support. It also seems clear to me that the lack of records about who married "whom, when, and where"—in addition to the constant geographical movements of individuals and families—is bound to result in a brother marrying a sister in the near future.

American Muslims also face potential problems as they seek to marry their children at ages lower than the legal limit and when they deal with Muslim youth who assert their rights to choose mates and to pursue their legal rights under U.S. law. Many Muslim families fear the "looseness" and permissiveness of U.S. society. Yet despite the increasing efforts of a growing number of Muslim camps and social events, American Muslim children are thoroughly indoctrinated in American society and culture. There are "runaways" from "oppressive" family conditions that require social agencies and the court system to intervene. In at least one instance, death has occurred at the hands of an irate and "dishonored" father over the "behavior" of his daughter.

Still another area of concern and legal deliberation is child-rearing practices, which vary widely in Muslim cultures. Love and protection of children is the norm in Muslim society. In some cultures, however, physical discipline is allowed, which by general American standards would be considered abusive (e.g., spanking with belts, shoes, etc.). When observed by non-Muslims, these practices have resulted in social service intervention. There also have been situations where standards of affection permitted in some Muslim cultures have met with disapproval in the American context. I am aware of one such case in which an open display of affection of a father toward his daughter (in ways acceptable in his own "conservative" culture) resulted in charges of sexual abuse. The subsequent intervention of various courts, both criminal and family, have cost this family almost everything they own, leaving them almost indigent. Even if they manage to get their children back, they will be in a desperate situation to care for them.

Spousal abuse and its general tolerance among Muslims—based on misinterpretation of one Qur'anic verse—is also a cause for concern. Immigrant women in marriages where abuse occurs tend to experience it as part of the normal course of life and submit—especially to verbal and emotional abuse—without complaint. Their daughters are more likely to be vigilant that the verbal abuse does not turn into physical abuse and to assert the threat of police intervention in an effort to modify their fathers' behavior. Increasingly, national conferences have sessions on family problems with discussions on abuse: what it is, what are possible resolutions to conflict, and the options when no resolution is possible. In some instances abuse has forced some women to seek the services of battered women's shelters. It is in some of these shelters that an additional concern has arisen for Muslim women: they are at times encouraged to convert to Christianity, and Islam, with its "sanction" of the beating of women, is presented as the problem.

As an aspiring scholar and community activist, I often find myself overwhelmed both by the enormity of some of these issues and the need for an American elaboration of a Muslim culture that is a synthesis of the old and new. My experience is that inside local Muslim communities, female scholars of anything Islamic are not seen favorably or are simply ignored. What such women can contribute to thinking about these new Muslim communities is also ignored. Yet they find themselves in constant demand by the non-Muslim community to explain what is going on at the grass-roots level. This situation puts scholars, who are generally invisible anyway—as Muslim women tend to be in their communities—in a dilemma. They have to be careful in their observations and assertions. They cannot afford the security or safety of belonging to only one community because it automatically decreases their perspective and capacity to "see" the larger community. Yet getting to know and observe Muslim communities requires at least a minimal level of acceptance as a visitor. Ironically, this is an extremely difficult position to maintain for the insider. Muslims, as with any religious community, can be hostile to their own if criticism and ideological challenge are suspected. Women scholars have to be measured and timely in their responses to inquiries because they understand that their answers can lead to danger and prejudice from within and without.

The Muslim scholar is also aware that although the community is not likely to know what has been said about it by the scholar, the community deserves to have its rights protected. Thus, the Muslim scholar, particularly if the scholar is a woman, is caught between her scholarly demands and the increasing requests for "expert Islamic opinion," on the one hand, and her own participation in the dynamics of growth and change in American Muslim communities, on the other, as Muslim communities forge an Islamic identity against the backdrop of their own "American" experience and culture. There is much work ahead.

PART THREE

Literature, Spirituality

7

Braiding the Stories

Women's Eloquence in the Early Islamic Era

MOHJA KAHF

Introduction: Nusaiba's Scar—
Women's Eloquence Infuses Early
Islamic Literature

❧ Women's words are woven into the whole range of early Islamic texts. Conditions in their own cultural milieu and in the cultural environments of the men through whose writings their words were transmitted obscure women's discursive presence in this material. How can this heritage be retrieved?

Um ʿAmara Nusaiba bint Kaʿb al-Najariya narrated accounts of the Prophet Muhammad, peace and blessings be upon him, and did many extraordinary things, extraordinary for men and, no doubt, more extraordinary for women: losing a hand in combat, for example, and taking the pledge to the Prophet at Aqaba with sixty-two men and one other woman. One of her best-known deeds is her combat in defense of the Prophet when the Muslims began losing the Battle of Uhud. Ibn Hajar (d. 449/852) cites al-Waqidi, one of the earliest authorities[1] for the following account:

---

1. The source he cites is *al-Maghazi* by al-Waqidi (d. A.H. 207 A.D. 822). When both Hijra and Georgian dates are given henceforth, the Hijra will precede the Georgian and the A.H. and A.D. will be dropped.

Um Saʿid bint Saʿd bin al-Rabiʿ used to say, I visited her and said, "Aunt, tell me [haddithini; in another version, akhbirini] your account of the Day of Uhud." Then she said, "I went out on the Day of Uhud with canteens filled with water, and we ended up beside the Messenger, peace and blessings be upon him, while he was in the midst of his companions, and the state and the victory were for the Muslims. Then, when the Muslims were losing, I made my way over to the Messenger of God, and I began direct combat, shielding them with the sword and shooting from the bow, until the wounds I sustained overtook me." Then I saw a scar on her shoulder with a deep hollowness so I said, "Who struck you with this?" She said, "Ibn Qamʾa."(Ibn Hajar 4:479)[2]

Ibn Hajar adds that ʿUmar bin al-Khattab (d. 24/644) reports the Prophet as saying, "I did not turn right or left on the Day of Uhud but saw her there fighting in my place." This adds another level to the multiple tissues of narrative composing the story of Nusaiba's scar. The Prophet's image of Nusaiba is one in which the woman's figure multiplies and fills the horizon in a whirl of activity just as Nusaiba's recounting activity fills a page in the histories.

Instead of multiplicitous presence, we have inherited an erased page of women's discourses in the early Islamic era. Recovery begins with Um Saʿid's interlocution, "Aunt, tell me your account." Um Saʿid is not just after news (information about the battle is available from other sources) but is fascinated by the way Nusaiba's scar is a mysterious mark to decipher and turns Um Saʿid into a reader. The verbs in her inquiry, haddithini (speak to me, fem.) or akhbirini (inform me, fem.), are richly connotative in early Islamic literature.[3] Haddithini/akhbirini describes the posture of researchers into the literary history of women in the early Islamic era: we become Um Saʿids.

Gathering up the scattered leaves involves a great deal of handiwork. Such anthologizing has been done, to some extent, and has not given women's literature staying power in the foreground of cultural memory,

2. He gives her two entries, one under "Nusaiba" and the other under "Um ʿAmara." This is from the "Um ʿAmara" entry. Her name may have been Naseeba. Um Saʿid may have been Um Saʿd.

3. Haddatha is related to hadith, "speech" or "report," and becomes the basic unit of Islamic historiography. Akhbirini comes from khabar, "news" or "report," imparting guidance or information (Khalidi 1994, 18).

with one or two exceptions. For permanent expansion of canon to happen, theoretical work must overcome the tendency to treat these texts as curiosities rather than as the compositions of contributors to literary discourse. The first step is to move from a narrow definition of literature and widen our scope to include all compositions identified as having rhetorical eloquence, *balagha*. Toward theorizing women's discursive contributions to the *balagha* of the early Islamic era, I suggest the idea of *mujadila*, "she-who-disputes," or "interlocutor." This theoretical construct pulls against the tendency to consider women's eloquent compositions as incidental, against prevailing winds that shatter women's discourses into isolated slivers of "so-and-so's wife said," "the warrior's mother cried," "a woman from Bani Hanifa responded." *Mujadila* is a rudimentary way to conceptualize women's compositions in the diffuse textual material of early Islam, compositions on the borders of the recognized genres.

The early Islamic period begins with the Hijra (the migration of the Prophet Muhammad and his followers to Madina in A.D. 622) and ends with the last of the "Righteous" caliphs forty years later. "Early Islamic literature" as taught in the Arab world conventionally includes, besides the Qur'an, *hadith* (utterances of the Prophet or narrations about him); sermons of the Prophet, the Rashidun caliphs, and a few other men; and the poetry of Hasan bin Thabit, Ka'b bin Malik, al-Nabigha al-Ja'di, and other men, with Khansa' often included as the only woman.[4] Because information about this period reaches scholars through records written in later times, research into this era must address the question of authenticity. Are we reading the actual unmediated words of women from the early Islamic era or purely the contrivances of men who wrote, beginning several generations later, the treatises in which those words are found? Many Arabic studies assume the former (Gharib 1984; Gharib 1985; Ma'badi 1983) and much Western-based scholarship assumes the latter; neither position is satisfactory. Denise Spellberg makes transmission the mother of all problematics in her meticulous study of that most articulate of women, 'A'isha (d. 50/670).[5] She finds no residual subjectivity for 'A'isha, as if her discursive traces were stitched together entirely by her classical Sunni and Shi'i com-

---

4. For a recent example of the conventional canon, see Hasan 1992.

5. 'A'isha bint Abi Bakr was married to the Prophet and is an important narrator of *a hadith* and a religious authority in her own right in the Sunni tradition.

mentators. Why is ʿAʾisha's role in recounting the life of the Prophet and the story of early Islam to be considered a technical matter of "preservation" devoid of creativity while the role of the men in the third A.H./ninth A.D. century who transmit ʿAʾisha's words is to be treated as if it were all that mattered (Spellberg 1994, 53–54)? Such a position owes much to the Joseph Schacht argument that *hadith* literature relied entirely on oral transmission until the late Umayyad era and ·is a product of the third/ninth century (1953).[6] This argument is disputed, most recently by Tarif Khalidi, who maintains that "written materials existed alongside oral transmission from the very beginning" (1994, 27).[7] Khalidi notes that "if these first-century materials were doctored in toto by later ages, all one can say is that it was a pretty bad doctoring job. The fragmented, often contradictory state in which these materials are found is perhaps the best proof that they were transmitted with only haphazard and generally recognizable doctoring, of the type and quantity that one may well expect in any similar body of traditions transmitted in both written and oral form. After having allowed for this doctoring (admittedly with the numerous problems raised therein) we still possess a body of materials, daunting in volume and constantly increasing, which needs careful and laborious examination" (Khalidi 1994, 27–28).

Khalidi's argument is useful in regard to the transmission of women's literature because we deal with the same source materials. Women's literature is in an even more fragmentary and haphazard state. The imprint of its transmitters is present in two "generally recognizable" ways. One is the tendency to bring the discourse of the early Islamic period in line with assumptions about political legitimacy dominant at the time the books were compiled. The other imprint of the transmitters is the obscuring of ways in which women in the early Islamic period engage in behavior different from what the authors of the later era could see as believable for a woman or acceptable in an early Muslim. That said, it is not reasonable to deny

6. See, also, Crone and Cook 1977; and Hawting 1986, 11–18.

7. See, also, Ismaʿil n.d., 13–29. Khalidi (1994, 19–20) describes the evolution from loose parchment pages in the early first century A.H. to specialized books in the early second century. The book explosion that produced most of the existing references on the early Islamic period occurred in the third and fourth centuries A.H. In addition to Khalidi's and Ismaʿil's arguments, see Farrukh 1984, 1:38.

altogether the discursive presence of the early Islamic women. Historian Leila Ahmed points out that women were "important contributors to the verbal texts of Islam, the texts that, transcribed eventually into written form by men, became part of the official history of Islam and of the literature that established the normative practices of Islamic society." She continues, this "means that early literature incorporates at least some material expressing the views of women fairly directly" (1992, 47). Extant texts represent an encounter between the editing men of the eighth through the fifteenth centuries A.D. and the composing women of the early Islamic era.

What texts are sources of women's compositions? Every classical (eighth to fifteenth century) Arabic text that inscribes material from the early Islamic period needs to be sifted for women's compositions. This sweep includes religio-historical materials and texts conventionally considered literary. Women's contributions to the privileged genre of Arabic literature, poetry, have been studied, to a modest extent, since classical times.[8] (This says something heartening about the men who collected women's poetry and the societies toward which they published it.) Modern scholarship (such as that of Salim al-Tanir 1988) continues to harvest women's poetry from the great behemoths of classical literature such as al-Aghani and al-'Uqd al-Farid, showing that these classical works are source books not merely for male representations of women as Fedwa Malti-Douglas has maintained (1991, 29–43) but for traces of women's compositions too. There are also modern studies of specific women such as Khansa' and Laila al-Akhyalia (poets who straddle the pre-Islamic and Islamic periods).[9] Religio-historical materials, including *hadith*, biography of the Prophet, histories, and biographical dictionaries, are rich with discur-

8. Al-Marzubani (d. 384/994) collects poetry in *Ash'ar al-Nisa'* (The poetry of women). Al-Suyuti (d. 911/1445) anthologizes women's poetry of his "modern age" in *Nuzhat al-Julasa' fi Ash'ar al-Nisa'*, leaving out pre-Islamic and early Islamic periods because, he says, there is too much women's poetry from those times for him to cover. A small number of poems by women can be found in the classical anthologies. The *Hamasa* of Abu Tammam (d. 241/846), the foremost anthology of this type, contains a few poems by women. The *Mufaddaliyat* of al-Mufaddal al-Dabbi (d.178/794) contains one, by an anonymous "woman of Bani Hanifa."

9. For Khansa''s collected poems with notes, see Khansa' n.d. For explication of her poems see al-Hufi n.d. For a full-length critical study of Khansa''s poetry, including her influence on modern Arab women writers, see al-Kawamila 1988.

sive traces of women. Women's compositions in the religio-historical corpus have rarely been treated to literary study.[10] Ibn Taifur (d. 280/893) comes closest to anthologizing these; he gathers prose, poetry, and miscellanies in his *Balaghat al-nisa'* (women's eloquences). The literary traces of women have been approached from two angles: as an incidental part of a study of gender or as a marginal part of a study of literature. Happily, a tiny number of people have a third approach that combines literary and gender analyses ('Abd al-Rahman 1958).[11]

Balagha/Eloquence

To begin theorizing the early discursive compositions of Arab women one must question the parameters of the term *literature.* The noun *adab* (literature) was not used by Arabs until the Umayyad era although it was used as a verb, *addaba,* to refer to the imparting of a moral education) (Husain 1991, 1:24–33). *Balagha,* however, is a classification generated from the early Arabic context, one which allows the inclusion of religio-historical and literary texts as well. *Balagha* is Arabic for "rhetoric," the art of eloquent composition and style. The etymological root is the verb *balagha,* "to reach," "to attain."[12] One meaning of the verb *balagha* is to come of age, to mature sexually, to attain legal majority, to reach adulthood. The noun *balagha* describes composition in which a message reaches its recipient in the fullness of its meaning. *Balagha* can apply to brief utterances whose eloquence is in part a function of their suitability to their contexts and to whole texts that can stand alone. It pertains to written as much as to oral discourse, to prose as much as poetry. *Balagha* is an effective concept with which to open a field of "early Islamic cultural studies" while maintaining rigorous criteria for the texts studied.

The ability to express oneself beautifully and effectively through the

---

10. 'Abd al-Halim Abu Shaqqa (1990) has collected *hadiths* narrated by women and hadiths mentioning women as well, facilitating research in this direction.

11. See, also, 'Abd al-Rahman 1970. Ahmad al-Hufi (1972) while writing about the image of women in pre-Islamic literature, also addresses the loss of women's literature. Khalif (1991) uses thematic, formal, and social-class analysis to produce fascinating insights on women's poetry.

12. *Al-Qamus al-Muhit* is a dictionary of ancient and classical usage compiled by al-Fairuz Abadi (d. 817/1415).

word was valorized in Arabic culture since pre-Islamic times (Mubarak 1981, 23). A modern linguist remarks that the Arab esteem for *balagha* from pre-Islamic times "explains to us why the wielders of the tongue, the poets and orators, were the heads of delegations among the Arabs, and their ambassadors and representatives; they were, among the Arabs, the shapers of opinion and decision-making." He adds that this love of eloquence "was widespread even among their commoners, and their women and children participated in it" (Mubarak 1981, 24).

Is *balagha* a gendered concept? How does the etymological meaning of *balagha* as reaching sexual adulthood act upon the possibility of women's *balagha* given the complex position of women in the pre-Islamic and early Islamic periods? If *balagha* was a route to power and influence, under what conditions did women's *balagha* have the social space in which to develop?

Cultures are heterogeneous compounds in which contradictory elements coexist. *Balagha* was indeed a universal ideal that claimed to allow participation of women and men as well, "objective" excellence of composition being the only standard. Women, however, were handicapped by the contradictory cultural ideal of feminine self-effacement, epitomized in the testament of Umama bint al-Harith to her daughter on her wedding day: "Beware of joyousness when he is sad, and of gloominess around him when he is joyous. . . . Know that you will not get what you want until you prefer his contentment over your contentment and his desire over your desire in what you love and what you hate" (Ma'badi 1983, 17). In this pre-Islamic situation that exists in Western societies as well, mother teaches daughter acquiescence to male domination. The ideal of feminine reticence coexists in tension with the ideal of expressiveness. The irony is that Umama's testament is widely cited (in places as varied as the classical al-'Uqd al-Farid to present-day school textbooks)[13] as an example of *balagha*.

The language in which *balagha* was evaluated often betrayed a male-centered bias: those deemed to be great poets were (and still are) sometimes called *al-shu'ara al-fuhul*, (the virile poets) although women could have this quality. Poetry that had *lin* (tenderness, pliancy) was feeble. With regard to prose, the term *asatir* (myths), generally a derogatory word, was

13. The United Arab Emirates' 1996–97 tenth-grade language curriculum, for example, contains Umama's testament.

applied to women's stories. Caliph Muʿawiya (d. 60/680) tells Arwa bint al-Harith, "Leave aside your women's tales [*asatir al-nisaʾ*]" (Ibn Taifur 1987, 42). There is no comparable phrase, "men's tales," although there is "tales of the ancients" (*asatir al-awwalin*).[14] Women who could counterbalance their gender handicap with other factors—high social class, for example— were more likely to be among those history has preserved as mistresses of *balagha*. Women of all classes were caught between clashing values when they attempted to bespeak themselves, whereas men, except the lowest in status, had less ambiguous encouragement to advance toward the podium.

Fuhula (virility) however, was not the only standard for the evaluation of poetry; *jazala*, meaning "lucidity" and "soundness," was a gender-neutral term that also applied. One can argue that every social class and group, slave or free, male or female, had a certain space within which its members could compose eloquence and express the self. Even female slaves had the realm of song.[15] And although examples of the disparagement of women's stories exist, so do examples of appreciative reception for these stories. One appreciative listener to women's tales is the Prophet Muhammad in the *hadith* about the eleven women (al-Mundhiri 1977, 442–44):[16] ʿAʾisha, versed in pre-Islamic folklore, narrates that "eleven women convened and contracted not to hold back anything about their husbands. The first said, ʿMy husband is the flesh of a flaccid camel on the peak of a mountain too grueling to climb and not worth the effort.ʾ" Each woman describes her spouse in pithy *sajʿ* (rhythmic prose). The eleventh woman waxes nostalgic over a nonpareil named Abu Zaraʿ. Although she has remarried since the dear man left her for another woman with breasts firm as pomegranates, he will always be her favorite husband. ʿAʾisha says that the Prophet, after hearing this racy pre-Islamic narrative, said to her, "I am to you what Abu Zaraʿ was for Um Zaraʿ." Here ʿAʾisha is acting as storyteller and transmitter while the Prophet is responding as amiably to her "Scheherazading" as to the characters in the story within the story.

Women's eloquence traditions, with roots in pre-Islamic Arab culture, thus flourished in the early Islamic period in a context shaped by the

14. For examples, see Qurʾan 6:25, 8:31, 16:24, 23:83, and 83:13.

15. For a full-length critical study of the connection of poetry to song in Makka and Madina, see Daif 1992.

16. It is in Muslim's *hadith* collection in the Book of the Virtues of the Companions under "ʿAʾisha's virtues."

tension between the acknowledgment of women's discourse and its marginalization. One reason why classical literature uses the term *balaghat al-nisa'* (women's eloquences) is because of the (assumed) scarcity of such a thing (Mubarak 1996). There is no such category as "men's eloquences." In retrieving this category of women's eloquence, does one reinscribe the separateness of women in the literary tradition or offer a way for women's texts to be reintroduced into the mainstream? One does both.

Mujadila/ Interlocutor

The concept of *mujadila* (she who argues or disputes) helps one gather those women's eloquences that are fragmentary and dispersed in the textual sources. One needs to add *mujadila* as a mode of coming into literary history because these compositions are not quite poems, orations, and folk tales, yet they have too much substance to be counted as proverbs. These compositions usually have an "interlocutory character," to borrow a phrase from work on African American women's writing (Henderson 1994, 258). The *mujadila*, or interlocutor, both interrupts and acknowledges the other to whom she speaks. She is both inside and outside the discourse that results from this encounter between herself and others; she both tells the story and is told by it.

The prototype *mujadila* comes from *hadith* material related to the chapter of the Qur'an called *al-Mujadala* (the dispute) or *al-Mujadila* (the woman disputant). The chapter begins:[17] "God has indeed heard the utterance of the woman who disputes with thee concerning her husband and complains unto God; and God hears your dialogue; indeed God is the all-seeing, all-hearing. Those among you who commit *zihar* upon their wives, their wives are not their mothers; their mothers are those who gave birth to them; they do but utter the abominable and false utterance; and God is the all-pardoning, all-forgiving." The next few verses prescribe the fines to be imposed on men who resort to *zihar*. *Zihar* was a pre-Islamic Arab custom of declaring to a wife, "You are to me like the back of my mother," thereby relieving the husband of sexual duties to her, leaving her with neither a proper divorce nor a proper marriage. The rest of the chapter addresses the challenges of facing the newly constituted community in Madina in envi-

17. The translation is my own modification of Ali 1994.

sioning a new society based on Islamic values, even charting the physical spaces of the community toward the cohesion of new social groupings: "O you who believe! When you are told to make room in the assemblies, make room; God will make room for you."

The *hadith* material behind these verses, as reported by Ibn Saʿd (d. 230/845) and others,[18] explains that Khawla bint Thaʿlaba was married to her crotchety paternal cousin Aws bin al-Samit. One day he lost his temper and said the *zihar* word to her. This put Khawla and Aws in an unhappy predicament: Neither wanted an end to the marriage, yet *zihar* in pre-Islamic times had been irreversible. Khawla hastens to find the Prophet, who was at ʿAʾisha's house. The Prophet sees no way out of ending the marriage. Khawla protests:

> O messenger of God, this is Aws whom you know. He is the father of my child and the son of my uncle and the most beloved of people unto me. You know very well how he is beset with dotage and the loss of his faculties, with dwindling strength and garbling tongue. And the person it most behooves to look in on him if she finds any way to help him is me, and the person it most behooves to look in on me if he finds any way to help me is him. He uttered a word. By the one who revealed the Book to you, he did not mention divorce. He said "You are to me as my mother's back." (Ibn Saʾd 1957, 8:378–80).

In another version she adds, "He has nothing and no one provides for him but me."[19] The Prophet still sees no other solution. Khawla persists, disputing the issue with the Prophet. Finally she says, "O dear God, I complain unto you of the severity of my predicament and of the hardship of parting; oh dear God, reveal through the tongue of your Prophet something that will have comfort in it for us" (Ibn Saʾd 1957, 8:379). Ibn Saʿd's version has ʿAʾisha saying at this juncture, "Then I wept indeed, and so did all who were with us of the Prophet's family weep in compassion and empathy for her." ʿAʾisha narrates the rest of the story of how the Prophet goes into a state of inspiration with Khawla waiting anxiously and returns

18. Versions of it also occur in al-ʾAsqalani 1909; Ibn ʿAbd al-Birr 1969 (d. 563/1070), and Ibn al-Athir n.d. (d. 630/1232), but Ibn Saʾd (1957) is the earliest source. There is some confusion over her name (e.g., Khawla or Khuwaila, daughter of Thaʿlaba and daughter-in-law of Samit, or daughter of Samit) among versions.

19. For a comparison of versions see ʿUmar Rida Kahhala, 1991, 1:382–84.

with the above verses. Khawla is so relieved she jumps for joy. She then counters every penalty the verses impose on the man guilty of *zihar* with a convincing reason for excusing Aws from it: He is too feeble to fast two months and too impoverished to feed dates to sixty poor people. Finally, the Prophet offers to donate half the dates. Khawla chips in with the other half, and between the two of them they get the sorry old fellow off the hook. Aws is reported to have said, "But for Khawla, I would have been done for." The whole story is framed, in Ibn 'Abd al-Birr's version, within a narrative of how the caliph 'Umar runs into an old woman outside the mosque. She says:

> Hey there, oh 'Umar, I knew you when you were little 'Umair running about in the 'Ukaz Market steering your sheep with a stick. The days had barely passed before you were called 'Umar, and then the days had barely passed again before you were called Commander of the Faithful. So revere God with your flock, and know that whoso fears the Promised Day, people draw near to him from far away. But whoso fears death dreads to forego. (Ibn 'Abd al-Birr n.d., 4:1831)

The man with 'Umar says something dismissive, but 'Umar responds, "Leave her [to speak]. Do you not know who she is? This is the Khawla whose utterance was heard by the One above the seven heavens." He adds, "This is Khawla bint Tha'laba about whom God revealed 'God has indeed heard the utterance of the woman who disputes with thee concerning her husband.' By God, even if she stood here till nightfall I would not leave her except for prayer times," or, in another version, "So 'Umar, by God, had better listen to what she utters."

Mujadila is an active participle and refers to a person. The root verb is *jadala*, "to coil or braid." The noun *al-jadal* means argumentation and skillful disputation, "maneuvering left and right in debate."[20] A *mujadila* (fem.) is one who argues or disputes skillfully. What I call *mujadila* discourse is rhetorically excellent composition forming part of a dialogue or a conversation. It is braided with the utterances or texts of others to produce a new meaning for the collectivity. In the *hadith* text at hand, narrated by Khawla, 'A'isha, and a number of others, Khawla's spoken compositions are braided into an account of the contextualizing history attached to the revelation.

20. There is even an erotic description of a woman by a woman (Ma'badi 1983, 23–24).

The exchange between ʿUmar and Khawla adds another sequence to the plait of the story.

The Qurʾanic chapter juxtaposes the problem encountered in Khawla's marriage with problems of transition from pre-Islamic to Islamic order faced by the Madinan community altogether, connecting the Khawla issue to a broader social context. The Qurʾanic response to Khawla's *jadal* is to increase the elasticity of the law. God's response to Khawla is followed by admonishment to the townspeople that their assemblies should be more inclusive; these are the private and public dramas of a society in transition in post-Hijra Madina.

Khawla's *balagha* lies in the overall fluency and lucidity and charm with which she articulates her thoughts, in her ability to move her listeners to empathy. The *mujadila* interrogates an other and wedges a lever into the culture. In this case, Khawla argues with the Prophet about the customary divorce law that he has too uncritically affirmed. Khawla's description of the particularities of her husband and her marriage are a protest against a literalistic status quo that has not taken the individual characteristics of this couple into account with any flexibility. Her opening sets up her claim for the primacy of kin and emotional relationships over the letter of the law. Her speech is a petition for a more compassionate alternative and has implications beyond the case at hand. The Qurʾanic text acknowledges Khawla's utterance and knits it into the *sura,* reflecting back Khawla's phrase "O dear God, I complain unto you" (*ashku ilaika*) in the verse, "God has indeed heard the utterance of the woman who disputes with thee concerning her husband and complains unto God" (*tashtaki ila allah*).

It is fair to ask if this is not making too much out of the speech of a woman who was trying to save her marriage, not necessarily compose eloquence. Yet she had to call up her aesthetic talents to argue for some-thing in a manner similar to those men who used the tongue to defend the tribe and earned the status of great orators of *balagha.* The nature of oral literature is that it is often composed under the pressures of the occasion. This does not mean it cannot exceed its initial motivation, nor does it mean it did not involve consciousness of aesthetic and craft. Just as there are examples of *balagha* that happen to be shaped around men's life ex-periences, her *balagha* is inspired by her concerns as a woman. Second, by the time of her speech to ʿUmar, she has clearly assumed a more self-conscious speaker's role. This is clear from her rhythmic prose (*saj*ᶜ, whose traits include rhyme, assonance, and short clauses). *Saj*ᶜ is a pronounced characteristic of the pre-Islamic Arabic prose of priestesses and priests. She assumes a diction that draws upon the traditions of pre-Islamic priestesses and Islamic styles of sermonizing as well. Third, this *mujadila* prototype sets up the speaking posture of the *mujadila* and allows one to cluster other examples around it toward theorizing women's contribution to early Islamic literature.

One can point to thematic categories. Khawla's description of her husband is part of a tradition of women's representation of men and masculinity. Khawla's critique of male religio-legal rulings links her to another position, best-known of ᶜA'isha, of the woman who disputes men's interpretation of the faith. Another category of *mujadila* compositions involves women accosting an authority figure with a petition or a challenge. The stories of the proto-Shiᶜite women accosting Muᶜawiya in his assembly are so numerous that a third-century A.H. treatise is devoted to relating sixteen of them (Akhbar al-Wafidat min al-Nisa' ᶜala Muᶜawiya, attributed to al-ᶜAbbas bin Bikar al-Dabbi). The degree of audacity in this type of *mujadila* discourse is directly related to social conditions of gender: women could get away with saying more because as women they were not seen as capable of posing a real threat to the authorities. Because these texts are so imbedded in Sunni-Shiᶜi polemic, they raise all sorts of issues too voluminous to be treated here. The proto-Shiᶜite and Khawarij *mujadila* discourses, however, must not be dismissed as male appropriations of women's eloquence in the service of great persecuted causes. It may be that when men try to appropriate women's voices, the process entails envisioning women as speaking subjects rather than as silent submitters and can activate unintended challenges to the gender status quo ante.

Gynocentric Portrayals of Manhood

Um Aban bint ᶜUtba was a prominent Makkan who moved to Syria with the first wave of the territorial expansion of Islam; her husband died in the Battle of Ajnadin against the Byzantines. Ibn Qutaiba, author of an encyclopedic collection of *akhbar* (accounts) that straddle both literary and historical writing, as do so many classical Arabic works, reports:

'Umar bin al-Khattab proposed to Um Aban bint 'Utba bin Rabi'a after her husband, Yazid bin Abi Sufyan, died, and she said, "He does not enter but scowling and he does not leave but scowling; he closes his doors and minimizes his bounty." Then Zubair proposed to her, and she said, "He has one hand on my temples and one hand on the whip." Then 'Ali proposed to her, and she said, "Women get no luck from him except that he sits among their four parts; they do not get anything else from him." Then Talha proposed to her, and she was responsive and he married her. So 'Ali bin Abi Talib visited her and said, "You rejected whom you rejected, and you accepted the son of the daughter of a Hadrami [southern Arab]!" She said, "Decree and destiny." He said, "Now then, truly you have married he among us who is most beautiful of face, most generous of hand, and the greatest in bounty to his family." (1925, 4:17).

The version reported in Ibn 'Asakir's history of Damascus adds this:

Then Talha proposed to her . . . she said, "I am well aware of his dispositions. When he enters, he enters laughing, and when he leaves, he leaves smiling. When I ask, he gives; when I am silent, he initiates; when I work, he thanks; and when I do wrong, he forgives." So after he had dwelled with her, 'Ali said, "Abu Muhammad, permit me to speak with Um Aban." He said, "Speak with her." So he said, "Peace be unto you, oh woman dear to herself." She said, "And unto you peace." He said, "The Commander of the Faithful proposed to you and you rejected him?" She said, "It was so." He said, "And I proposed to you and you rejected me although I am from the Messenger of God?" She said, "It was so." (Kahhala 1991, 1:21)

We have caught a glimpse, in 'A'isha's story of the eleven women, of a tradition in which women create a critique of masculinity, delineating ideal men and lampooning male foibles as they perceive them. Here Um Aban offers a completely woman-centered perspective on four men who have extremely high status among the Companions of the Prophet in terms of the new standard of *sabiqa,* or precedence given according to how early a person came to Islam and how close to the Prophet he or she was. Although Talha was also a prominent and early Companion of the Prophet, the other three are traditionally considered more eminent than he. Um Aban, who comes from a group of three sisters known for their

verbal audacity and lateness to Islam, is deliberately oblivious to this criterion of virtue, displacing it with woman-centered criteria of men's merits.
She elegantly paints miniature character portraits of each man, her contributions to the gallery of the eleven women. Positive as well as negative
portraits form this tradition, which offers a cultural counterweight not
only to men's depictions of women but to men's depictions of the ideal
man. Um Aban's first suitor is bad-tempered and tight-fisted. The second
is rough and demands too much hard work of a wife, and so on. Her
criterion for ideal manhood is entirely woman-centered (not to mention
delightful): the good husband is generous, solicitous, appreciative, and
easygoing with his wife. A striking feature of her description of Talha is
the syntactical equality and reciprocity suggested by "When I ask, he
gives; when I am silent, he initiates; when I work, he thanks; and when I
do wrong, he forgives."

Um Aban's eloquent lines are parts of a dialogue not only with each
man who proposes to her but with the implied eavesdroppers, the community that is interested in her responses, finally represented by ʿAli in the
story. Because the topic is marriage, she does not have to struggle to enunci-
ate her right to speak as a woman. She does, however, take that brief moment in which people are interested in what a woman has to say and use it
to add to the cultural repertoire through the power of her *balagha,* a new way
to be a woman—the woman dear to herself. It is ʿAli's phrase. ʿAli correctly
reads and interprets Um Aban's interlocutions as articulating the self-worth
of a woman, her feeling of personal dignity, great enough to overcome both
the cultural value of wifely self-abnegation and the cultural value put on
women's silence. As an interested reader and interpreter, ʿAli adds a fitting
twist to the braid of the story of Um Aban. The woman who rejects a
number of suitors is a motif in classical literature. It has been suggested that
when the suitors are prominent political figures, the stories are actually encoded political arguments (Roded 1994, 37). Um Aban's rejection of figures
venerated by both Sunnis and Shiʿis does not support reading the account as
a product of the legitimacy debates. Reading this for male-centered legitimacy politics does not work. Reading it as a woman-centered critique of
masculinity opens it to a rich context of similar discourse by women.

Um Maʿbad ʿAtika bint Khaled al-Khizaʿiya is another contributor to
women's verbal portraits of men. Um Maʿbad was an elder who provided
food and drink for people in the vicinity of the Kaʿba. Her claim to elo-

quence is a representation of the Prophet reported in Ibn Taifur's *balaghat al-nisa'* with a chain of transmission leading back to her son. The story is that on his way out of Makka during his migration, the Prophet stops at her tent along with Abu Bakr and their guide, seeking refreshment. All she has at the moment is a dry old goat. Upon being stroked and prayed over by the Prophet, the animal provides bowl after bowl of milk; they drink and go on to make Hijra history. Later that day, her husband comes home and, marveling at the milk and hearing its story, asks her to describe the man. "Many men have described the Prophet, peace and prayers be upon him," says a present-day literary historian, "kings of utterance and princes of clarity, but not one of them has reached the height that a Bedouin woman such as Um Ma'bad has achieved" (Ma'badi 1983, 15):

> I saw a man of distinct purity, serene face and comely physique. Neither thinness of hair nor frailty of build mars him. He is graceful, grand, handsome. Dark are his eyes, thick are his lashes, husky is his voice, bushy is his beard, and long is his neck. Houri-eyed, kohl-rimmed, join-browed, well-built he is. When silent, a gravity dignifies him, and when he talks, he soars and ascends. He is the most beautiful and the most radiant among people from afar and the sweetest and most excellent of them up close. His logic is engaging, neither too overwhelming nor too sparse; his logic is like pearls in a pattern, rolling down. He is of medium height, neither so tall as to annoy nor so short as to disgust. A branch between two branches, he is the most blooming of the three in his appearance and the best of them in proportion. He has comrades who cherish him; if he speaks, they hearken to his speaking, and if he commands, they hasten to his command. Neither stern nor feeble, he is well served and observed and obeyed and well arrayed. (Ibn Taifur 1987, 67)

Ibn Taifur adds that a man asked 'Ali (d. 40/660) why no one had described the Prophet as well as Um Ma'bad. 'Ali replies, "Women describe men with their desires, so they excel in their description." 'Ali's comment clues the reader to the charming sensuality of Um Ma'bad's portrait, in case one missed it. Sensual description of women by men abounds in Arabic literature (Ma'badi 1983, 23–24). Um Ma'bad's portrait fills in the sparser category, women's physical descriptions of men.

Ibn Taifur describes Um Ma'bad as a *"barza, jalda"* woman. In the etymological dictionary *Al-Qamus al-Muhit, jalda* means sturdy and *"a barza* woman is one who has prominent merits, or a conspicuous, dignified elder who appears before the people, and they sit with her and converse, and she is chaste" (Abadi 1993, 646). Um Maʿbad, then, is described in terms that suggest a public speaking role for her. Some consciousness of her verbal portraiture as craft is also indicated by the fact that she draws upon the *sajʿ* (rhythmic prose) stylistics of the pre-Islamic priestesses (Ibn Saʿd 8:289).

Male-authored images of women in early Arabic literature have been studied ad infinitum. The eloquent compositions of Um Aban and Um Maʿbad offer gynocentric aesthetics of manhood that can be compared with androcentric literature about womanhood and with the cult of male beauty among women as well.[21]

Qaila's *Kitab*

Qaila bint Makhram narrates a story of a woman on the edges of the new Islamic society trying to make her way to its center both physically and discursively. She offers a unique perspective on the dramas of social transition so central to the early Islamic era. Qaila recounts:

> I was married to a man of Bani Junab bin al-Harith bin Juhba bin ʿAdiy bin Jundub bin al-ʿAnbar, a man who was called al-Azhar bin Malik. He died and left behind girls, one of them al-Fuzaira'; she was the youngest of them. . . . So I went out searching for traveling companions heading for the Messenger of God; this was in the infancy of Islam. Then al-Hudaiba' wept for me, and I pitied her and carried her with me on my camel, hiding from her paternal uncle Athwab bin Malik. We left, slowing our camel when a rabbit bolted out at us. Al-Hudaiba' the well-born said, "By the Lord of the Kaʿba!" And she uttered something when the fox jumped in front of us. And al-Fuzaira' said, "By the Lord of the Kaʿba, your heel is still higher than Athwab's heel." Then the camel kept faltering, even though it was clear, and took fright. So al-Hudaiba' said, "It has found you out, and the trust is for Athwab's taking." I said, "I was compelled to it; what shall I do?" She said, "You will turn your clothes belly out and turn your saddlebags belly out and turn yourself back to front." So I turned over a woolen garment of hers and turned it belly

21. The appreciation of the beauty of Joseph by the city women comes to mind; see the Qurʾanic chapter "Joseph."

out. I did all she ordered. Then the camel rose and straddled and uri-
nated, and I replaced its equipage on it. Then we left cautiously. Sud-
denly there was Athwab, in pursuit of its tracks, sword in hand. We fled
from him into a huge tent. The camel humbled itself in the hearth of the
house. I lunged into it with the girl, and he struck me with his sword and
hit me on the side of my temple and said, "Throw down my brother's
daughter to me, you foul one!" I flung her to him, for I knew him better
than anyone, and the people had mustered around him. And I left, going
to my sister who was married into Bani Shaiban, to look for traveling
companions heading for the Messenger, blessings be upon him. While I
was with her of an evening, she thought I was asleep when her husband
came in from banquet and said, "By your father, I have hit upon a traveling companion for Qaila, an honest companion and true." She said,
"Who is he?" He said, "He is Harith bin Hassan, returning in the morn-
ing as the delegate of Bakr bin Wa'il to the Messenger of God, blessings
be upon him." She said, "Woe is her, do not tell her that. Of all the
people who can see and hear on earth, that she will be following the
brother of Bakr bin Wa'il, and no man from her people with her!" He
said, "Do not mention that to her and I will not mention it." So when I
woke, having heard what the two of them had said, I tugged my camel
along and I went out to Harith bin Hassan. I asked about him and there
he was with his mounts, so I asked for his company to the Messenger of
God and he said, "Certainly, and generosity." So I left with him, an
honest companion and true. We arrived at the Messenger of God and
entered the mosque just as dawn wasbreaking. The rise to prayer was
called and the prayer was made while the stars blurred together and
people could barely be distinguished from each other in the gloom of
night. So I lined up with the men, and I was a woman new to the era,
still ignorant. The man beside me said, "Are you a woman or a man?" I
said, "A woman." He said, "You almost ruined me; you should join the
women behind you." Sure enough, there was a line of women which
began by the chambers, which I had not seen when I entered. So I lined
up with them, and after we had prayed, I looked around to find the man
of distinction and composure so I could find the Messenger of God,
until a man came near and said, "Peace be upon you, O Messenger of
God." And there he was sitting in a squat, hugging his knees to his chest,
wearing two fine garments dyed in saffron. Then he arose and in his
hand was a palm branch stripped of all but two leaves near the top, and
he said, "And upon you be peace, and the mercy of God." When I

beheld the Messenger of God and the gravity in his assembly I took deadly fright. A bystander said to him, "The poor woman has taken fright." So he said with his hand, "O poor one, serenity be upon you." And what I had felt of fear went from me. Then my companion advanced, the first to advance, and pledged Islam for himself and on behalf of his people, and he said, "O Messenger of God, write us title (*kitab*) to [the waters of] al-Dahna' so that Tamim cannot overrun it for us, except for a traveler or a neighbor." He said, "O young boy, write him title (*kitab*) [i.e., giving his tribe proprietorship] to al-Dahna'." When I saw that, I was disturbed, for it was my home and my homeland. So I said, "O Messenger of God, he has not asked you for the fair thing in this affair. This Dahna' with you is a tethering spot for camels and a pasturing spot for sheep, and the women of Tamim and its sons stand behind that." He said, "You have spoken truly. Stop, young boy. A Muslim is brother to a Muslim; the water and the trees suffice them all; they cooperate over what portions are left, like this." And so, when Harith saw that he was going to go without writing the title (*kitab*), he clapped one hand on the other and said, "You and I were, as they used to say, a weakling carried its own demise on its hooves." So I said, "Now then, by God, you were a guide in the gloomy night, openhanded in travel, chaste with your captive, and an honest companion and true, all the way to the Messenger of God. I can seek my business if you can seek your business." He said, "And what is your business with al-Dahna'?" I said, "It is the tethering spot of my camel; ask your wife's camel." He said, "I do make the Messenger my witness, that I am a brother to you as long as I live; if I go back on that, I will have to face him." I said, "If you begin it, then I will live up to it." Then the Messenger of God said, "What is to prevent a son of hers from breaking the plan and attacking from behind the rock?" I wept and said, "By God, I bore Huzam, and he fought with you on the Day of al-Rabdha, then he set out for Khaibar, and provided for me from there, but was struck with a fever and died. And he left the women in my care." The Messenger of God said, "If you were not a poor one, I would have dragged you on your face or ordered you to be dragged on your face. Is it common that one of you accompanies her intimate companion in this world fittingly, then when they are separated—who else does it behoove to take his place?" I said, "O Lord, reward me for what I have passed, and help me with what I have coming. By the One in whose hands is Muhammad's soul, I urge you all to fall into a love like mine and then have your intimate companion stripped from you. Therefore, o worshippers of God, do not persecute your brothers." Then he gave the order, and I was given the title (*kitab*) on a piece of red leather: "For Qaila and the women Qaila's daughters, they shall not be oppressed in any right, nor shall they be forced to any marriage, and every Muslim believer is their champion as long as they do good and do not do wrong." (Ibn Taifur 1987, 184–188)

Appended to this with a separate chain of transmission, and serving the compiler as further proof of its authenticity, is an epilogue:

"I knew of one of Qaila's daughters in the time of Hajjaj. A man from the people of Syria asked for her in marriage and she refused. Hajjaj [the caliph's deputy] sent after her to force her to marry the man, so she took refuge in the written title (*kitab*), and it was in her hand, saying, 'It is in our *kitab* that we cannot be forced to marriage!' But he paid no attention to her title and pushed her toward the Syrian."

Qaila's story is so obscure and rough-hewn, and so completely unrelated to issues of political succession, that it seems to be a fairly straightforward transmission of a woman's narrative. Qaila is on the margins of the new Muslim community in many ways. The community was urban centered, based in Madina, and she was nomadic. She does not appear to be of high class and so has no pre-Islamic privilege on which to capitalize, nor does she have any Islamic *sabiqa,* "precedence," or prominence coming from early conversion or service to the Prophet. Qaila has been badly treated by her husband's clan; her husband and son have died, and she is left to find a means of providing for her daughters. Their uncle seems to want neither to support them properly nor to let their mother leave with them. She enters Madina alone of her people, without ally or sponsor in the town, as a woman "new to the era." Her sense of emergence from an old way of life is reflected in the way the phrases "I left" and "I went out" (both translations of *kharajtu*) reverberate through the first half of her story, whereas her sense of strange newness and awe at the dawning era infuses her description of "arriving at the Messenger." Not only is she "new to the era," but Islam itself is on the wobbly legs of its "infancy," still a fluid, unsettled shape. Its stars are blurry; its people cannot be distinguished yet; its Prophet is not recognizable as a leader by the old signs of kingly body posture but must be detected by the phrase "Peace be unto you."

From what sources does Qaila scrape up the courage to speak in the Prophet's forum? Obviously, her personal experience of pre-Islamic life has not been one that has given her much although she has been able to seek refuge from its cruelties (represented by Athwab) in its generosities (represented by her sister and her husband and by the honest companion and true). Equally obvious is that she is a woman of abundant inner resources, including *balagha*. The story is as much a story of her coming into her speaking voice as it is about an intertribal water dispute.

Qaila constructs a podium for herself out of several disparate materials. First, what impels her to speak out is "home and homeland." This is a woman's experience of homeland, of informal rights of access to water and pasturage claimed by the women and children of both tribes in an old order that was no longer living up to its ideal of protecting the weak. She is fighting for the survival of fragile women's spaces in the pockets of Bedouin life. Painfully able to see the flaws of the old way, Qaila is a prime candidate for the new faith, with its critique of brute might and its ideal of universal brotherhood ostensibly supplanting tribalism. The other thing that enables her to stand and deliver is the Prophet's assurance of serenity, *sakina*, a grammatically feminine quality with etymological connections to dwelling and abode (*sakana*). The Prophet, who is the goal of her quest from the beginning of the story, provides refuge from the blows of the old system. The Prophet's blessing, however, is only a temporary stay against a tide of change that was more than a change in religion but a transition to centralized government, urbanization, and sedentarization. The languages of the two social orders that she straddles intertwine in her narrative; the language of folk beliefs and "belly out" rituals and "the Lord of the Ka'ba" spoken by al-Hudaiba', on the one hand, and the language of abstract ideals of brotherhood and writing rituals and "Allah" spoken by the Prophet, on the other. Her narrative does not try to smooth these lumpy elements into one homogenous language. The fragility of Qaila's women's space is underlined by the epilogue; her daughters are unable to hold against the misogyny of the succeeding kingdom the rights guaranteed them in writing during the "infancy" of Islam.

Is the type of discourse collected under the concept of the *mujadila* unique to women? Obviously, as in Qaila's case, men were involved in arguing positions too. First, it is the source literature itself that sets off what these women say as examples of women's *balagha*. This has to do with the ghettoizing of women's eloquence. Second, there may be something in the connection of *mujadila* discourse to the social conditions of gender. Women could petition authority figures in a way that men might avoid for fear of being seen as vulnerable. To return to Khawla and Aws, Ibn Saʿd reports that at first Khawla tells the husband to go to the Prophet, and Aws replies, "I would be ashamed before him to ask him about this; you go to the Messenger of God, peace be upon him. Maybe you will gain some good for us from him that will relieve what we are in, out of what he knows best" (Ibn Saʿd 1957, 8:379). Arguing his case would involve revealing the doddering state of his tongue and other embarrassing things that Khawla does not hesitate to describe. Women produce discourse in the *mujadila* mode in part because of marginalization from other routes of access to power. Qaila comes from an outlying Bedouin tribe in which a dispute like hers might have been more readily solved by the sword than the word, had there been a man in her family able to take up arms. In addition to the *mujadila* position being imbued with gender qualities considered to be outside the masculine range, such as an ability to discuss the private underbelly of life, it is often related to the defense of an "underdog" position. The cultural emphasis on women's reticence was more likely to be overcome by opposing cultural values when a woman's reason for speaking was defense of an oppositional group or political movement, which lent her legitimacy. This was the case with the proto-Shiʿite *mujadilas*. Being oppositional, such a group would be less organized, its podiums less formalized, and, hence, less excluding of women than that of the authorities. *Mujadila* discourse emerges from gendered conditions. Qaila's discourse speaks for an unorganized, unrecognized social cluster—the Bedouin women who use the waters of al-Dahnaʾ.

Asma's *Khutba*

Qaila may speak in defense of informal women's spaces without articulating her position specifically in terms of gender, but Asma bint Yazid al-Ashhaliya speaks from a position of full-fledged gender consciousness. If the social organization of gender roles gave men literal podiums from which to make orations (*khutba*), Asma bint Yazid steps into a speaking position self-consciously modeled on that of the male orator (*khatib*). Asma "was dubbed the orator [*khatiba*] of the women" (Ibn Hajar 1909, 4:234). Asma approached the Prophet while he was among men and said:

> I am the messenger [*rasul*] of those who are behind me of the congregation of Muslim women. God Almighty sent you to men and to women. So we believed in you and followed you. We, the company of women, are encircled and enchambered, biding in your houses and satisfying the lusts of men and carrying their children. And men earn merit over us in congregation, attending funerals, and *jihad*. And if they leave on *jihad*, we preserve their property for them and we rear their children. So do we share in the reward, O Messenger of God? (Ibn ʿAbd al-Birr n.d., 1787–88)

The Prophet is reported to have turned his full face to the throng of men with him and said, "Have you ever heard the expression of any woman more excellent than her inquiry into her religion?" Then he turns his full face to Asma and says, "Go, O Asma, and inform the women who are behind you that the good wifeliness of a woman for her husband and her efforts toward his happiness and her following his assent do equal all that you mentioned for men."

Asma's style fuses some pre-Islamic elements with Qurʾanic diction. The sajʿ (rhythmic prose) is not pronounced; although there are some internal rhymes, they are subordinated to the flow of ideas. One hears distant echoes of Sura al-Nur's vocabulary (see 24:60) in Asma's "biding in your houses" (qawaʿidu buyutakum), and sees shades of the "chaste-eyed" (*qasirat al-tarf*) houris of numerous *surahs* (e.g., 37:48, 55:56, 38:52) in her women "encircled and enchambered" (*maqsurat mukhdirat*). Asma begins by introducing herself using the generic/masculine form of "messenger." She carefully lays the postulate she wants to test: that God sent the Prophet to men and women equally. Then she describes the social conditions of being a woman in the specific experience of the women whom she represents and how these conditions hamper women's ability to seek religious merit as measured in the quantitative terms (e.g., number of congregational prayers performed, number of funerals attended) that seem to dominate. She describes men's activities from a woman-centered perspective to show the hidden ways in which men's meritorious actions depend on the underappreciated daily work of women, then poses the question that sums up this sophisticated gender analysis: How will God redress the unfairness of standards for religious merit that do not take into account that the de facto social conditions of women limit their access to activities considered meritorious? The Prophet's answer is that God will redress it through a comparable worth policy that neither mandates women's domesticity nor demands that it submit to androcentric notions of merit. The Prophet's response pragmatically acknowledges the pressures placed on women in the type of marriage that predominated in his times and attempts to raise the value of the woman's work within it but does not imply that such "marriages of subjugation" (as Amina Wadud terms them) dictate a universal norm.

Assigning equal value to women's traditional domestic roles does not suggest that women must limit themselves to those roles, as this incident is conventionally read. A typical reading from a book on literature of the early Islamic period mentions the incident as an example of how "even" women participated in oratory: "It is narrated that a woman went to the Messenger of God (peace and blessings be upon him) and said, O Messenger of God, I am the delegate of the women to you. Then she mentioned the reward that men get; then she asked, So what do we get from this, O Messenger of God? So he said, Inform the women you meet that obedience to the husband and recognizing his right equals that, and it is few of you who do it" (Hasan 1992, 107). The author does not name Asma or report the body of her speech. His summary of the Prophet's response assumes that any prescription for good spousely behavior of wives toward husbands is the same as a prescription for obedience. The power of her critique of gender roles is obliterated. It is subordinated to the conservative assumption that Muslim women in the idealized era of early Islam could not have challenged traditional gender roles. One is, apparently, to believe only contemporary Muslim women capable of such challenges; one is, perhaps, to find ways for blaming such thoughts in contemporary Muslim women on so-called Western influence.

The extent to which Asma's oration offers a pointed critique of the traditional domesticity of women and not a normative portrayal of it is evident in view of her own life. Among other things, she participated in the Battle of Yarmouk, where she is reported to have killed nine Byzantine soldiers with her tent pole (al-'Asqilani 1909, 4:234–35). Without glorifying the disturbing level of violence of her world, I believe it safe to say that a woman who is prepared to do feats of that sort has not had embroidery on her mind most of the time. If she exaggerates the constraints on women when her own life shows that women were not all that completely enclosed and enchambered, it is because she is chafing under them. Unlike Um Ma'bad, Asma is in the prime of womanhood here. She underscores her sexuality when she says "we" women are the satisfiers of the "lusts" of men. Her striding forward to the Prophet while he is among the men to make this particular speech must be seen as a conscious challenge to the sexual politics of public space. This challenge may explain why the first thing the Prophet does is help legitimate her presence and her speaking as if to stave off possible hostility from the men. Muslim men in subsequent generations would try to prevent potential Asma's from crossing those lines.

Conclusions: *Akhbirini/haddithini*

The work of reconstructing the literary history of women in the early Islamic era begins with Um Sa'id's inquiry, *akhbirini/haddithini*: "Aunt, tell me your account." The inquiry yields neglected compositions by women that fall into established genres of poetry and oration and harvests texts that do not take forms normally recognized as literature. These short compositions are marked in Arabic culture as eloquent. What can one call these women if they are not poets, orators, or storytellers, yet provide compositions that are more than short proverbs? I offer as a working concept the idea that they are *mujadilas*, interlocutors. The idea that women participate in braiding an interlocutory discourse in the texts of the early Islamic era allows one to retrieve these difficult-to-reach texts and recover them for women's literary history in the Arabic tradition. These eloquences add exhilarating spaces to the range of early Islamic culture. The examples I have included here create a discourse of manhood in woman-centered terms, record women's experiences in the dramas of early Islam, and initiate a critique of androcentric attitudes toward religion. What other constellations of women's eloquence will come into focus in this still indistinct field? What will it all mean for understanding gender relations, literature, and values in this highly contested place in Muslim culture?

8

Reading the Signs

Unfolding Truth and the Transformation of Authority

RABIA TERRI HARRIS

> We shall show them Our signs in the horizons and in them-
> selves until it becomes clear to them that it is the truth.
>
> —Surah *Ha Mim,* 51

New Truth

> Say: The truth has arrived, and falsehood neither creates anything
> new nor restores anything. (Surah *Saba,* 49)

❧ For Muslims, Islam is supposed to be *din al-haqq,* "the religion of truth." Truth is *the way things are,* as opposed to the way we pretend them to be. Of the way things are, some aspects are *evident,* and some aspects are *not evident* (in Qur'anic terms, *shahadah* and *ghayb*). Guidance is sent to us concerning those aspects of the way things are that are not evident. It is sent to us because it is relevant to us: to function properly, we need to be responsive to what lies beyond us.

A principal content of this guidance is that the reality one knows and experiences contains pointers to the reality that one does not know and has not yet experienced. In the Qur'an these pointers are called *ayat,* "signs." The verses of the Qur'an themselves are also called *ayat,* "signs." The two sets of signs are declared to be mutually confirming. Whoever

172

reads them together approaches the highest knowledge of truth. That knowledge brings together this world and the next, the spiritual and the material, the evident and the hidden. Nearness to truth generates faith and action. And faith and action generate human fulfillment.

> But give good tidings to those who are faithful and work righteous-
> ness that for them are gardens beneath which rivers flow. Every time
> they are fed with fruits therefrom, they say, "Why, this is that with which
> we were fed before!" (Surah *Baqarah*, 25)

In the context of human existence, in whatever realm, truth is recognizable when it appears. There is no mistaking the "ring of truth"—what the Qur'anic image portrays as the *taste* of truth. Truth is not only recognizable, it is coherent across circumstances, and it nourishes us: truth is the food of the soul. The truth of this world, "with which we were fed before," will be consistent with the truth of the next world, and truth that comes to us from elsewhere is consistent with truth we possess. Yet we only grasp the truth in new experience to the extent that we have eaten and assimilated the truth we have met already.

> The closest to the believers in affection are those who say, "We are
> Christians" because there are priests and monks among them who are
> not arrogant. And when they hear what was sent down to the Messenger,
> you will see their eyes overflowing with tears because they recognize part
> of the truth. They say, "Lord, we believe; inscribe us among the wit-
> nesses." (Surah *Ma'idah*, 82–83)

Those priests and monks could receive the impact of Islam because they had received the impact of Christianity. Because they had learned the taste of truth in one place, they could recognize it in another. They had made use of their religious experience: they had knowledge.

Knowledge is both the fruit and the seed of experience. It is the concentrated essence of experience. True knowledge is not necessarily intellectual knowledge, susceptible to intellectual proof. Revealed knowledge in this *ayah* spoke to the heart so that eyes overflowed with tears; those tears were the best proof of the truth of that moment. But true knowledge always creates changes, causes the soul to grow.

You shall surely travel on from stage to stage. (Surah *Inshiqaq,* 19)

The truth in our lives is not a fixed quantity. *Lived truth* is a subtle and fugitive *quality* arising when the knowledge we receive from elsewhere is transformed, in us, into recognition and work. Knowledge, however, *is* quantifiable: it may be more or less. It may gather or fragment . . . and it will. People and societies may grow or wither, but they cannot remain indefinitely the same.

To every people is a term appointed. (Surah *A'raf,* 34)

More knowledge is better than less, and an understanding that is whole and integral is better than one that falls to pieces. We will find these principles affirmed by both experience and revelation, inevitably, for the expansion and assimilation of knowledge are at the root of the human task.

Islam is supposed to be the religion of truth. At least, it is in the Qur'an. It was, in the words and actions of the Prophet. Is it, in the lives of Muslims today? Why does "Islamic reality" so often seem like a smaller, poorer, and more uncomfortable space to occupy than "regular reality"? Why is "the Islamization of knowledge" a project going nowhere? Why are so many believers so defensive, or so offensive, about their faith?

The West—the phenomenon misidentified as "the West"—came as an awful shock to our parents, grandparents, our great-grandparents. It was a shock that would not go away. We have discussed this among ourselves, ad nauseam, for the past two hundred years: the way things are no longer fits our sense of the way things ought to be. Where did we go wrong? How can we fix it? The diagnoses are always either "To much religion" or "not enough," and the cures, either "less religion" or "more." But the Qur'an says about confusion,

No, indeed: they called the truth a lie when it came to them, and so they are in a confused affair. (Surah *Qaf,* 5)

It does not say "the *shari'ah*" or "the *din.*" It says "the truth."

We knew God said He would reveal no further scripture. We thought that meant He had put a lid on truth. But

If all the trees in the world were pens, and the ocean stretched by seven other oceans [were ink], yet the words of your Lord would not be exhausted. (Surah *Luqman*, 27)

We were satisfied with the understanding we already had. Allah Glorious and Exalted was not. The truth that came to us and was rejected consisted of new signs that we had not attempted to read.

Signs in the Horizons

Have We not made the earth as a wide expanse, and the mountains as pegs? (Surah *Naba'a*, 6–7)

Do you not see how Allah has created the seven heavens in layers? (Surah *Nuh*, 15)

In the year 1979 of the common era, Shaykh ʿAbdul-ʿAziz Ibn Baz, *Mufti* of Saudi Arabia, issued a *fatwa* that the earth was flat and that anyone who said otherwise was a *kafir* (an unbeliever). Nevertheless, just a few years later, Prince Sultan Salman al-Saud of Saudi Arabia, while helping to aim a camera toward a possible black hole at the center of the galaxy, orbited the planet neatly quite a number of times.[1]

The Ibn Baz episode, which produced vast embarrassment in nearly every Muslim who heard of it—and scornful merriment in everyone else—is worthy of closer consideration. It offers pointed lessons about our dilemma. For three things about this scholar's action are of great interest: his readiness to issue decrees of *takfir*, his ignorance of the facts, and the ease with which he derived a false conclusion from the Qurʾan.

Takfir, proclaiming someone to be an unbeliever, is a device for excluding persons and ideas from the community. It amounts to a blanket invalidation: *kafirs*, by definition, have chosen falsehood and, therefore, are to be dismissed personally, spiritually, and intellectually. *Takfir* is the most serious of charges among Muslims, and the Holy Prophet strongly disapproved of it. He also warned that making such accusations was intrin-

---

1. The Discovery mission during which Sultan Salman as-Saud launched the Arabsat communications satellite and assisted with an x-ray observatory took place between June 17 and June 24, 1985. See *New York Times* June 19, 1985, sec. 2, 6:1 and June 25, 1985, sec. 3, 6:1.

sically dangerous. "If one of you calls his companion a *kafir*," he cautioned, "the charge is sure to be true of one of the two!" (Muslim 1976, 41).

In religious circles *kafir* has come to mean "untouchable." But in the Qur'an and in Prophetic usage, *kafir* means something else. The *kafir* is the one who disguises, hides, or actively avoids the truth. The contemporary cliché for this is "being in denial." The *kafir* does not want to know and does not want *you* to know. Because knowledge is the threat, the desperate effort of such people is to try and get rid of knowledge. This strategy does not work. But although the habit of denial may harden, becoming unbreakable by anything short of a disaster, it may also be a temporary state. When that is the case, it is our responsibility as Muslims to try and help people out of it.

One might well ask how the product of any current educational system—for Shaykh Ibn Baz is indubitably educated—should happen not to know that the earth is round. The answer is that in the vast majority of traditional madrasas, the knowledge of *kafir* outsiders is not admitted. If everything is in the Qur'an—and it is a point of faith that everything is in the Qur'an—then it is a waste of time to look elsewhere for information. Just study the text: with time and patience and Allah's grace, all will be revealed. And if some fact should not be so revealed, then that is clearly something we really ought not to know.

But the Holy Prophet was instructed to pray, "My Lord, increase me in knowledge" (Surah *Ta Ha*, 114), not "suffice me with knowledge!" He said, "Whoever strikes a path to seek knowledge therein, it opens a path for him into Paradise" (Jawziya). He said, "Knowledge is the stray camel of the believer: wherever he finds it, he is entitled to it." *Wherever* he finds it! The Qur'an warns us against things that we ought not to *do*, not things that we ought not to *know*.

The concept of forbidden or perilous or evil *knowledge* is a product of medieval power politics, which bequeathed to us a strategy of government that legitimates force by means of ideology. This strategy requires limits to be placed on thought because alternative ideologies present a threat to order. Because new ideologies arise from new interpretations of reality and new interpretations of reality arise from new data, what data are admissible must be rigidly controlled.

The easiest way to keep facts under control, as history teaches, is to condemn independent reflection and to ban books. The determined cultivation of complacency through self-congratulation is also quite effective, given the right circumstances. Fortunately, as He tells us time after time, Allah Exalted and Glorious does not accept any of this indefinitely.

> If you say, "Believe in what Allah has sent down," they say, "We believe in what Allah has sent down to us," rejecting all besides, even if it is truth confirming what is with them. (Surah *Baqarah*, 91)

A closed system cannot afford to credit an unregulated truth. If it is not already owned, a fact may turn out not to be ownable—that cannot be allowed, for the great fear of official custodians of reality is that new data will *not* confirm what is with them. Is the treasure they have been guarding really brass? When people's religion is constructed of indoctrination and blind imitation, if they have never developed the "taste for truth," then they very well may not know. One unauthorized observation places a whole world of dogma at risk: Galileo must be put down because if the Bible admits to contradiction, Christianity might crumble! Well, Christianity did not crumble, but church hegemony in Europe crumbled; and the world, and the church, are much better for it. "Nevertheless, it moves."

Christianity did not crumble because there is, in fact, a good helping of truth in it: truth that can be proven in social relations and upon the touchstone of the heart. Yet intellectual truth and the facts of the natural order are no longer sought through the expositors of the Bible, except by the least sophisticated of Christians. Those domains have been ceded to scientists, who are as jealous of their hegemony as the old priests ever were. The most generous-minded of these secular clergy propose a double reality: that there is a moral and religious, and also a scientific truth, the two of which can never meet. Such a formulation is congenial to the spiritual/temporal split tolerated by Christians, but it will not do for us Muslims, who are proponents of *tawhid*.[2]

---

2. *Tawhid* means unity, specifically the divine unity; the concept has seen extensive and profound theological development. In terms of practice, *tawhid* is the declaration or explicit acceptance of the divine unity as expressed in the first statement of the Islamic profession of faith: *la ilaha ill' Allah*, "There is no god but God." This acceptance, together with an acceptance of the office of the prophet Muhammad as servant and messenger of God—*Muhammad 'abduhu wa rasuluhu* (frequently summarized as *Muhammad rasul Allah*)—when freely offered before witnesses, constitute a person a Muslim. The Holy Prophet himself allowed that a

We know that the status of the Qur'an and the status of the Bible are not the same: the former has accumulated none of the complications and irregularities of transmission undergone by the latter. And we often pride ourselves on how various Qur'anic *ayats* reflect or foreshadow the latest discoveries of science. But it is noteworthy that all those discoveries have been made by scientists and not by *ulama*. Shaykh Ibn Baz is a perfectly good 'alim. He declared the earth to be flat because he read in the Qur'an that the earth is flat. So we cannot avoid the question: If the world is really round, why did Allah talk about it as flat?

In the famous description in Surah *Al-'Imran,* 7, the Qur'an says of itself:

> It is He who has sent down upon you the Book. From it are decided-upon signs [*ayat muhkamat*]—they are the Mother of the Book—and others, mutually resembling [*mutashabihat*]. As for those in whose hearts there is aversion, they will pursue that of it which resembles, wishing discord and wishing to reduce it to its origins [*ta'wil*]. None knows the reduction to its origins except Allah, and those firmly grounded in knowledge, they say, "We believe in it: all of it is from our Lord." And none will remember except those who have a center. [This translation is not standard, but it is faithful.]

The portrayal of the earth as flat, then, must obviously be a *mutashabihah,* an irreducible metaphor, rather than a *muhkamah,* a definition. But that is obvious to us only through our own experience: it was not obvious to Shaykh Ibn Baz. The Qur'an itself provides no criteria by which to sort the *muhkamat* from the *mutashabihat. We have no guarantee of what is a metaphor and what is not.* What seems to us to be *muhkam* is precisely that: what *seems to us* to be *muhkam.* We know that some signs *are* definitive, and we do well to make an effort to establish them: we are better off basing our practice upon what is clear to us, rather than on what is obscure. But the work of clarification is never done. The signs that present themselves as obvious and indisputable will vary from era to era and from place to place, changing with the state of human knowledge. The flat earth turns out to be round, and *then* we discover the heavenly bodies "swimming in their orbits"

---

battlefield "conversion" consisting of the first statement only was sufficient to make an opponent unlawful for a Muslim to engage.

in the Qur'an (Surah *Anbiya'*, 33; Surah *Ya Sin*, 40). When reading the sacred words in pursuit of knowledge, we will fail if we dispense with the world outside.

This is not a flaw in the absoluteness of revelation. It is essential to its function as a guide. What are we being guided through, if not our actual world? Over and over again the Qur'an commands us: *Travel* through the world. *Examine* the heavens and the earth and all that is between them. *Use your minds.* Then read the signs.

Qur'anic scholarship has declined to travel or examine. Western science has obligingly done it for us. And the challenge of science to traditional forms of Qur'anic reading is very simple: How can your text be true, and our observations also be true, in the same way, at the same time, when text and observation no longer coincide?

But the challenge is formidable only when the Qur'an is regarded of as a fixed object, rather than as a dynamic process.

Many of the signs set as examples in the Qur'anic text were much clearer to their first audience than they are today. How many of us really get the point of, say, "Do they not look at the camels, how they are made?" (Surah *Ghashiyah*, 17). But the Prophet's Arab listeners did and could use what they thereby learned to draw closer to truth. Through studying the Qur'an, we can assimilate how they did it, *so that we can do it ourselves.*

> Allah has not created the heavens and the earth and all that is between them except with truth. (Surah *Hijr*, 65)

The extraordinary claim being made here—and it is made over and over in the Qur'an—is that *wherever* human knowledge takes its cross-section of the creation, the signs of God will be revealed. The universe is *built of truth*—on every scale, top to bottom, inside and out—and *all* truth bears witness to Allah.

The signs of Allah are "clear." They are clear because they are really present in the knowledge and experience of the perceiver. Consequently, whenever the *actual state of human knowledge* shows that the world is flat, its flatness will provide a sign. And whenever the *actual state of human knowledge* shows that the world is round, its roundness will provide a sign.

Ibn Baz was not wrong to believe that the earth is flat. It *is* flat, in the concrete experience of practically everyone. He was wrong to believe that, therefore, it is *only* flat.

The great thing about the profound spiritual discipline that erupted in the West in reaction to the constraints of a developing church absolutism—that discipline now called science—is that it has proven two points beyond doubt. The first is that the witnessable world, the *'alam ash-shahadah,* is both accessible and *really real.* The second is that our descriptions of it are only provisional.

The emergence of Einsteinian physics did not invalidate Newtonian physics; it merely illuminated the limits of the earlier vision. The one is discovered to be a subset of the other.

The knowledge and experience of a round earth does not invalidate the knowledge and experience of a flat earth. It invalidates the finality and sufficiency of the earlier knowledge. The earth is not just flat. It is also round. *It may be other things too.*

Far exalted is Allah beyond what they describe! (Surah *Anbiya',* 22)

Yet even when we know that our reading cannot possess the text, we do not lose our obligation to read it.

Signs in Ourselves

Does not man see that We have created him from a drop of liquid— and lo, he is an open disputer! He has coined similitudes for Us, and forgotten his own creation. (Surah *Ya Sin,* 77–78)

We know more, now, about how children are made than we did just a little while ago. About the *ghayb*—the immaterial dimension of the process—we have no more (or less) direct knowledge than we have ever been allowed. But the realm of the *shahadah*—where we can observe events and where we are called upon to bear witness—has been expanded for us. Signs that were veiled here, before, are quite explicit now. As a consequence, we must readjust our vision in order to serve the truth.

The new seeing that is asked of us is difficult because it is so fundamental. Male and female are not what we thought they were.

For millennia, men and women have felt that the procreative act is equivalent to planting a seed. The aspiring mother is equivalent to the earth; the aspiring father, to the farmer—the husbandman—who sets the seed in the earth to unfold and be fed in its life-giving depths. The Qur'an refers to this deep image when making a common-sense argument against superstition in sexual practices—"Your wives are a tilth for you"—but its resonance echoes from outside of revelation. Even in the putative Golden Age of gender equality that certain feminists postulate before the onset of patriarchal religion, the priestess impersonating the goddess Inanna in rites of sacred marriage would demand, "Who will plow my high field?" And the prescribed answer was, "I, the king, shall plow your high field" (Wolkstein and Kramer 1995, 69). The agricultural metaphor does not necessarily imply oppression, and it defined the boundaries of our knowledge for a very long time.[3]

One development of this felt relationship suggests that if the aspiring mother is equivalent to the earth, then the aspiring father is equivalent to the sky, which makes the earth fruitful with rain. And, indeed, there is a great deal to be absorbed through human experimental participation in the Sign of Heaven and Earth, a sign that is intricately woven into the entire fabric of the Qur'an. But the next step in this line of analogy is calamitous, and revelation urgently warns against it: for if we agree that woman is spiritually approximate to Nature and then decide that heaven is absolutely superior to earth—that life comes always from above, never from below—then maybe man is superior to woman and approximate to God.

The step may be calamitous, but it has certainly been taken with gusto by learned authorities from Aristotle through the rabbis and the church Fathers right up to and including many of our own ʿulama, even today. Yet the reddest of red flags should go up for every Muslim at the merest hint of this proposition. *Shirk!* To propose any equivalence to Allah means departing from the truth: guaranteed. Our image ceases to be a sign and becomes an idol. And an idol, no matter how revered, is a species of lie.

So something must be wrong with the metaphor—either with attribut-

---

3. The advice to husbands from Surah *Baqarah,* 223—"Your wives are a tilth for you, so approach your tilth however you wish"—is often taken as demeaning to women. Such a valuation is not intrinsic to the metaphor, as observed here; nonetheless, the valuation and the image frequently become linked. As for the advice, the early commentators report that this *ayah* was revealed when a family dispute highlighted a tribal notion that rear-entry intercourse produced cross-eyed children.

ing the masculine to the sky or with attributing the divine action to the sky, or both. The Qur'an says little about the first attribution but advises us clearly about the second. We must not localize the divine action. Allah is "Lord of the Heavens and the Earth and all that is between them" (Surah *Maryam*, 65). The Presence of Allah will not be limited to any one focus, any one point of view. "Withersoever you turn, there is the Face of God" (Surah *Baqarah*, 115).

But it can be made to sound so rational, the Pharaonic claim of "I am your Lord, the Supreme" (Surah *Nazi'at*, 24). After all, woman is earth: she must be substance, body. It is man who is the conduit of form, whose act makes life happen; it is he who is the sacred channel of spirit. The body exists to serve the spirit, right? So woman exists to serve man and to carry out the orders he issues, and only in the perfection of her obedience will she find fulfillment; so a people exists to serve its leader, who alone has the right to command it and who alone can provide it with greatness; so men have the right to abuse the creation for their private purposes in order to "make something out of it," turn it to account; and so on and on and on.

Except that form is not male. Allah has shown us now, very clearly, that living form—vehicle of spirit, provider of harmony and order—is only partly male. Entranced by the fantasy of supremacy, men have "coined similitudes for Us, and forgotten their own creation." It is not their role to determine the shape of things. Form that is only male becomes deranged.

The Qur'an speaks variously about the "drop of liquid," the *nutfah*, the life-spark out of which Allah shapes us as living persons. Surah *Qiyamah*, 36, offers a savage satire on arrogance and stupidity and clearly refers to it as "ejaculated"; in the more ecstatic and celestial context of Surah *Dahr*, 2, the *nutfah* is described as "mingled." Other *'ayat* employ the word without qualifying it or with ambiguous qualification. There is no requirement that we read *nutfah*, in most circumstances, as "sperm" although that is generally how it is translated. It is probably better that we avoid such a reading today because we know now that is not how procreation works.

The male generative substance is not the source of life. although the male triggers the process in the female, *there is no passivity in reproduction*. Life does not originate on one side of the bed to be passed to the other like the Olympic torch. Women do not offer themselves for occupation; male and female join through mutual sacrifice. Twenty-three parental chromosomes must be lost, twenty-three gained, from each side, to make a child occur. Order is not unilaterally imposed upon substance. Form arises from two directions at once.

We must conclude from this fact, which we cannot conceal without doing violence to our own consciousness, that the old emanatory picture is no longer an adequate image for the creativity of God. *Systems of control based solely upon it will no longer yield a sufficient degree of truth.*

We know that now and cannot pretend otherwise. Not all of us know it yet, of course. In a recent *New York Times* report on an African escapee from genital cutting, the young woman's paternal uncle—her technical guardian after her father's death—expressed his consternation at her mother's collaboration in the escape. "She acted as though the child were hers!" he remarked, appalled (Dugger 1996, B6).

Once in every ten thousand or so conceptions, we receive a demonstration of that absolute unilateral authority still idealized by so many. It is called a molar pregnancy (Berkowitz, Goldstein, and Bernstein 1991, 40–44). Inside a fertilized egg the father's genetic material does not unite with the mother's genetic material but instead duplicates itself and replaces it. The feminine ovum is then really and exclusively the material host for a masculine genetic form. The result is that *no fetus develops.* Instead, the placenta grows explosively, digging its feeding fingers ever more deeply into the maternal blood supply. Unless this now dangerous and pointless organ is surgically excised, it will eventually rupture and the mother will bleed to death.

> When the Earth shivers and casts off her burden, and man says, 'What is the matter with her?'—on that day she will relate her tidings, for her Lord will have inspired her. Then people will come forth shattered to see their deeds. And whoever has done an atom's worth of good shall see it, and whoever has done an atom's worth of evil shall see it. (Surah *Zalzalah*, complete)

Perhaps we are entering upon the situation described here, and perhaps not: only Allah knows the *ghayb.* The day of reckoning may not be yet. But an adjustment in our lives is necessary, in accordance with the signs.

Divine Order

Then He directed His design toward the heaven, and it had been smoke. He said to it and the earth, "Come together, willingly or un-willingly." They said, "We come willingly." (Surah *Ha Mim*, 11)

We are now obliged to digest this sign: that fruitfulness arises among us only through full mutual participation in the creative act. Yet we are accustomed to thinking of order as a condition imposed by a more power-ful entity upon a lesser. Many of us cling to that; it seems "right" and secure. But it is no longer right *enough*. These days, it may even incline us to disaster.

The use of force is a great temptation for human beings, especially for males. There are certainly emergency circumstances in which the need for it is inescapable, and so Allah has endowed us with the capacity to employ it. Such circumstances are not common. Yet not only do we overemphas-ize those few that exist, we regularly seek to increase their number. There is a dreadful intoxication in coercion. Allah Exalted and Glorious tells us, "My mercy far overpowers My wrath."[4] Why, then, do so many of us choose wrath?

It is seductive, our belief that we should govern how things will be. When we find we do not succeed at this, we try harder.

In *Stopping Rape: A Challenge for Men* Rus Ervin Funk writes:

I am feeling out of control, so I'll grab hold of this person's hand to demonstrate that I am in control. But it's not working, she isn't under my control yet. . . . I feel more desperate to get her under control, but I am feeling more out of control due to having to resort to such an inane attempt at being powerful. . . . So I grab hold tighter. . . . But it still doesn't work. But to be a "man" I'm supposed to be "in control," but I'm losing control of myself and this situation . . . but this is the only way I know how to take control so I need to get bigger and more controlling but it doesn't work. (Funk 1994, 45–46)

Uneasy people, particularly men, all too readily lapse into violence when they feel that the other party ought to obey, but will not. Rarely, in

---

4. This is a very famous *hadith qudsi*, or non-Qur'anic divine utterance transmitted by the Holy Prophet. It is considered fully authenticated and may be read in Muslim 1976, 1437.

our frustration, do we ask ourselves whether there might be a reason for that. Who is doing the commanding and to what? Who is supposed to be in control and of what?

Islam is surrender. It means learning to cede control.

This is difficult to do until we recognize that someone else really is in charge and that the best form for a situation may not be the form we had in mind.

There are two kinds of command, *amr*, delineated in the Qur'an. One is the command of the Devil or of *an-nafs al-ammarah bi-su'*, the evil-commanding ego. The other is the command of Allah. One way to differentiate between them is that the former sort of command brings out the worst in us, and, although threatening catastrophes for disobedience, has no power to make us act without our own capitulation. If we capitulate, our obedience degrades us.

The latter sort of command simply *is*. When we hear it, our obedience exalts us.

His command, when He wishes a thing, is only to say to it, "Be!"—and it becomes. (Surah *Ya Sin*, 82)

Allah's command requires no enforcement. It develops out of the interior nature of things. It is entirely irresistible. When one person attempts to dominate another, the result is tyranny. But when Allah commands that heaven and earth should come to order, they both come willingly.

Sometimes we resist the idea of surrendering control because we confuse trust in God with a rejected passivity. And sometimes we like the idea only because we are timid, lazy, or weak. But the person who trusts Allah is not permitted to be passive. We know that *jihad*, effort, is necessary to our well-being.[5] Human beings are created to act: without action there can

---

5. Muslims grow weary explaining that *jihad*—routinely translated into European languages as "Holy War"—actually means no such thing. The only appropriate translation of the term is "struggle," or "effort." Talk about *jihad* is talk about *action*. In the time of the Prophet, some of the action the community was obliged to undertake was, in fact, warfare. The Qur'an addresses individually the many conflicts that arose during that complex and dangerous period when the survival of Islam was in the balance, but it never limits the significance of action in aid of religion to fighting for it.

be no divine service. Allah prefers us to employ our will, as He prefers us to employ our intelligence, in His service:

> Allah coins a similitude. Two men: one of them dumb, incapable of anything; a wearisome burden is he to his master. Whichever way he turns him to face, he brings no good. Are they equal, he and one who commands justice and is upon a straight path? (Surah *Nahl,* 76)

In the service of Allah, then, passivity by choice can only be ignorance. But passivity by constraint is oppression, and we are bidden to command justice.

Social action (*al-jihad al-asghar,* the lesser struggle) is directed toward alleviating forced passivity. It cannot be directed toward imposing it. Exterior *jihad* must be undertaken when people are prevented from coming to Allah willingly. It cannot be undertaken to make them come. The exercise of force and submission to the divine order are *not compatible.*

> Let there be no compulsion in religion. Right guidance is clearly distinct from error. (Surah *Baqarah,* 256)

We do not have to make the universe work. We need only to allow it to work. It is trying to force things to work that creates the problems. Justice indeed *works,* in the way that physics *works.* Allah never invites us to what does not work.

Finding Power

> Have you not seen the one who disputed with Abraham concerning his Lord because Allah had given him worldly power? So Abraham said, "My Lord is the one who causes life and death." He said, "I cause life and death." Abraham said, "Allah makes the sun rise in the east. Make it rise in the west!" (Surah *Baqarah,* 258)

Although it is certainly power that drives events in the world, apparent power and real power are not the same. Apparent power is something I can wield. Real power is something only Allah can wield. It is easy to be misled, to take the apparent for the real as long as we refuse to read the signs.

Sometimes Allah allows us a particular capacity to see if we will lay claim to it and go astray. This is called *makr,* the divine ruse (Surah A'raf, 99). The opponent of Abraham (peace be upon him), was permitted to taste power: power is a reality. He thought it was his own power, his own reality and was destroyed.

It is a subtle and delicate situation that confronts us, for we are called upon to act, and yet not act of ourselves. There is a vast difference between an attribute that I take to be my own and an attribute that is known to be Allah's. The former, no matter what it is, is useless. The latter, no matter what it is, is priceless.

Islamic spiritual tradition views the attributes of God as falling into two broad categories. There is *jamal,* "beauty," which supports existing forms, and there is *jalal,* "majesty," which overcomes them. The balance between the two is called *kamal,* "perfection." Human being has the quality of a mirror, and the reflection of the totality of the divine attributes is our unique inheritance. It is our business, through *al-jihad al-akbar,* to actualize these attributes in their finest form by gradually removing identifications that obscure them. This removal is a form of evolution.

He sends down water from the sky, and the channels flow, each according to its measure; the torrent carries off a rising scum. And from what they heat in the fire, desiring ornament or useful tool, there is a scum like this: thus Allah limns truth and falsehood. As for the scum, it is cast forth as futility. And as for what benefits humanity, it remains in the earth. (Surah Ra'd, 17)

Actualizing an attribute is a refining process, like smelting a precious metal out of a raw ore. The starting material that is given to us determines what the finished product will be, but the two are far from the same. The dross that must be separated out in order to free first the silver of virtue and then the gold of *tawhid* is our own self-regard.

This is as much the case for *jalali* attributes as it is for others. Courage and strength must be trained up out of cruelty and rashness and judgment wholly purified of vindictiveness and rage before they can begin to serve as divine mirrors. Yet the *jalali* in us is seldom subjected to refinement, and unrefined, its quality is dangerous. *Jalal* seeks to prevail. Ego also seeks to prevail. The *jalal* in us may attract the ruse of God. We must, therefore, be extremely careful to avoid laying claim to it. Yet we somehow feel there is glory in laying claim to it.

Some Muslims choose to assign the formidable divine majesty specifically to males while assigning the comforting divine beauty to females (see Murata 1992). Convenient though it may be as an occasional description, this metaphor lacks the criteria of a sign. There is neither any Qur'anic reference for it nor convincing proof of it in our own experience. Are men only men when they manifest power? Do women who manifest power cease to be women? Such an argument "makes unlawful what Allah has made lawful" in human nature. And it serves as a tacit justification for severity in men and societies that ought not be so easily allowed.

Perhaps the *raw materials* for *jalali* attributes are more naturally concentrated in males than in females, in the "powerful" than in the "powerless." If so, it does not matter. Raw material is not the point. When we consider spiritual stature—which means attunement to the divine order—the natural starting position is irrelevant. One half ounce of pure gold is worth a small mountain of unrefined ore. The possession of extra resources, of any kind, is not a sign of divine favor. The real question is, How will they be used? It is refinement versus unrefinement and not male versus female—or any other dichotomy—that counts.

Perhaps this gender generalization is popular because men feel less anxious when they encounter only *jamali* attributes of gentleness, kindness, mercy, and forgiveness in their women! But women, too, feel less anxious when they meet with *jamali* attributes in their men. The *jalali* traits, except in the ardor of mutual passion, are wholly out of place in the intimate realm. Yet all of us profit through their cultivation in our character.

Still, whoever we are, we are wise to be wary of how we pursue our *jalali* tendencies. They are not easy to refine, and they have not received the divine preference. A predominance of *jalali* traits in a personality or a society may be looked upon as "manly." We cannot, merely on that account, take it to represent an ideal state of affairs.

For the signs are otherwise. Allah carefully described the role of our living ideal as *rahmatan lil-ʿalamin*, "a mercy to the worlds" (Surah *Anbiyaʾ*, 107). The name of God that the Prophet introduced to his people, the unique one that they had never heard before, was ar-Rahman, the Most Merciful. And in His Qur'an, Allah begins every surah but one with the invocation of the Most Merciful and the Most Compassionate: two *jamali* names. These are the way we consecrate our acts.

Two names of mercy are prescribed for our constant recollection, *not* one of mercy and one of severity. Perhaps we might seek for some help with gender there. And we received one hundred and thirteen *surahs* crowned with the *basmala*. There is only one without. Perhaps that is the ideal balance of *jamal* to *jalal* in our societies and our lives, the proportion that would best accustom us to the divine order, 113:1, mercy far overpowering wrath.

Allah knows best. But it is worth thinking about.

Human will exists. The question for every Muslim is whether its exercise is to reflect the style and the ends of the ego or the style and the ends of Allah. To teach us to identify the former, the Qur'an shows us pharaoh, Nimrod, Abu Jahl, and tyrannical societies that collapse.[6] To teach us to identify the latter, it shows us free obedience enlightening heaven and earth.

Interpretation and Authority

> O you community of jinn and men! If you can pass beyond the portions of the heavens and the earth, then pass! Not without authority shall you be able to pass. (Surah *Rahman*, 33)

Authority is not the same as power. It is the *right* to act, the *right* to decide. In this sign from Surah *Rahman*, we read that the limits of what we know are impassable—unless we are granted permission to pass them. The word for this in the Qur'an is *sultan*.

Muslims generally agree that in the era of prophethood, authority lay solely with the prophets. They had a very special knowledge. They held the right to decide in a unique way, inaccessible to any person now. They had an indisputable *sultan*.

6. Pharaoh is known to all. Nimrod, "a mighty hunter" in the Bible, is the name traditionally assigned by Muslims to the tyrannical opponent of Abraham (peace be upon him). Abu Jahl was a representative of Meccan high society and one of the foremost enemies of the Holy Prophet. The Qur'an contains a great number of references to particular corrupt and exploitative societies that ignored specific advice that might have saved them.

The age of the prophets is sealed, and we are its heirs.

To us are left the Prophetic example and *al-Qur'an al-Karim*, the Generous Reading, for guidance. There is still authority there. But who is entitled, in this later age, to apply it? Who may interpret what God has said and done?

What a vexed question that one has been, over all these years! For all along we have assumed that a true interpreter has the right to demand obedience. Yet there is precious little evidence to support such an assumption in the text, and there is less and less in the world.

If interpretation does not legitimate force, if nothing but tyranny legitimates force, then why should interpretation not be open? For if there is no implicit demand that we agree, then no claim is being made of "I am your Lord, the Supreme." Surely those who must be guided, to whom the message was sent, are the ones who are intended to absorb it. And surely Allah is capable of speaking to the people we are, to *all* of the people we are, just as we are capable of speaking to each other. Allah has designed us for hearing from the beginning.

> He said, "Am I not your Lord? And they said, "Indeed!" (Surah *A'raf*, 172)

Either we listen or we do not. In Surah *Baqarah*, Moses (peace be upon him) tells his people that God commands them to sacrifice "a cow." Rather than picking out a cow and offering it up, they insist on knowing *which* cow God has in mind. Moses keeps asking, God keeps limiting the field, and the sacrifice step by step becomes a more painful one to make as the people still continue to refuse to make it. How dare they choose, themselves, among so many alternatives? Someone has to tell them what to do.

> They said, "Beseech your Lord for us to make clear to us what she is; all cows are similar to us [*tashababa 'alayna*]; if Allah wills, we will be guided. (Surah *Baqarah*, 70)

But they have already declined to be guided; they have rejected the freedom Allah gave them spontaneously to respond. They have demanded to be constrained. Only when the definition of one particular cow has become so specific as to be unavoidable—when one heifer, as it were, has been singled out of the herd of *mutashabihat* to be the *muhkamah*[7]—do the people finally consent to understand. And even then, "they almost did not do it" (Surah *Baqarah*, 71). They could have done it at any time. *Any* heifer could have been the decided-upon, the precise one, the *muhkamah*. It was up to them.

Our demand for the restriction of our interpretive freedom is indulged, but not approved, by our Creator. We see in the story of the cow that narrowness and rigidity in religion are a direct consequence of not wanting to listen, of unwillingness to take responsibility for listening. But when we listen, meaning surfaces to meet us; it seeks us out, insofar as we seek it out. "Walk toward Me," we read in a *hadith qudsi*, "and I will run toward you!" (Graham 1977, 175–76).

If we sincerely feel that we lack sufficient knowledge to understand what we are told, we are obligated to search for that knowledge. And if we sincerely feel that we have sufficient knowledge, then we must act. But "sufficient knowledge" *changes*. Understanding the revelation is not a passive accommodation to a pattern imposed from above. It, too, forms from two directions at once. It is a divine act in which we act as well. If truth were not constantly recreating its meanings, if it did not call constantly to be reheard, there would be no point in checking in with it five times a day.

Every day He is upon some business. (Surah *Rahman*, 29)

From moment to moment and from case to case, we may be ignoring or rejecting the present truth; manipulating it; or embracing it. But as Muslims, our appointed object is more and more dependably to come to embrace the truth: to be *faithful* to it. This goal requires a vigorous and unrelenting examination of ourselves, our world, and our guidance. And it is here that the social project of sincerity runs into its greatest difficulty, for such examination requires a degree of energy that many people are unwilling or unable to devote.

The desert Arabs say, "We are faithful." Say, "You are not faithful—so say, 'We submit'; for faith has not entered your hearts. But if you obey

---

7. *Mutashabihat*, "those mutually resembling," may sometimes be read as "metaphors," as noted earlier. But the one significance scarcely exhausts the full resonance of the Qur'anic term.

Allah and His messenger, He will not discount any of your deeds, for Allah is profoundly forgiving, most merciful." (Surah *Hujurat,* 14)

The simpler course *works,* but only as long as the sum of knowledge available to a community remains a given quantity that some person or persons can possess. Then we may, in good faith, resign the mastery of that knowledge to those people whose vocation draws them to it; grant them the authority to decide for us; and go about our business, confident of our harmony with the way things are.

But in times like these, when uninvited knowledge is thrust upon us from every direction, far more involvement is required. Living truthfully, now, requires a more conscious effort. Though we will always be in need of teachers—because we are always in need of education—the prophets are gone, and no one can take their place. No specialist's vision can adequately mediate times like these; no scholar can wholly digest them for us. There is nothing for it but to do what the prophets urged us to do in the first place: to follow their example. We must now, ourselves, acknowledge the taste of truth and learn to be literate in the words of God.

Many modern thinkers have intuited an urgent call for the direct spiritual responsibility of ordinary people. Quite a few of them hold that achieving this end means abandoning the religion of the past. But the Christian case is the Christian case, and the Muslim case is the Muslim case. Radical separation from tradition is not necessary for us. (Indeed, it is a large part of what ails us.) What we must do is to claim the living thread.

Hold fast together to the rope of Allah, and do not fragment. (Surah *Al-ʿImran,* 103)

Muslims are called, not to doctrinal formulation, but to reading the signs of God. We do ourselves no favors by attempting to establish a tidy little church, our own exclusive ideological club, more than two hundred years after the concept failed. Nor do we honor the great interpreters who preceded us by binding ourselves to their conclusions while forcibly shutting our own eyes. Most of them would be horrified to catch us at it! For that is not at all how they confronted their own time.

> O humanity! We have created you from a male and a female and made you into nations and tribes so that you may recognize one another. The noblest among you, with Allah, is the most conscious of God. (Surah *Hujurat*, 13)

Truth is not property. Revelation cannot be owned, only heard and answered for. Its readers, too, form tribes, who need to recognize one another.

Once we make that recognition, we can take down our defenses. When we are free to consider that many readings may simultaneously be true, we are likewise freed to work in common toward the reading that seems truest to us now, the reading that is "most conscious of God." And when we can admit that even our best reading is always provisional, we shall discover that the dignity of the Qur'an remains eternally above events. Then we can stop trying to protect God, and let God protect us.

For it is only by clinging to the rope of Allah—the existing, all-sustaining unity—that we are saved from turning into a whole multitude of tiny pharaohs; of little tin messengers each proclaiming a solipsistic divinity and demanding the worship of all the rest. That condition is the very taste of hell.

> Indeed that is true, the mutual recrimination of the people of the Fire! (Surah *Sad*, 64)

It is arrogance that sets us at each other's throats, that warps our vision into self-glorification and that prevents us from reading Allah's signs—either in the world or in the text—when we are most in need of being warned.

> Those who wrangle over the signs of Allah without any authority granted them, there is nothing in their breasts but a greatness they shall not achieve. Take refuge in Allah; it is He who hears and sees. The creation of the heavens and the earth is greater than the creation of humanity, but most people do not know. (Surah *Mu'min*, 56–57)

Yet we *can* know, if we open ourselves to learn. God has spoken through the prophets of the *ghayb* and speaks still through the *shahadah*—in the universe and also in ourselves.

By the Lord of the heavens and the earth! This is truth like your speaking with one another! (Surah *Zariyat,* 23)

The signs in the Qur'an and the signs in the world are an attempt to engage us in conversation. They transmit to us information that we can use: "a promise and a warning." They help us to orient ourselves in the extraordinary complexity of the human situation. And they mark out the path for us, wherever we may be, that allows us to travel safely from what we know into what we do not know. "Not without authority shall you be able to pass!" The signs of God are road signs.

Yet "none will remember except those who have a center" (Surah *Al-'Imran,* 7). Recognizing the eternity of the Qur'an—rather than simply positing it—calls for us recognize the eternity in ourselves. "Indeed, we are Allah's, and to Him we are returning" (Surah *Baqarah,* 156). Recognition requires that each traveler come to order around his or her center. It requires *ulul-albab*—people who have a pith, a core, an essence; people who have a point. Holding that center is not tied to any obscure mystical experience. It is tied to not being frightened by the flux of life. And why should we be frightened, who have been guided, who know where we are and why, and how to proceed?

Of course, we are "only human," and fear change. But the fear of change is not the fear of God. Truth lasts, and faith is founded upon that. "Do not curse Time," Allah told us, who is the First and the Last, the Evident and the Hidden. "For I am Time."[8]

God knows best. So blessings upon our Master Muhammad, and upon his family and companions, and peace. And all praise belongs to Allah, Lord of the Worlds.

8. Citations in Wensinck and Mensing 1943 include *Muslim,* Alfaz 4,5; *Bukhari,* Adab 101; *Muwatta',* Kalam 3; Ahmad, 1:259, 272, 275, 318, 934. The most common variant runs, "Say not, 'Oh, the disappointments of the time!' For Allah is Time."

PART FOUR

Activism

9

Striving for Muslim Women's Human Rights— Before and Beyond Beijing

An African American Perspective

GWENDOLYN ZOHARAH SIMMONS

⌘ In this chapter I explore some of the issues confronting contemporary Muslim women who question many of the traditions and views regarding the role of women both in Islam and in society in general. Foremost in my focus are the educational and organizing activities of Muslim women in several parts of the world related to securing human rights for women within Islamic societies. I will give a brief overview of some of the currents and themes underway around the issue of *Women and Islam* in modern discourse. Described also are some Muslim women's activities related to securing human rights for women in Muslim societies as articulated at the Fourth World Conference on Women (FWCW) held in September of 1995 in Beijing, China, in which I was a participant.

Prologue

It has become more of a practice now for academicians writing about social, political, or anthropological issues to state up front the grounds on which they stand and the perspective they bring to their research and writing. I shall follow that practice. I am a practicing Muslim and an Islamic scholar, presently pursuing both a doctorate in Islamic studies and a certificate in women's studies at Temple University in Philadelphia, Pennsylvania. In part of 1996 and 1997 I spent fifteen months in Jordan and, to a lesser extent, in Palestine researching the women's movements there. My research activities were made possible through a United States Information Agency Near and Middle East Research Training Act (USIA NMERTA) Fellowship granted through the American Center For Oriental Research (ACOR) and a Fulbright dissertation research fellowship. A fair amount of the progressive women's movement activities that I observed in both countries were directly related to their earlier work in preparation for Beijing and their follow-up activities to secure implementation of the Platform For Action (PFA) ratified at the FWCW. I led an American Friends Service Committee (AFSC) delegation of nine women to Beijing. There I was actively involved with various Muslim women's workshops, especially those related to securing human rights.

For me as an American woman convert to Islam, engaging in the research and writing of this chapter is more than an academic exercise. This is an issue of real concern to me as I navigate my way through the spiritual, cultural, and legal aspects of my religion. I am also a feminist and an activist. I began my activist work in the U.S. Civil Rights movement in the 1960s. I was both a leader and a foot soldier in that historic struggle for justice and equality. I grew up in the Jim Crow South (Memphis, Tennessee) where I experienced the United States's own brand of racial apartheid. In my early life I was relegated to the back of the bus, to the "colored" toilets, water fountains, theater balconies, and hamburger joints (if at all). I was accustomed to not having hotel accommodations when traveling or entrance to the public library or the zoo (except on designated days; in Memphis, Thursdays were "colored" people's day). There were many other indignities I experienced but never accepted, such as whites routinely calling me *"nigger"* or *"gal"* and the ever-present fear that I might be the victim of a racially motivated hate crime with little hope for justice. As a black woman, there was the added fear of being the victim of white male sexual assault with the knowledge that if it occurred, justice was not likely to prevail.

What I now know in retrospect is that the worst part of being an African American person in that era was the almost complete erasure of my people's heritage and contributions as actors on the grand stage of history. Racist white America had worked thoroughly to delete Africa and its children from the history books, movies, and television programs. For the most part, I thought, then, that my *"real"* history began with slavery, for which it was suggested I should be thankful because the slavers had *"res-cued"* my ancestors from a *"barbarous and uncivilized land and life"* in the jungles of Africa. Because my knowledge of Africa was largely gleaned from Tarzan movies that I saw in sequel every Saturday at the black theater in my neighborhood, there was a subtle and hidden shame for being so visibly a descendent of the *"dark continent."* (I am a dark brown woman with African features.) I internalized the racist history and ideology and secretly longed to be other than myself. Seeing my reflection in the mirror often caused me pain.

My journey to full personhood was accelerated with my recruitment by the Student Nonviolent Co-ordinating Committee (SNCC) workers to join the demonstrations to desegregate the restaurants, hotels, public libraries, train and bus stations, and other public places from which African Americans were barred. Repeatedly confronting the racist establishment owners and workers besides the Atlanta police forces (defenders of injustice) gave me a newfound pride and courage. From these beginning assertions of full personhood, I increased my involvement and commitment to securing justice for me and my people. Jailings, beatings, vicious racist attacks, and the courage of my compatriots, some of whom were only in junior high, heightened my resolve to continue in the struggle. When I made the decision to go to Mississippi in the summer of 1964 as a participant in the Mississippi Freedom Summer Project, I went against my family's wishes and my own fear of the worst state in the Union for blacks. All of my life as a child in Memphis, Tennessee, I had heard of the horrors of Mississippi. My family knew blacks who had literally escaped from plantations where they had been held in virtual slavery (as indentured servants) as late as the fifties and sixties. Because I had become part of the student leadership of SNCC, I had participated in the SNCC decision to do the project. *"To crack the state"* was the goal of the summer project, Bob Moses, state director of the Mississippi project, would often say.

I knew the death toll of blacks in the state. The *Jet Magazine* picture of the swollen body of thirteen-year-old Emmit Till, when it was pulled from a river in Mississippi (he was killed, tied to weights, and thrown in a river for allegedly whistling at a white girl) when I was ten or twelve years old, is indelibly imprinted in my memory. I knew about Medgar Evers (the brilliant civil rights leader who was shot down on his front porch in Jackson, Mississippi, for his efforts to secure black rights), too, and several others whose deaths were reported in the Memphis black press. Yet, I *had* to participate fully in the movement to make blacks *"free"* in spite of my fear. What had been a three-month commitment to Mississippi turned into almost two years. I, by default, became the project director of the Laurel, Mississippi, project (the original director was arrested and run out of town). I could not leave at summer's end because our work was only beginning, and the local folks needed a few of us "outsiders" to stay to help keep the fledgling movement growing. Although I gave my all in that project, I went away with much more than I gave. Any internalized myths and stereotypes about blacks' happiness with the status-quo or our inability to organize potent movements for change were eradicated. Dispelled also were all embedded stereotypes about women's weakness, lack of skills, and inability to lead. Of course I was already aware of the strength of women as religious and political leaders from my exposure to women of power and courage throughout my life, beginning with my own grandmother, Rhoda Douglas. It was during this period in Mississippi that I began identifying myself as a feminist. The African American women of Laurel and the whole state of Mississippi were the backbone of the Freedom movement. Their involvement outnumbered the men's. And in most instances, their commitment and endurance were greater. They were both leaders and foot soldiers. The Fanny Lou Hammers, Victoria Grays, Eunita Blackwells, Annie Devines, Euberta Spinks, Susie Ruffins, Carrie Claytons, and many others too numerous to list are etched in my heart and memory forever. I was favored by God to get to know and to work closely with these strong women in helping to build the Mississippi movement. These women helped mold and shape of my character.

As a result of my years in the Civil Rights movement and the Black Power movement that it helped to ignite, I learned that most, if not all, of what I had imbibed of white racism as a child were lies perpetuated by a system hellbent on keeping my mind enslaved, even if it had grudgingly and partially *"freed"* my people's bodies. The lies and stereotypes about women as the "weaker sex" were also exposed for what they are, men's efforts to maintain power over women through systematic brainwashing. Religion, tradition, and culture, I learned, have been used historically to convince women of their inferiority and their second-class status just as it had been used to convince African Americans of the same.

Over the decades spent in the various movements of my time (civil rights, peace, and women's), I have engaged in a deprogramming process, an unlearning of all the internalized oppressions ingested since my childhood. Little by little, I have been able to stand tall and take my place as a full-fledged human being at life's table. This has meant divesting myself of racist and sexist images of divinely decreed inferiority. I had thrown off much of the internalized racism and sexism before becoming a Muslim in the mid-1970s. Clearly, I had no desire to reoppress myself as a woman in the name of religion. I found unacceptable the notion that woman is a secondary creation made for man's use.

Therefore, my relationship with my chosen religion, Islam, has been wrought with ambivalence and tension. My biggest problem has been with the traditional depiction of women and our role in both the religion and in society. You may ask how I came to a Muslim given the above brief biographical account and given the stereotypical depiction in the West of Islam as the most misogynist of the three Abrahamic Traditions.

My conversion to Sunni Islam was through the example and guidance of a Sufi teacher from Sri Lanka, Sheikh Muhammad Raheem Bawa Muhaiyadeen. I was drawn to the religion by its mystical and spiritual aspects as taught by him. The beautiful prayer rituals, the month of fasting, the pilgrimage to Mecca (which I was recently graced by God to make), the particularly Sufistic practices, such as *dhikr* and the *maulids*, and the Sufi stories of mystical quests leading to union with God drew me to the religion. Bawa, as he is affectionately called by all of his disciples, taught an Islam of love, compassion, wisdom, and human unity. His own life mirrored what he taught. He was a wise, compassionate, and loving human being. In his daily discourses which he gave for more than fifteen years of his life here in the United States, Bawa pleaded with his racially and gender mixed audiences to love one another, eschew violence, racial intolerance, separations, egotism, anger, and injustice. He urged his followers, who were from a variety of religious traditions, to come into their true birthright and live as *"real human beings"* (*insan al-kamil*) and to exemplify in their every thought, word, and deed, the *"three thousand gracious qualities of Allah"* and His *ninety-nine attributes,* which include patience, tolerance, and compassion. In the forward to Bawa's book, *Islam and World Peace: Explanations of a Sufi,* Annemarie Schimmel, retired professor of Indo-Muslim culture at Harvard University, wrote, "Real Islam is a deep and unquestioning trust in God, the realization of the truth that there is no deity save God' and of the threefold aspect of religious life: that of *islam,* complete surrender to God; *iman,* unquestioning faith in Him and His wisdom; and *ihsan,* to do right and to act beautifully, because one knows that God is always watching man's actions and thoughts (Muhaiyaddeen 1987, iii).

Bawa taught that true Islam is "equality, peacefulness, and unity"; that it is exemplified in the human being's life by "inner patience, contentment, trust in God, and praise of God." This person will become God's representative on earth. That person in his or her own life will demonstrate God's qualities, God's action, and God's conduct. Bawa made it perfectly clear that this was a spiritual state accessible to human beings of both genders, equally.

This was the Islam that I embraced unequivocally and joyously. For those who sat with Bawa and understood his message, there is no question about equality between males and females (spiritually or intellectually). From the very beginning Bawa picked women for leadership roles in the community, a practice that continues to this day. Women and men work freely together in an atmosphere of sisterly and brotherly love. Although modesty and chastity are observed, this is done without rigid enforcement of gender segregation. Nor is there a need for hierarchical gender arrangements. Women perform tasks that are often said to be "male" jobs and, likewise, men perform tasks mistakenly thought to be "for women only." For example, women head many of the Fellowship's departments; one of the organization's three presidents is a woman; the executive secretary who runs Fellowship operations is a woman; several women sit on the organization's board and on the Mosque Committee. Women often head the committees that oversee the ʿIds and other religious and commemorative festivals that are observed. Women also often lead the weekly public meetings, presenting their interpretations and understandings of Bawa's teachings. Women serve as presidents of some of the Fellowship branches (chapters) located around the United States. In his discourses Bawa often used feminine images in his descriptions of God's care for his creation and in his descriptions of his relationship to members as their sheikh. He often referred to himself as *"having given birth to all of us, his disciples,"* and he would say that he was *"nursing us from his breast of wisdom."* He constantly reiterated the "feminine" qualities of Allah, His *compassion* and His *mercy* for his creations as being two of the most important of Allah's attributes.

Bawa, believed by many to be a *Qutb* (a reviver of the faith and a divinely inspired wise man) was not interested in returning his disciples to a culturally Arab seventh-century Islam. His was a twentieth-century Islam that adhered to the foundations and to the eternal and universal principles of the religion while it embraced the knowledge and understanding of this era. A saying that the Chinese Women's movement popularized some years ago—"Women hold up half of the sky"—is amply exemplified in the Fellowship Community.

As a Muslim woman, when I remain within my own religious community, for the most part, there is no problem with overt sexism or exclusion. But once I venture out into the larger U.S. Islamic community or into the Islamic practices that I found in parts of the Middle East, I find a very different situation, a difficult one for me to accept. Here in the States, many *imams* and other religious leaders, including some in the African American Muslim community, seem to embrace the most conservative views when it comes to Islamic interpretations of the role of Muslim women. Practices are embraced here that are either severely questioned or even under attack in the Muslim Middle East and other parts of the Islamic world by progressive Muslim men and women. Examples of these expanding practices in the States include the following: growing numbers of polygamous marriages, young women being encouraged to marry early, produce many children, and even give up their schooling to do so, the discouraging of women's participation in the public prayers in the mosque, the urging of women's withdrawal from public life, the insistence that their only role is that of mother and homemaker, increased face veiling, unquestioned obedience to male family members, and rigid gender segregation. I have also found that some of the more misogynist passages from the *hadith* and sexist interpretations of Qu'ranic texts are often quoted as the justification for the views and practices being embraced. I find these trends troubling and unacceptable for me personally.

In addition, there is widespread resistance to a public exchange of ideas within the Muslim community, especially when initiated by women, who are expected to simply "accept" male perspectives and interpretations. These conservative interpretations defy what I, and many other progressive Muslims, see as the essentially egalitarian message of the Holy Qu'ran and of the early Islamic community. These conservative views deeply offend my notion of what is just. Furthermore, given the historic role that African

American women have played in women's struggle for justice, it is unbelievable that African American male Muslim leaders seek to marginalize women in the Islamic community, attempting to relegate them solely to domestic and silent roles. In my opinion, such practices will only accelerate the growing decline in impoverished African American communities at a time when it needs its best religious minds (male and female) engaged in the project to rebuild inner city communities and to rescue large numbers of children from crime, drugs, and despair. *"No Nation can rise higher than the status of its women"* is an old proverb that is as true today as it ever was. I fear that this attempted relegation of women to domestic roles is a manifestation of male egotism and an expression of the long-held belief by black men that black women have too much power. Unfortunately, this is an old issue in the African American community, long predating the black largescale entry into Islam. I experienced it often in the Civil Rights and in the Black Power movements. It was rife in what was called the Black Nationalist movement of the seventies and eighties. Many black men have longed to participate as full members in the *patriarchy.* This *"right"* was taken from them as the result of slavery and its aftermath. In its own horrible way, slavery put enslaved African males and females on the same level as far as work and responsibility were concerned. After slavery, economics demanded that black women continue to work to help maintain their families. This gave black women a semblance of independence, which has long been resented by some black men. I fear that Islam is being used as a cover to continue this age-old struggle to bring black women under black men's control.

Many leaders in the Muslim world have discovered that it is very difficult to build modern national states while oppressing one-half of the population. It would be good if African American male Muslim leaders could learn from these leaders' experiences about the negative consequences to the whole society of oppressing more than half of their population.

Muslim Women Struggle for Human Rights: The Context

Most non-Muslims credit Islam as being the root cause of the oppression of women in the Muslim World. In a special Middle East report,

"Women's Rights in the Arab World", authors Ramla Khalidi and Judith Tucker write:

> For many Westerners, the issue of Arab Women's rights and the broader problematic of gender and power in the region can be neatly summed up in one word, "Islam." The image of Islam as the fount of unmitigated oppression of women, as the foundation of a gender system that categorically denies women equal rights and subjects them to men, recurs in the movies, magazines and books in our popular culture as well as in much academic discourse. (Khalidi and Tucker n.d., 2)

But, of course, it is not that simple. A growing number of Muslim women scholars and activists have begun to challenge the notion that Islam is synonymous with the oppression of women. These women, many of whom consider themselves feminists, are questioning the male and often misogynist interpretations of the sacred tenets of Islam. They are focusing a women's, or feminist, lens on Islam's canon, and they are deriving different interpretations from those that have prevailed for centuries. As the two authors quoted above write: "[Seeing] a single essence or 'spirit' of Islam, a single blueprint for gender roles . . . proves difficult. Islam is not one thing, but is rather a set of beliefs and values that has evolved over time in rhythm with changing historical conditions and local customs and practices with which it came into contact" (Khalidi and Tucker n.d. 2).

It is these women scholars and activists who are bringing this insight and information to the forefront. They argue convincingly that Islam is not a monolithic structure etched immutably in stone for eternity. They are seeking to separate Islam, the religion, from culture, tradition, and social mores. They are calling for, and are themselves reinterpreting, the sacred texts. They are reviewing the history of the religion, at times bringing to the foreground the interpretations of earlier sects or groups in Islam who were labeled heterodox and their views dismissed. Just as happens among Christian and Jewish feminists, some Muslim women express anger toward religious institutions that undergird the oppression of them and their sisters. But, for the most part, these women want to work within their religious tradition and seek to reinterpret, reconceptualize, contextualize, and historicize Islam and their societies' rituals and practices. All of the women activists with whom I have spoken or whose materials I have read realize that they have a difficult task before them. Thirteen centuries of belief and cultural traditions are difficult to change.

As many, if not most, of the Muslim feminists see the need to change their societies within an Islamic context, they question Western feminist paradigms. There is also the problem of the heritage of colonialism. In the nineteenth and early twentieth century, colonial powers repeatedly used the issue of gender to advance their own agendas in the region. They argued that the oppression of women justified colonial intervention and that the imperial project would elevate women to the standard of equality putatively present in northern Europe. As Khalidi and Tucker point out, "the linking of gender issues to Western intervention and the invocation of Western standards to which all must aspire left a bitter legacy of mistrust. This legacy continues to cloud relations between women in the West and women in the Arab [Muslim] world" (Khalidi and Tucker n.d., 2).

Women here in the West use certain benchmark aspects in a society to measure the position of women within it. These include legal equity, reproductive freedom, and the opportunity to express and fulfill the individual self through work, through art, or through sexuality. But are these the only criteria by which one should assess the status of women in a particular society? Are these the universals of "feminism"? If one looks at what the women in the Muslim or Islamic world say are their main concerns, one gets a somewhat different list of priorities. They want legal equity, political participation, education, health care, and the right to employment (Khalidi and Tucker n.d., 2). Although there are similarities and overlap, what is quite obviously missing is the emphasis on the opportunity to express and fulfill the *individual self* through work, through art, or through sexuality.

On a group trip to the Middle East in October 1994, we met with a Muslim woman feminist psychologist on the faculty at the University of Jordan in Amman, Dr. Arwa al-Amry. She spoke with us about the state of women in Jordan. Although she noted that there had been great strides in education, health care, and equal pay for equal work, there had been little advancement in the area of gender relationships, particularly on the domestic front. Dr. al-Amry said that the model of gender relations in the Western world was not attractive to women in her part of the world. She spoke of the commodification and appropriation of women's sexuality and their bodies for commercial purposes in the West. She described the way that they see it: "Males in the Islamic world control women by veiling them and keeping them secluded; in the West, males control females by stripping them naked and exposing their nudity for sexual gratification and commercialization." For Dr. al-Amry and her feminist colleagues at their Women's Center, both positions are objectionable.

Two main factors must be understood in assessing gender issues in the Muslim world. One is the Islamic view of gender, which is, of course, based upon the sacred texts of Islam. First is the Qu'ran, considered the divine revelations from God to the Prophet Muhammad, which is, for the most part, uncontested. The Qu'ran does prescribe gender differences in terms of responsibilities and rights. The *surah* (chapter) most often quoted to support male control and domination is *Surah* 4:34. A traditional interpretation of it states: "Men are the protectors and providers (*qawwamma 'ala*) of women." Muslim women scholars, such as Amina Wadud and Azizah al-Hibri, are questioning this translation and the interpretation of this particular verse. Muslim women scholars say that many of the Qur'anic verses upon which women's subjugation is built are difficult to translate and are subject to varying interpretations (Wadud 1992; al-Hibri 1985). The Qu'ranic verse most often used to impose dress codes on women, "women cover your adornments" (Sura 24:31), can be understood as mandating veiling for the good Muslim woman or simply as requiring reasonably modest dress.

The question of equality in the Qu'ran is mixed. The sacred book clearly equates the genders in the spiritual or religious realms. Men and women have equal religious responsibility and will receive the same reward or punishment for their behavior. Yet there are statements that seem to indicate differences between men and women that disadvantage women and privilege men over them: for example, that women's legal testimony is worth one-half a man's or that women's inheritance is one-half that of their male relatives. Some Muslim feminists say that although these stipulations had their reasons and, perhaps, justification in the middle of the seventh century, there is no need or justification for a continuation of these practices in the last decade of the twentieth century. Herein lies the controversy. Of course, this argument brings these women interpreters into conflict with a hugh number of people in the Muslim world who believe that the Qu'ran, as the immutable and unchangeable word of Allah, is the *literal truth* for all times. This prevalent view holds that the interpretation of the holy book is not subject to context or history but is to be accepted literally as a whole. This is a major issue that Muslim feminists who hold a different view will have to struggle with for some time to come. Many of the women activists with whom I worked and spoke saw this issue of "literal" interpretation versus a contextual and historical interpretation of the sacred Islamic texts as a large and difficult matter with which to contend. Many of them even dread having to face it and are actually avoiding it for as long as possible. This was true in both Jordan and Palestine. The issue of textual interpretation is a potentially volatile one, and these women, for the most part, are handling it gingerly if at all. Yet most will acknowledge that it will be next to impossible to avoid it in the effort to change the public's perceptions of women's roles in society.

The second issue to be understood is the relationship of women's rights to the development of modern Arab states. In her "Women, Islam and the State" Deniz Kandiyoti writes: "All Muslim societies have had to grapple with the problem of establishing modern nations states and forging new notions of citizenship. Diverse processes of nation building have produced a spectrum of distinct shifting and actively contested syntheses between cultural nationalism and Islam. Women's rights were debated and legislated in the search for new ideologies to legitimate emerging forms of state power (1991, 4–9).

Kandiyoti gives an overview of these changes in several Islamic countries. Turkey, for example, has taken the most radical of all steps, secularizing all aspects of their society by adopting a secular civil code in 1926 and giving women the vote in 1934. Iran attempted sweeping reforms, including more rights for women. The shah was unable to control the Shiʿa clergy, who came back into the political arena in the 1960s, overthrew him, and returned Iran to an extreme form of traditionalism under the Ayotollah Khomeini. (Of course, it would seem that the pendulum is swinging more toward center with regard to women's rights in Iran as evidenced by the election of the moderate cleric, Muhammad Khatami in the August 1997 presidential elections—largely as a result of women's support.)

It is interesting and noteworthy that many Islamic societies by and large have been able to accept all types of reforms permitting states educational and juridical autonomy from religious authorities, but *"shariʿa inspired legislation in family and personal status codes persists even where secular laws have been adopted in every other sphere"* (Kandiyoti 1991, 10). John Esposito in his *Women in Muslim Family Law* explains the impact of the personal status or family law phenomena on women's citizenship status. He comments on the fact that personal status laws undermine the protection and guarantees of citizenship for women that are putatively guaranteed under the state constitutions in most Muslim countries (Esposito 1982). Kandiyoti, writing about this same phenomena states, "Equal citizenship rights of women guaranteed by national constitutions are circumscribed by personal laws granting men special privileges in the areas of marriage, divorce, custody, maintenance and inheritance" (1991, 10).

Kandiyoti also raises the important question: "Does this conservatism in the areas of women and the family derive from the centrality of Islam to Arab cultural nationalism and represent an attempt to preserve Arab cultural identity in the face of Western Imperialism as many Arab Commentators maintain?" (1991, 10). In my opinion the answer to this question is an unfortunate yes. Fatimah Mernissi has documented this phenomenon in several of her books (Mernissi 1987, 1991, 1996). She gives an historical overview of how this process has occurred and how the notions of "male honor," Muslim identity, and self-determination are borne on the bodies of women in the Muslim world. It is not only a political and sociological problem, it is a problem that affects people at deep psychological levels also. As an American who has spent eighteen continuous months in the Middle East, I experienced firsthand how deeply the notions of gender separation and male proprietary rights over women are held. Just walking down the street as a visible foreigner, one feels it all the time. Sexual intimidation and harassment are commonplace. Men as the "owners" of public space screamed out at me every day as I went about my daily activities in the streets in the Middle East. It was quite unsettling at first. (Initially, I thought that perhaps the level of intimidation was the result of my visible foreignness. But local women told me that they experienced the same thing whether in Western or traditional Muslim dress.) I also learned that wearing traditional Islamic clothing (an *abaya,* a long overcoat) with full head covering, did not protect me from blatant sexual harassment. The prevailing notion seemed to be that if you as a woman are in public space (male space) alone, then you are subject to harassment and intimidation; this is the cost for being out of "place."

Muslim women, like all women in the world, are experiencing rapid changes in their lives. By and large, women in most societies are living longer, having fewer children, and increasingly having a paid job. Concurrently, women make up the majority of persons living in poverty and are the least educated. Of the 1.2 to 1.3 billion persons living in poverty in the world today, 70 percent are women. Sixty percent of the world's work is done by women, yet they earn only 10 percent (some reports say only 5 percent) of the world's income and own less than 1 percent of the world's land. Presently two-thirds of the world's 800 million illiterate adults are women. The Middle East has one of the worst records in this regard although there have been considerable improvements in the education of women in the past two decades. Almost one-half million women die every year from pregnancy-related causes. Eighty percent of the refugees or persons displaced because of conflict are women and children. Religious fundamentalism and conservatism in several parts of the world are moving to deprive women of basic often hard-won rights such as the right to education, employment, freedom of expression, or control of fertility. (Afghanistan, under Taliban rule, exemplifies this trend in the extreme [UNESCO Sources 71, July–Aug. 1995].) Although it is acknowledged that there have been rapid changes in the economic, political, and certain social aspects of women's lives in most of the world, the cultural codes comprising religion, tradition, and customary practices continue to impede women's progress toward full participation in the political, cultural, and social life in many societies. These codes still lock women into second- or third-class status and buttress their oppression. Muslim women who participated in the Beijing conference and in the many meetings, seminars, and other activities leading up to it addressed this issue head on. There was an urgency for many of these women, given the rise and spread of conservative Islamist movements in many of their countries.

Although the focus of the reports from Beijing is on Muslim women activists striving for U.N.-defined human rights, it should be noted that there were at least two other distinctly different Muslim women perspectives heard in Beijing and some of the preparatory meetings I attended. A number of women present espoused and defended a "traditionalist," or Islamist, view. This view affirms the position that women were given all their rights through the divine revelations of Allah enshrined in the Holy Qu'ran. In their view, nothing additional to these prescriptions is needed.

Many of these traditionalists concede that Muslim women have not been given all their rights in most Islamic societies and, therefore, educating Muslims about their (Islamic) rights is the area of focus they advocate. They wanted definitions of women's rights on the basis of Islamic principles. A second less-acknowledged group, but clearly present, were the Muslim women activists who were suspicious of economic and political motivations behind "universalist" U.N.-backed definitions of women's oppression. These women wanted attention brought to the suffering women around the world experience as a result of U.S. foreign policy and Western hegemonic interest. Glaring examples raised by these women included the plight of Palestinian, Iraqi, and Bosnian women. Muslim women addressing these forms of oppression joined with their sisters from across the Third World who spoke about women's suffering caused by Structural Adjustment programs (SAPs) imposed by the World Bank and the International Monetary Fund (IMF).

Those Muslim women who are specifically working for women's human rights within a universalist or U.N.-defined context uphold the view that women's rights are inalienable, universal, and a fundamental necessity for the development of women's full human potential. They firmly believe that women's rights are human rights and that these rights cannot be abrogated on the basis of religion, tradition, or culture. These activists are gravely concerned that several Muslim governments who are on record as being in support of the Universal Declaration of Human Rights in 1948 moved away from this support at the United Nations Vienna Conference in 1993. One such human rights advocate, Mahnaz Afkhami, executive director of the Sisterhood Is Global Institute (SIGI), describes in *Faith and Freedom: Women's Human Rights in the Muslim World* how these Muslim governments moved away from support of universal norms of human rights for women:

> They changed their position on the grounds that "universal human rights are Western parochial concepts used as weapons of cultural imperialism" [and they argue] that to judge Muslim societies by these standards injures Muslim Communal Rights, and that for Muslim countries Islam provides the basic elements of a just society including the fundamental rights of women. In short, they rejected women's human rights, as defined in international documents. (1995, ix)

Muslim women who are alarmed by their governments' behavior and its implications for their futures see much of this movement away from support of women's rights as the result of growing Islamist movements in these societies and the subsequent need for these governments to emphasize their own commitment to orthodoxy and the need to yield to the demand of some of these movements that "trespassing women" be contained" (Kandiyoti 1995, 23).

Those women, who have no intention of standing by and passively watching their hard-won gains for human rights be lost, are working to make their voices heard both within their own societies and at the international level in a myriad of ways. They are speaking out; they are writing books, pamphlets, and other tracts as part of their public education efforts in their home countries and abroad. They are developing local, regional, and global networks of Muslim women that advocate for women's full participation in all aspects of public and private life, including gaining the franchise in those countries that have not granted women the right to vote. They are running for elected office, sometimes against incredible odds and social opprobrium. Muslim human rights activists are, when possible, working to expose the instances of oppression and violence, state, religiously motivated, or domestic, against women. They are gathering petitions, drafting legislation, and, where they have made inroads into the political structures, introducing legislation to change or outlaw some of the more overtly discriminatory features of the family codes, particularly those sections dealing with divorce, polygamy, inheritance, and custody of children. Women in Muslim countries are organizing domestic abuse and sexual abuse hotlines and in a few cases shelters for women attempting to escape abusive husbands and/or other male relatives.

Muslim women from all of these tendencies (traditionalists, secularists, etc.) are engaged in educating themselves and the women in their communities about Islam. They are scrutinizing those passages in the Qurʾan and *ahadith* that are most often used to justify the subjugation of women. Close readings and different interpretations of these passages are being written and disseminated. In numerous cases Muslim women lawyers and others are educating women living under Islamic law about their rights as enshrined within religiously derived law and how to use them.

The four issues that emerged in Beijing as pressing for Muslim women were (1) women's rights as human rights, (2) the impact of Islamist movements on women's ability to gain human rights, (3) violence against women, and (4) economic justice.

Reports of Present On-the-Ground Work on Behalf of Women in Selected Areas of the Islamic World

The Maghreb (North Africa)

In the Maghreb the organization called Collectif 95 Magreb Egalité is a network of women's associations, intellectuals and researchers working in defense of women's fundamental rights in the Maghreb. Its membership is composed of women from Algeria, Morocco, and Tunisia. They state that among those obstacles to women achieving equality are (1) the socio-economic recession resulting from Structural Adjustment programs (SAPs) imposed by the world's monetary funds and (2) the rise and growth of the "fundamentalist" movements (their words) that eclipses the real reasons behind the crises of their societies and casts guilt on the just struggle of women for equality.

Collectif 95 in its work affirms these principles: Human rights are a universal and indivisible principle. Women's rights are human rights. Equality between men and women before the law is a basic principle. Finally, respect for women's rights is an essential prerequisite for the achievement of a democratic and just society.

Collectif 95 denounces the following as detrimental to women exercising their fundamental rights: (1) claimed "preservation" of Islamic culture and identity to support continued discrimination against women, (2) a judicial system that discriminates against women within the family, (3) use of religion for political agendas, (4) use of religion to support discriminatory practices, (5) laws against women that lead to their exclusion from public life, and (6) persistence of violence against women and the official silence that surrounds it.

Collectif 95's list of demands to their governments includes the ratification by their governments, without reservation, of the "Convention on the Elimination of All Forms of Discrimination Against Women" (CEDAW) and all other international instruments related to women's rights and the introduction of international laws for human rights into their national legal systems. They have introduced a One Hundred Measures and Provisions program that calls for an egalitarian codification of women's judicial status and family rights that will put an end to women's legal inferiority, permit women to work outside the home and to have control over all aspects of their health, including their reproductive health and sex life, and allow women to be actively involved in the political and economic lives of their societies, including the running for elected offices and serving if elected.

Morocco. The Union de l'Action Feminine began in 1983 and is a Moroccan nongovernmental organization (NGO) whose aim is the institution of effective legal equity between men and women in daily life, the integration of women in the development process, and women receiving adequate salaries—in short, the recognition of women as full-fledged citizens. Their main activities include a literacy campaign, support to women victims of violent acts, the creation of economic projects for women, and a national campaign for the amendment of the Personal Status codes. They have also launched a national campaign against violence. After a decade of activity aimed at sensitizing women and the public to the problems brought about by the application of the Code of Personal Status, which they say is discriminatory and unjust to women, and a decade of study and research on the codes, the Union launched a national campaign calling for the amendment of the Code of Personal Status. They collected one million signatures during their petition drive in three months, which they forwarded to the king, who acknowledged the unjustness of the code and the legitimacy of the women's struggle. The king urged religious leaders and the women to amend the code. Some articles were amended, but the women felt that problems continued even after the amendments. Because of their dissatisfaction with the amendments, the group launched their Program of Urgent Claims, which maintains (among other things) that the family should be seen as an institution based on equity and equality between men and women, that women should be granted majority status at twenty-one years of age, that women should receive the right to give themselves into marriage, that the same rights and obligations should be granted to husbands and wives on equal footing, that discrimination against women who apply for divorce should be abolished, that polygamy should be abolished, that women should be given guardianship over their children, that education and work should be considered as a legitimate and inalienable right of which women cannot be deprived by the husband, and that women should be given the right to obtain a passport and to travel without the husband's permission.

The Near East

Jordan. The Jordanian Women's Union is an NGO whose primary focus is on human rights and violence against women. Their issues include the right for women to obtain a passport and to travel without their husband's or male guardian's permission and the right of a women to give her nationality to her children, a right she does not currently have in Jordan and numerous other countries. One of the most critical campaigns in which they are engaged is the issue of deadly violence against women in the form of "honor killings." In Jordanian society over the last three years, women's groups have caused unprecedented exposure to the number of so-called "honor killings" that plague the kingdom. Jordan has a small population of some four million people; "everyone knows everyone else." Although "honor killings" were never confirmed, they were whispered about. The Union and other women's organizations have set about to change this situation. They have obtained and made public the police records that show that "crimes of honor" have ranked the highest among all murders in Jordan for the past ten years. Fathers and often younger brothers kill girls or women for such things as the girl running away from home, getting pregnant out of wedlock, and, sometimes, just because they "suspect" that a girl is behaving "immorally." Women's organizations have exposed that on average some thirty to sixty girls and women each year die at the hands of their families for supposedly "shaming them." The Jordanian penal code in some sense supports these honor killings because it states, *"He who discovers his wife or one of his female relatives committing adultery and kills, wounds, or injures one or both of them is exempt from penalty."* Jordanian law also reduces penalties for those men who kill their wives or female relatives who are found in an "adulterous situation." Women who are battling this issue know that it is an uphill battle to change this type of law in a society that indirectly condones killing women for reasons of a man's "honor." The effort to bring this matter to public attention has been aided by woman reporters in Jordan who write about each new "honor killing" incident in the newspapers. It should be noted that "honor killings" are not prescribed by the Qu'ran and are really a cultural tradition. In fact, they are in direct opposition to the Qur'anic injunction that there be actual witnesses to an act of adultery or fornication before any prosecution can take place and that these witness are required to testify about what they saw. Often these girls and women are killed on suspicion alone.

Other major efforts related to securing women's rights in Jordan include increasing women's economic power through training women entrepreneurs and providing start-up funding for women's economic enterprises and increasing the number of women elected officials through training and support for women candidates at local, regional, and national levels. During 1997, most of the women's groups were involved in this activity. Seventeen women from across the country stood for election in the November 1997 parliamentary elections; unfortunately, none of them won. Even the one woman who was running for reelection, Toujan Faisal, lost. She was the first woman ever elected to that post. Some of the most progressive activists and their supporters organized a campaign to establish a women's quota in Parliament. This initiative was not supported by the king, the government, and many in Parliament, and it died as a result of nonaction.

Legislation to change the more discriminatory aspects of the Personal Status laws, including some alteration in the divorce provisions of the *shari'yah* law, is being drafted and submitted to Parliament. Most of the submissions are weak and still leave an inordinate amount of power in men's hands. For example, they do not challenge men's right to unilateral divorce nor to their unabridged right to marry four wives without justification. There are two functioning hot lines for abused women staffed by women lawyers and social workers: one (noted above) run by the Jordanian Women's Union and the other by the Business and Professional Women's Club. (These are two of the few hot lines in the Arab world.) Many consciousness-raising and empowerment workshops and seminars for women across the country are being run on a regular basis.

Palestine. Although Palestinian women's organizations are engaged in projects similar to those of their counterparts in the region, the suffering caused by the continued Israeli occupation colors and is the ongoing context for much of their work. Numerous workshops at the NGO Forum addressed the exacerbation of women's suffering caused by Israeli policies on the West Bank and Gaza Strip. These policies include border closings, blockades, curfews, school closings, continued appropriation of Palestinian land to make space for more Israeli settlements, seizure of Palestinian property, and demolition of Palestinian homes. Palestinian women spoke about the increased family violence they endure in their homes that is directly related to the mounting political tension and the economic crisis in the territories resulting largely from border closures and men's inability to work.

Although the new Palestinian state has not been established, Palestinian women are working hard to make sure that they will live under laws granting them justice in their independent state. Legal discrimination is a real problem for women here. The Women's Centre for Legal Aid and Counseling held a series of six open workshops focused on women and the law in Ramallah in 1994. Their published report on the sessions, *Towards Equality—An Examination of the Status of Palestinian Women in Existing Law* (1995, 10), affirms "blatant dejure discrimination against women in law and defacto discrimination against women [exists] in the application of the law." Women are working in the West Bank, in Gaza, and in Jerusalem to draw up legislation for the Palestinian National Authority (PNA). Although only one woman, Intisar al-Wazir, was appointed by PNA president Arafat to a ministerial post, more than one dozen highly political women hold important deputy positions in culture, education, and youth ministries. Five women were elected in the 1996 national Palestinian elections. The well-known Hanan Ashrawi, a Christian, is one of these. The other four elected women are Muslims: Dalal Salame of Nabulus, and Intisar al-Wazir, Jamileh Saidan, and Rawjah al-Shawa of Gaza. Palestinian women activists have set up a highly specific agenda that will require protection by law. It includes equal pay for equal work, protection against dismissal from employment because of marriage or pregnancy, the right to breast-feeding leave, and provision of adequate day-care centers for working mothers. They also want labor rights education integrated into school curricula. A minimum age of eighteen years for marriage for women is proposed. (Currently, in some of the refugee camps the average age of marriage for women is fourteen years.) The women are also asking for a Personal Status Code that will allow civil marriage, something in the Islamic world that only exists in Turkey, and even there this practice is under attack. An attorney at the Women's Centre said that they understand that this is a long-range goal. They expect that it could take up to ten years to achieve civil marriages in Palestine, something that is not permitted in Israel either. Clearly, for many women, civil marriage is seen as the most immediate way to prevent the injustices allowed under the "traditional" religious marriage.

Palestinian women are also very concerned about violence against women and the so-called "honor killings," both of which are very sensitive issues and ones the feminists say the PNA is not ready to handle. Women's organizations have been set up to provide counseling, medical help, and legal assistance for women who are victims of spousal and family abuse. Abuse hot lines have been developed, and at least one shelter for abused women is operating—the Jerusalem Shelter for Battered Women. This shelter serves both Palestinian and Israeli women and has staff from both nationalities. There is also a Haifa Rape Crisis Center in the region. Women's NGOs are drafting legislation that will protect women from violence inside their homes, and they are calling on the PNA to sponsor legal protection, emergency hot lines, and abuse shelters for women seeking refuge from male violence. In the area of education, Palestinian women want to make school mandatory until the age of eighteen. Presently, many girls in the rural areas and refugee camps drop out of school after the sixth grade.

Israel. Another important development in the region is the burgeoning progressive women's movement in Israel. One of the most visible of these at the NGO Forum was Bat Shalom. They describe themselves as "a feminist center for peace and social justice [whose] aim is to work toward a democratic and pluralistic society in Israel, where women will be of more influence" (Bat Shalom 1997). Bat Shalom brings together women peace activists, women educators, and women community leaders to raise one another's consciousness and to create a culture of peace and social justice in Israel. Bat Shalom works closely with a Palestinian women's group, the Jerusalem Center for Women of East Jerusalem, to end the Israeli occupation and to secure the just rights of both the peoples who share this land. A coordinating committee oversees the two organizations' joint activities, called the Jerusalem Link. The organization's Women's Joint Venture for Peace is a program whose goal is "to promote women's political, social and cultural activities and leadership in the service of women's rights and the realization of peace on the basis of justice and equality" (Bat Shalom 1997). Their joint projects include working for human rights in the transitional period through women's joint pressure group efforts directed toward eliminating human rights violations in the Occupied Territories, developing leadership seminars to enhance the effectiveness of women's leadership in both the Palestinian and Israeli communities, and holding lectures and discussion on feminist theories for Palestinian and Israeli women to examine various feminist theories and their unique reading in the Middle East.

They are training young Palestinian and Israeli women to lead the joint encounters and activities of the Link, such as publication of *Jerusalem 1948—The Female Voice*, which is a collection of Palestinian and Israeli women's life histories from the period of the 1948 war.

Egypt. Egyptian women human rights activists state that the most serious enemy of women's empowerment in Egypt is the rising tide of "ultra-orthodox Islam." They maintain that this trend is no longer confined to the militant movements that opt to drag women back into seclusion and to subject them to full patriarchal authority but has penetrated the state's religious establishment. An indication of the truth of this assertion is that since the beginning of 1995, al-Azhar, Egypt's prestigious and powerful Islamic university, has battled ferociously against a proposed bill to ban the practice of female genital mutilation to which it is estimated that some four thousand girls are subjected daily (this is another pre-Islamic custom with no basis in the Qur'an). In the spring of 1995, the grand sheikh of al-Ahzar issued a religious ruling stating that female genital mutilation is "a duty on every Muslim woman," arguing that the ritual checks a woman's sexual drive and, thus, makes her virtuous. The law on banning female circumcision, which thousands of women worked to have introduced into their legislative process, was supported by Egypt's ministers of population and justice. None, however, chose to discredit publicly the grand sheikh's views. A prominent human rights activist, Nigad El-Broai, secretary general of the Egyptian Organization of Human Rights (EOHR) stated, "The government likes to appease the official Islamicist because it wants to concentrate on its battle with militant Islamicts who are trying to topple the regime and establish a theocratic state." Nigad says that women are fighting back. The EOHR sued the grand sheikh of al-Azhar for his ruling. Fortunately, women won a great victory at the end of 1997 on this front. On December 28, 1997, Egypt's highest court upheld the ban on the genital cutting of girls and women (*New York Times*, Dec. 29, 1997, 27).

Another positive development in Egypt was the [then] new regulations regarding women and the marriage contract. Among other provisions in this new contract is that women planning to marry now have the right to sign a marriage contract that allows them to leave a bad marriage with greater ease. It also requires that both parties be tested for AIDS. This provision already has the support of the grand mufti of Egypt. Women have been working for this contract for more than ten years. Why? Men in Egypt can still have more than one wife and women are still unable to travel without their husband's permission, nor can women obtain a passport on their own. Many women, once married, are unable to continue their education or to work outside the home because their husbands will not give their permission as is the case in most of the Muslim Arab world. According to Mona Zulficar, an Egyptian attorney and one of the framers of the new contract, under the existing laws men in Egypt can divorce their wives "in one minute," whereas women have to suffer for up to seven years, trying to prove "damage" to obtain a divorce. This new contract also prohibits polygamy, settles the ownership of the home in the event of divorce, and the specific amount of money to be given when a wife is divorced against her will.

Iran. The most highly visible Iranian women human rights activists in Beijing were exiles, forced out of their country, they maintained, by the harsh religiously based laws put in place since the creation of the Islamic Republic in 1979. These Iranian exiles waged a fierce public education campaign in Beijing. They have organized a worldwide network of Iranians in exile who are lobbying for the governments of the world to censure Iran for what they call "flagrant discrimination against women and abuse of their human rights." The November 1994 report of the Parliamentary Human Rights Group entitled *Iran: The Subjection of Women* (n.d.) states, "In the Islamic Republic of Iran, women are third class citizens. They are inferior in law, subordinate to their husbands, denied equal entry to the professions and politics and forced to wear clothes specified by the religious establishment. . . . In Iran, . . . the idea that men and women are equal is systematically denied. . . . Discrimination against women . . . has found vehement ideological, legal and official backing in the clerical establishment."

Within months of the establishment of the Islamic Republic, Ayotollah Khomeini issued directives requiring women to wear the veil and a decree to dismiss all female judges and bar all females from pursuing legal studies. Men were regranted the universal right to divorce and permitted again to marry up to four wives with almost no restrictions. And according to the January 1, 1994, edition of the weekly publication, *Zan-e-Rouz*, the age of marriage was reduced to nine for girls and fifteen for boys. Women were barred from admittance to scientific and technological fields. Women and men were no longer able to walk or talk together in public unless they were able to prove they were married or closely related. Even at the universities, the only educational facilities in which coeducation has not been banned, the classrooms were separated by a curtain to prevent any contact between male and female students (Saadatmand 1995, 1). Ayatollah Khamenei has laid down what women can do: "Women's major role, which is in fact the product of their special functions, is bearing children; fostering and safeguarding the children's lives; providing comfort and satisfaction for men and moderating the family environment" (Parliamentary Human Rights Group 1994).

Iranian human rights advocates are fighting back. They assert further that freedom of religion or belief may not be asserted to shield sectarian religious laws and practices based often upon irrelevant sources and interpretations, depriving women's status of international scrutiny and monitoring. In their recommendations they urge vigilant and concrete action, including the documenting of human rights violations by the U.N. High Commissioner for Human Rights, the Special Rapporteur On Violence and Women, and other concerned international institutions. They further urge the publicizing of these findings and the pressuring of those governments that violate women's human rights to make their laws and regulations compatible with international norms. If this should fail, these NGOs asked that Iran be confronted with economic and other sanctions and that international condemnation against the regime should be used as it was used successfully against South Africa.

From media reports during 1997 it appears that the Iranian government is moving toward a more centrist position with regard to the rights of women. Iran's new president, Muhammad Khatami, won by a landslide over the government-favored candidate as a result of the huge turnout and support from women and youth. Since taking office in August 1997, Khatami has made moderate statements about a range of issues and has appointed several women to high-ranking posts within his administration.

Southeast Asia

Malaysia. The All Women's Action Society (AWAM) and the National Women's Coalition (NWC) are two of the human rights for women groups in this country. Both groups held consultations in both grass-roots and indigenous communities with women workers in rural and urban areas to prepare for the FWCW and to present their findings to the Malaysian government. Out of these consultations five major concerns were identified: violence against women, health, culture and religion, land, and labor. The premise of the consultations was that women are central to the process of nation building, yet they are the group that has benefited the least from opportunities and resources for national development. They state that women have been denied equal access to unionization, key decision making at any level, adequate legal protection, and quality health care for the specific needs of women.

They have launched an anti-Violence Against Women (VAW) campaign to educate the public on the pervasiveness of rape, domestic violence, and sexual harassment in Malaysia. They maintain that their society tends to overlook the seriousness of these problems and their broader implications. They state, "VAW limits a woman's personal growth, her productivity, her socioeconomic roles, her physical and psychological health, and the family. Most of all, it negates the right of women to be human" (AWAM and NWC, n.d.). In their view the fundamental issues underlying VAW are women's inferior position in the society and the unequal power relationship between men and women. They also see men's wish to exert their position of power over women and the lack of fundamental respect for women as the factors that have led to dehumanizing violence against women, who are deemed to be "weaker." Traditional, cultural, and religious beliefs also aggravate the situation by maintaining that women are subservient to men. They point to the negative images of women in the media as also serving to perpetuate violence against women by portraying women as objects of desire to be used by men for their own needs. Victims and participants of VAW are found in all levels of society, all socioeconomic classes, all ages, and all races in Malaysia, they assert.

These two organizations have used a number of strategies in their campaign against VAW. These strategies have included advocacy (to make VAW a crime and to include the issue in their country's national agenda) and awareness, or consciousness raising (focused on how VAW reinforces patriarchy and the subordination of women). They also focus on educating the public about the seriousness of wife battering. There were two major campaings related to VAW. One was to increase the penalty for convicted rapists, which passed Parliament in 1989. Another was the Domestic Violence Act designed to make domestic violence illegal. This did not succeed and was tabled in Parliament in 1994.

As a result of the success of the campaign in raising Malaysians' awareness of VAW, the police department has set up an all-woman rape squad at its headquarters in Kuala Lumpur, and several training sessions have been held for police officers regarding the handling of rape survivors. A few shelters and counseling services have been set up by NGOs in a few cities. Because of a lack of resources and inadequate programming services for women, however, these programs have not been able to expand and serve more women who need help.

Sisters in Islam (SIS), an Islamically based human rights organization, has produced a sharp and insightful critique of the view that Islam is synonymous with the mandatory enforcement of *shari'ah* law, especially the *hudud* punishments. It is a group of Muslim women studying and researching the status of women in Islam; these women "have come together as believers because they want to achieve the rights granted to us by Islam." This group believes that both men and women make up the Islamic community and that both must participate as equal partners in developing an understanding of Islam as a comprehensive way of life. They see Islam historically as a liberating religion that uplifted women's status, but that in spite of this, Muslim practices today often oppress women and deny them the equality and human dignity granted in the Qur'an. Two of the most popular booklets in the series of educational materials that they have produced are *Are Women and Men Equal Before Allah?* and *Are Muslim Men Allowed to Beat Their Wives?* SIS organized panels and workshops and disseminated their literature broadly at the NGO Forum.

Conclusion

My time in Beijing—listening to the Muslim women activists and learning about their work—and my eighteen months living in the Middle East freed me of any residual Western stereotypes of Muslim women as uniformly veiled and oppressed, passively accepting patriarchal norms and dictates in their religion or in their societies. Although in many cases there were huge differences in background and life experiences between me and my Muslim sisters, there were many commonalities. Included in those experiences held in common were the legacy of gender stereotyping and overt sexism and the internalization of those oppressions. Similar also was our struggle to deprogram ourselves of the internalized feelings of inferiority based on ethnicity or gender. I found that I could relate completely to the struggle that these women were waging in their efforts to secure their human rights and their Islamic rights, both of which have been denied them under the guise of religion, tradition, and culture.

Being in the Middle East and experiencing the effects of thirteen centuries of women's subjugation made me painfully aware of what is occurring in my own country to many African American women who have embraced Islam. Women and men being taught the most conservative interpretations of the role of women in Islam and in society are of particular concern to me. Many of the Islamic converts here are young African American teenagers. Some of them equate being a Muslim with the wearing of a face veil, *khimar,* and/or *hijab* and, for the females, subjugation to the Muslim males in their lives—*imams,* husbands, boyfriends. These young women are being encouraged to marry early and to produce many children. In today's world this is bad advice, and in the United States it is disastrous.

Few will lead productive lives in this country without a high level of education or technical skills. No one in the world can afford to bring large numbers of children into the world today, least of all those with minimal amounts of education and technical know-how. To advise women to return to the way of life of seventh-century Arabia, or even the Middle Ages, is counterproductive. I understand and am likewise concerned about issues of modesty and chastity, particularly among the youth in American society who give birth to many children out of wedlock. Many are promoting early marriage as an antidote to the huge percentage of youth engaged in sexual activity. Pushing girls, however, into teenage marriages, sometimes polygamous ones, clearly is not the solution. We in the African American Muslim community must find ways to encourage both our male and female youth to remain chaste without pushing girls into dead-end situations that can ruin their lives forever. Nor should we suggest to them that their primary role is a maternal one. Women have brains as well as wombs. At the early stages of their lives, their brain is the most important organ they should be encouraged to use. Parenting should come later for both genders after they are prepared for such responsibility.

Rigid gender segregation, hierarchical gender relations, relegation of women to primarily domestic roles, marginalization of women's theological/religious participation in the interpretation of Islam, and advocacy of unmodified patriarchy are not what is needed to produce a full flowering of Islam in America. I long to see the promotion of an egalitarian, compassionate, merciful, and peaceful Islam where male and female believers grow in the *three thousand gracious qualities and ninety-nine attributes* of the living God. I hope to engage in whatever work I can do to promote a universalist, egalitarian, and pluralistic Islam.

10

Is Family Planning Permitted by Islam?

The Issue of a Woman's Right to Contraception

RIFFAT HASSAN

Sources of the Islamic Tradition

✌ Before one can speak meaningfully about family planning in the context of the Islamic tradition, it is necessary to clarify what one means by "the Islamic tradition." This tradition—like other major religious traditions—does not consist of, or derive from, a single source. Most Muslims, if questioned about its sources are likely to refer to more than one of the following: the Qur'an (the Book of Revelation believed by Muslims to be the Word of God revealed through the agency of Archangel Gabriel to the Prophet Muhammad); *sunnah* (the practical traditions of the Prophet Muhammad); *hadith* (the sayings attributed to the Prophet Muhammad); *fiqh* (jurisprudence) or *madhahib* (schools of law); and the *shari'ah* (the code of life that pertains to all aspects of Muslim life). Although all of these "sources" have contributed to what is cumulatively referred to as "the Islamic tradition," it is important to note that they do not form a coherent or consistent body of teachings or precepts from which a universally agreed upon set of Islamic norms can be derived. Many examples can be cited of inconsistencies among various sources of the Islamic tradition. There are, for instance, inconsistencies between the Qur'an and the hadith literature, which are considered to be the primary sources of the Islamic tradition. Inconsistencies can also be found within the body of the hadith

226

literature and the literature of the Schools of Law. In view of this fact, it is scarcely possible to speak of "Islam" or "the Islamic tradition" as if it were unitary or monolithic. Its various components must be identified and examined separately before any generalization is attempted on behalf of the tradition as a whole.

It is obviously not possible, within the scope of this short chapter, to engage in a comprehensive discussion of the complex issue of family planning in the light of all of the above-mentioned sources of the Islamic tradition. In the brief account that follows, attention however, I draw to those ideas and attitudes in the sources of the Islamic tradition that I consider significant and pertinent in a contemporary reflection on a subject of increasing importance both in the Islamic world and the world in general.

Family Planning and the Qur'an

Theoretically, without a doubt, the Qur'an is the highest and most authoritative source of normative Islam. A clear Qur'anic statement on any subject is regarded by the overwhelming majority of Muslims as decisive and beyond questioning. The Qur'an is not, however, a book of laws and regulations that deals directly with every conceivable issue or problem. Rather, it is a book of divine wisdom meant to guide human beings so that they can actualize their potential as human beings made "in the best of molds" (Surah 95: At-Tin:4) and become God's vicegerents on earth. Although no clear text or texts in the Qur'an focus directly on the contemporary issue of family planning, the Qur'an does establish, through its teachings, the ethical framework in which this issue—like other contemporary issues—can be discussed in all its multifaceted complexity.

Often, progressive Muslims who support family planning, say that the Qur'an is silent on the issue of family planning and they take this silence to be a sign of affirmation rather than negation. For instance, Fazlur Rahman has pointed out that "in the verses of the Holy Qur'an one finds nothing which gainsays the view that we should control our population, for a time, to remedy our present situation (Rahman 1972, 94)." By contrast, conservative Muslims, such as Abul 'Ala' Maududi, insist that "the Qur'an is not silent" (Maududi 1974, 83) on the subject. They point to the Qur'anic condemnation of the practice of burying female children alive, which was prevalent in pre-Islamic Arabia (Surah 81: *At-Takwir*: 8–9; Surah 16: *An-Nahl*: 57–59), and to the Qur'anic verses in which the "killing" of children is prohibited or censured (Surah 6: *Al-An'am*: 137, 140, 151; Surah 17: *Al-Isra'il*:31; Surah 60: *Al-Mumtahanah*:12). Further, they refer to verses such as the following to support their contention that procreation is a blessing from God:

> O people! fear your Lord who has created you from a single soul and from it created its mate and from these He raised up many men and women. (Surah 4: *An-Nisa'*:4 in Rahman 1972, 94)

> And remember (the time) when you were few, and (how) He made you many. (Surah 7: *Al-A'raf*:86, in Asad 1980, 216)
>
> And, truly, We sent forth apostles before thee, and We appointed for them wives and offspring. (Surah 13: *Ar-Ra'd*:38, in Asad 1980, 368)

> And God has given you mates of your own kind and has given you, through your mates, children and children's children, and has provided for you sustenance out of the good things of life. (Surah 16: *An-Nahl*:72, in Asad 1980, 406–7)

> And who pray:"O our Sustainer! Grant that our spouses and our offspring be a joy to our eyes." (Surah 25: *Al-Furqan*:74, in Asad 1980, 558)

Opponents of family planning also cite Qur'anic verses, such as the following, which state that all sustenance comes from God who provides for all creatures, particularly blessing those who have trust in God:

> Do not kill your children for fear of poverty—(for) it is We who shall provide sustenance for you as well as for them. (Surah 6: *Al-An'am*:151, in Asad 1980, 198)

> There is no creeping being on earth but that upon God is its sustenance (Surah 11: *Hud*:6, trans., in Rahman 1972, 94)

> And unto everyone who is conscious of God, He (always) grants a way out (of unhappiness) and provides for him in a manner beyond all expectation; and for everyone who places his trust in God, He (alone) is enough. (Surah 65: *At-Talaq*: 2–3, in Asad 1980, 872)

Addressing, first, the arguments used by conservative Muslims to contend that the Qur'an is opposed to the idea of family planning, I state the following:

1. The references in the Qur'an to the killing of children (who—according to the testimony of both "sacred" and historical texts—were female, not male, offspring) are to *children already born* and not to unborn children. Hence, they are not relevant in a discussion of whether, according to Qur'anic teaching, birth control is permissible.

2. The references in the Qur'an to the "killing" of children may not, in all instances, point to actual slaying of offspring but could be symbolic of ill treatment of children. As pointed out by Ghulam Ahmad Parwez in his lexicon of the Qur'an, the Arabic root word *q-t-l* means not only to slay with a weapon, blow, or poison but also to humiliate and degrade or to deprive of proper upbringing and education (Parwez 1961, 1338–40).

3. Although the Qur'an repeatedly refers to God as the creator and sustainer of all creation, it does not absolve either individuals or communities of responsibility for their survival and well-being. Rather, it constantly reminds human beings (a) that "for itself lies every soul in pledge" (e.g., see Surah 52: *At-Tur*:21; and Surah 74: *Al-Muddaththir*:38) (b) that reason (ʿaql), is what elevates human beings above all other creatures and enables them to become God's vicegerents on earth; (c) that right belief (*iman*) is inseparable from righteous action (ʿamal), which involves continual striving (*jihad*) for overcoming inner and outer obstacles to making the world the abode of justice and peace, which is the goal of Islam; (d) that God will not change the condition of human beings until they change what is in themselves (Surah 13: *Ar-Raʿd*:11). Using the Qur'anic references to God's power or promise to sustain all creation to argue "for an unlimited population in proportion to the economic resources" is—as pointed out by Fazlur Rahman—"infantile." The Qur'an certainly does not mean to say that God provides every living creature with sustenance whether that creature is capable of procuring sustenance for itself or not" (Rahman 1972, 94).

Addressing, next, the argument used by progressive or "liberal" Muslims in support of family planning, namely, that the Qur'an is silent about the subject, which means, at the very least, that it is not opposed to the idea of birth control, I respond as follows:

1. The absence of war does not necessarily imply peace just as the

absence of sickness does not necessarily imply health. The fact that the Qur'an does not say anything against the idea of birth control does not, likewise, necessarily imply that it supports family planning.

2. Many present-day Muslims, having heard all their lives that "the Qur'an is a complete code of life," expect to find in the Qur'an specific or direct statements pertaining to all the issues or subjects that are important to them. When they do not find such statements, they assume that the Qur'an has nothing to say about these issues or subjects. This perceived "silence" of the Qur'an regarding a number of significant "modern" issues, such as the issue of family planning, creates a theological and ethical vacuum that different persons and groups fill in different ways. What needs, urgently, to be done is a critical review of the idea that the Qur'an is a complete code of life. In what way is the Qur'an a complete code of life? Certainly, it is not an encyclopedia that may be consulted to obtain specific information about how God views each problem, issue, or situation that may confront human beings. Nor is the Qur'an "a legal code" as pointed out by Muhammad Iqbal (1962, 165). By regarding the Qur'an as a book in which they will find ready-made laws, regulations, prescriptions, or assessments relating to everything in life, a large number of Muslims have lost sight of the main purpose of the Qur'an. This purpose, as stated by Iqbal, is "to awaken in man the higher consciousness of his relation with God and the universe. . . . The important thing in this connection is the dynamic outlook of the Qur'an" (1962, 165–66).

Although the Qur'an does not address the issue of family planning specifically, or directly, its teachings shed a good deal of light on how this issue and other contemporary issues may be understood, or dealt with, within the ethical framework of normative Islam. For instance, the Qur'an puts great emphasis on the preservation of what one commonly refers to as "fundamental human rights," such as (a) the right to be respected for one's humanity (e.g., see Surah 17: *Al-Isra'il*:70); (b) the right to be treated with justice and equity (e.g., see Surah 4: *An-Nisa'*: 135–36, Surah 5: *Al-Ma'idah*:8; (c) the right to be free of traditionalism, authoritarianism (religious, intellectual, political, economic), tribalism, classism or caste system, sexism and slavery;[1] (d) the right to privacy and protection from slander, backbit-

---

1. For instance, see Surah 2: *Al-Baqarah*: 177, 256, 282; Surah 3: *Al-'Imran*: 79, 159; Surah 4:

ing, and ridicule;[2] (e) the right to acquire knowledge;[3] (f) the right to work, to earn, to own property (e.g., see Surah 4: *An-Nisa'*: 11–12, 31); (g) the right to have a secure place of residence in an environment in which one's possessions and covenants are protected and in which one can move freely;[4] (h) the right to leave one's place of origin under oppressive conditions (e.g., see Surah 4: *An-Nisa'*: 97–100); (i) the right to develop one's aesthetic sensibilities and to enjoy the bounties created by God;[5] and (j) the right not only to life but to "the good life," which is possible, according to Qur'anic perspective, only in a just society because justice is a prerequisite for peace and peace is a prerequisite for self-actualization (Hassan 1982, 51–65; and Hassan 1992, 463–95).

For Muslims, the Qur'an, being God's Word, is the primary and most authoritative source of Islam. As mentioned above, the Qur'an strongly affirms and upholds fundamental human rights. It follows, therefore, that these rights must be acknowledged and protected in all Muslim societies and communities. Given the unhappy sociocultural, economic, and political conditions of much of the present-day Muslim world where the increase in the birthrate is amongst the highest in the world, the need for family planning may be regarded as self-evident. *The right to use contraceptives, especially by disadvantaged masses whose lives are scarred by grinding poverty and massive illiteracy, should be seen—in the light of the Qur'anic vision of what an Islamic society should be—as a fundamental human right.* This is particularly applicable to Muslim women who, although more than five hundred million in number, are among the most unrepresented, or voiceless, and powerless "minorities" in the world.

An-Nisa': 36, 92, 135, 136; Surah *Al-Ma'idah*:89; Surah 6: *Al-An'am*: 107, 108; Surah 9: *At-Tawbah*:60; Surah 10: *Yunus*:99; Surah 12: *Yusuf*:40; Surah 16: *An-Nahl*:82; Surah 18: *Al-Kahf*:29; Surah 24: *An-Nur*:33; Surah 42: *Ash-Shura*: 21, 38, 48; Surah 47: *Muhammad*:4; Surah 58: *Al-Mujadalah*:3.

2. For instance, see Surah 4: *An-Nisa'*: 148–49; Surah 24: *An-Nur*: 16–19, 27–28, 58; Surah 33: *Al-Ahzab*:53; Surah 49: *Al-Hujurat*: 11, 12

3. For instance, see Surah 9: *At-Tawbah*:122; Surah 20: *Ta-Ha*:114; Surah 39: *Az-Zumar*:9; Surah 96: *Al-'Alaq*: 1–5.

4. For instance, see Surah 2: *Al-Baqarah*:229; Surah 3: *Al-'Imran* 17, 77; Surah 5: *Al-Ma'idah*:1; Surah 17: *Al-Isra'il*:34; Surah 67: *Al-Mulk*:15.

5. For instance, see Surah 7: *Al-A'raf*:32; Surah 57: *Al-Hadid*:27.

Family Planning and the Hadith Literature

In pre-Islamic Arabia birth control was practiced mostly by "coitus interruptus" (ʿazl). As pointed out by Fazlur Rahman, contradictions may be found in the *hadith* literature on the question of whether Islam permitted or prohibited ʿazl (Rahman 1989, 113). There are three well-known *ahadith* on the subject of ʿazl, and they are mutually contradictory.

According to one of them, the Prophet is reported to have referred to ʿazl as a "lesser infanticide" (Rahman 1989, 113). This *hadith* is contradicted by a second one that narrates that a man came to the Prophet and said, "We practice ʿazl, but we have some Jewish neighbors who say that this is a lesser infanticide." The Prophet responded by saying, "They are lying. It is not a lesser infanticide. You may practice it, but if God has predetermined for a child to be born, it will be born." After some time, this man told the Prophet that his wife had become pregnant, and the Prophet said, "Did I not tell you that if a child is predetermined by God to be born, it will be born?" (113). The third *hadith* is inconsistent with both of the above. It states that a companion of the Prophet said, "We used to practice ʿazl (during the Prophet's lifetime), and he knew about it while the Qurʾan was also being revealed, but the Qurʾan did not prohibit it" (114). According to Fazlur Rahman, the last-mentioned *hadith* "seems to have a ring of historical authenticity about it. . . . It therefore seems plausible to hold that the common pre-Islamic practice of contraception was allowed to stand by the Prophet as it was, without his saying anything about it, although it would have been possible for him to ban it, if he had thought fit" (114).

Because two of the three *ahadith* cited above indicate that the Prophet gave either verbal, or tacit, approval to the practice of ʿazl, progressive or "liberal" Muslims adopt the position that the *hadith* literature sanctions family planning. To refute this view, conservative or "traditional" Muslims cite the Qurʾanic verses in which offspring are referred to as a blessing from God, and to *ahadith* that report the Prophet as exhorting his followers to get married,[6] procreate, and increase in number and as saying as that on the the Day of Resurrection he would be proud of how large his commu-

---

6. It is widely believed by Muslims that the Prophet had said that whoever gets married completes half of the *din*, or "faith," of Islam.

nity was in comparison to other communities (Rahman 1989, 114). Here, it may be noted that neither getting married nor begetting children is considered mandatory in Islam. Although the Qur'an refers to offspring as a blessing, it also states that they could be a source of *fitna*, or mischief, in the world. Further, the Qur'an is far more concerned about the righteousness (*taqwa*) of Muslims than about their numbers. This concern is also echoed by the *hadith* that says that the few who are virtuous are superior to the many who are undesirable (Engineer 1992, 5).

In the context of family planning and the *hadith* literature, it is important to mention that although the *hadith* according to which the Prophet heard directly about the practice of 'azl and did not disavow it is found in *Sahih al-Bukhari* and *Sahih* Muslim—the two *hadith* collections that Sunni Muslims regard as the most authoritative—the *hadith* condemning the practice of 'azl is generally regarded as a "weak" (as opposed to *sahih*, or "sound") *hadith* (Osman 1960, 197). Here, it is also of interest to note that according to the *hadith* collections compiled by Ahmad ibn Hanbal (the *Musnad*) and Ibn Majah and Abu Dawud (the *Sunnan*), the Prophet forbade the practice of 'azl *without the wife's consent* (197).[7]

Family Planning and Schools of Law/Muslim Jurists

All the five major Schools of Law in Islam, namely, the Hanafi, Maliki, Shafi'i, Hanbali, and Ja'fari, permit the practice of 'azl (Bowen 1991, 10). Whereas the Shafi'i School "allows contraception unconditionally *to the husband,*[8] who need not do it with the consent of the wife" (Rahman 1989, 114), the other four schools permit the practice of 'azl only with the wife's consent (al-Zuhayli 1984, 331–32, in al-Hibri 1993a, 5). The practice of contraception is forbidden only by the medieval Spanish Muslim Ibn Hazm's Zahiri, or "literalist," School, which had few followers (Rahman 1989, 114). It is allowed by the Zaidi and the Isma'ili Schools (Bowen 1991, 10).

Among the Muslim jurists whose views on contraception have had the most widespread impact is al-Ghazali, who was a preeminent philosopher

---

7. The emphasis is the author's.
8. The emphasis is the author's.

and Sufi besides being a Shafi'i legal scholar. Fazlur Rahman has summarized al-Ghazali's position on contraception in the following passage:

> Al-Ghazali held that a truly pious person who has attained to "trust in God" (among the highest spiritual "stations" of Sufism) cannot resort to contraception because he or she knows that God, who has created a soul, will not leave it without sustenance. Therefore, for such a person to exercize conception control is unlawful. But people who have this kind of trust in God are very rare, while the average person is always haunted by worldly considerations. For such people, it is permitted to exercize conception control to free them of economic worries. Further, if a person fears that having children might force him or her to obtain livelihood by foul means like stealing or robbery, it is *mandatory* that he or she avoid having children in order to avoid the distinct possibility of committing sins. Al-Ghazali goes so far as to hold that a man who fears that if his wife has children, her health or good looks might be affected and *he might come to dislike her* should refrain from having children. (Rahman 1989, 115)

A Note on Abortion

Here, it may be of interest to mention that several medieval jurists permitted not only contraception but also abortion within four months of pregnancy before the "ensoulment" of the fetus (Rahman 1989, 118). In general, Muslim jurists have held two opposing views on abortion. The first is that it is totally forbidden. This view is held by the majority of the Maliki School, whereas a small minority permits abortion within 40 days of conception. The Ja'fari School also prohibits abortion. The second view is that abortion is permissible until "ensoulment," which is generally believed to occur after 120 days of conception. This view is held by the Hanafi School, the Shafi'i School, the Hanbali School, and the Zaidi School although there are differences in opinion among individual jurists regarding the time of "ensoulment" and whether a compelling reason is required for abortion (Bowen 1991, 10–12). Among the compelling reasons may be mentioned danger to a mother's life or a nursing child and the probability of giving birth to a deformed or defective child (Omran 1988, 322, in Bowen 1991, 11).

Reflections on Women's Health and
Well-Being in Muslim Societies

Based on the overview of sources of the Islamic tradition that has been presented in the foregoing pages, it can be stated with confidence that there is much support for family planning within the religious and ethical framework and the legal and philosophical literature of Islam. Despite this fact, in practice, family planning programs continue to fare badly in most of the Muslim world. It is beyond the scope of this chapter to examine all the factors responsible for this state of affairs. I mention here two factors, however, that have, in my judgment, contributed greatly to the large-scale ineffectiveness of family planning programs in Muslim societies and communities.

The first and most important factor is that women, who are the persons most obviously and directly affected by family planning initiatives (only they can become pregnant), are regarded in nearly all Muslim societies as being less than fully human. In several of my writings I have shown how the idea that women are inferior to men, who alone are fully human or autonomous, is built into the Islamic—as in the Jewish and Christian—tradition on three fundamental theological assumptions. (1) that God's primary creation is man, not woman, because woman is believed to have been created from man's rib and is, therefore, derivative and secondary ontologically; (s) that woman, not man, was the primary agent of what is customarily described as "man's fall" or expulsion from paradise and, hence, "all daughters of Eve" are to be regarded with hatred, suspicion, and contempt; and (3) that woman was created not only *from* man but also *for* man, which makes her existence instrumental and not of fundamental importance. The major reason why these assumptions, which are not warranted by a correct reading of the Qur'an, have remained unchallenged for so long is not only because the masses of Muslim women are steeped in poverty and illiteracy but also because even privileged and educated Muslim women—like their counterparts in other major religious traditions—have been systematically denied the opportunity to acquire the critical tools whereby they can examine the roots of their tradition and discover how they became so disadvantaged. They are, therefore, unable to refute the arguments that impose unjust laws and restrictions upon them in the name of Islam.

Here, it is important to note that women have been the primary target of the "Islamization" process that has been initiated by governments in a number of Muslim countries in recent years. To understand this phenomenon it is necessary to know that Muslims in general see educated or emancipated women as symbols not of "modernization" but of "Westernization." Whereas the former is associated with science, technology, and progress and is largely approved, the latter is associated with emblems of "mass" Western culture such as promiscuity, the breakup of family and community, latch-key children, and drug and alcohol abuse and is largely disapproved. Caretakers of Muslim traditionalism feel a strong and urgent need to put women in their "proper place." They seek to do that by confining them to their homes and by reducing them systematically—almost mathematically—to less than a fully human status.[9]

Muslim women are subjected not only to physical and economic subjugation but also to moral, intellectual, and spiritual degradation through a misrepresentation of the essential message of Islam. Thus, they are told that according to Surah 2: *Al-Baqarah*:223, the wife is the husband's "tilth" so he can "plow" her whenever he so desires, that according to Surah 2: *Al-Baqarah*:228, and Surah 4: *An-Nisa'*:34, men have "a degree of advantage" over them and that they have the right to control and confine and even to beat women who refuse to be totally subservient and obedient to their husbands, who are referred to as *majazi khuda,* or "God in earthly form."

Having spent twenty years researching women-related passages in the Qur'an, I know that the Qur'an does not discriminate against women. In fact, in view of their disadvantaged and vulnerable condition, it is highly protective of their rights and interests. But this protectiveness does not change the fact that the way Islam has been practised in most Muslim societies for centuries has left millions of Muslim women with battered bodies, minds, and souls. Lacking any sense of self-worth, self-esteem, or self-confidence, they find it very difficult to resist the pressure put on them by conservative, widely influential Muslims, such as A. A. Maududi, who tell them repeatedly that family planning is demonic in intent and con-

9. In this context reference may be made, for instance, to the Hudud Ordinance (1979) or the Law of Evidence (1984), which were implemented in Pakistan as part of the "Islamization" process initiated by General Muhammad Zia-ul-Haq. Both of the above were very discriminatory toward women and have had a markedly negative impact on the lives of many women (especially disadvantaged) in Pakistan.

trary both to God's wishes and society's welfare. Maududi's observations, cited below, are typical of the conservative line of thinking that is thwarting the success of family planning programs throughout much of the Muslim world:

> Co-education, employment of women in offices, mixed social gatherings, immodest female dresses, and beauty parades are now a common feature of our social life. Legal hindrances have also been placed in the way of marriage and on having more than one wife, but no bar against keeping mistresses and illicit relationships, prior to the age of marriage. In such a society perhaps the last obstacle that may keep a woman from surrendering to a man's advances is fear of illegitimate conception. Remove this obstacle too and provide women with weak character assurance that they can safely surrender to their male friends and you will see that the society will be plagued by the tide of moral licentiousness. (Maududi 1974, 176)

Without a radical change in the way in which Muslim women perceive themselves, there is no chance that family planning will ever become an integral part of Muslim social and domestic life. How this change is going to be brought about is the challenge that needs to be faced by everyone who is concerned about the future of the Muslim *ummah* (community) and of the world at large.

The second factor that has been responsible for the failure of many development projects, including family planning projects, in the Muslim world is the attitude toward religion in general that exists in the minds of those who design these projects. A bias that is widely prevalent in development "experts"—most of whom have a Western, secular, orientation—is that "the issue of development does not involve theological debate; it relates to entirely other issues" (Sobhan 1993). I disagree very strongly with those who regard religion as being irrelevant to development issues. Even those who concede that religion may be one *of the factors* to be considered in development projects do not understand the reality of present-day Muslim societies. Certainly, in the context of the Muslim world, it is essential to see that *Islam (in all its complexity) is not just one of the factors involved in development issues but the matrix in which all other factors are grounded.*

Appendixes
Glossary
Works Cited
Index

APPENDIX A

Human Rights
in the Qur'anic Perspective

RIFFAT HASSAN

To many Muslims the Qur'an is *the* Magna Carta of human rights and a large part of its concern is to free human beings from the bondage of traditionalism, authoritarianism (religious, political, economic, or any other), tribalism, racism, sexism, slavery, or anything else that prohibits or inhibits human beings from actualizing the Qur'anic vision of human destiny embodied in the classic proclamation: "Towards Allah is thy limit"[1] (Qur'an 53:42).

In the section entitled "General Rights," which follows, an account is given of the Qur'an's affirmation of fundamental rights that all human beings ought to possess because they are so deeply rooted in our humanness that their denial or violation is tantamount to a negation or degradation of that which makes people human. From the perspective of the Qur'an, these rights came into existence when people did; they were created, as people were, by God so that human potential could be actualized. Rights created or given by God cannot be abolished by any temporal ruler or human agency. Eternal and immutable, they ought to be exercised because everything that God does is for "a just purpose."[2]

---

1. See Iqbal 1971, 57.

2. For instance, see Surah 15: *Al-Hijr*:85; Surah 16: *An-Nahl*:3; Surah 44: *Ad-Dukhan*:39; Surah 45: *Al-Jathiyah*:22; Surah 46: *Al-Ahqaf*:3.

General Rights

Right to Life

The Qur'an upholds the sanctity and absolute value of human life (e.g., Qur'an 6:151) and points out that, in essence, the life of each individual is comparable to that of an entire community and, therefore, should be treated with the utmost care (e.g. Qur'an 5:32).

Right to Respect

The Qur'an deems all human beings to be worthy of respect (e.g., Qur'an 17:70) because of all creation they alone chose to accept the "trust" of freedom of the will (Qur'an 33:72). Human beings can exercise freedom of the will because they possess the rational faculty, which is what distinguishes them from all other creatures (e.g., Qur'an 2:30–34). Although human beings can become "the lowest of the lowest," the Qur'an declares that they have been made "in the best of molds" (Qur'an 2:30–34), having the ability to think, to have knowledge of right and wrong, to do good, and to avoid the evil. Thus, because of the promise that is contained in being human, namely, the potential to be God's vicegerent on earth, the humanness of all human beings is to be respected and considered to be an end in itself.

Right to Justice

The Qur'an puts great emphasis on the right to seek justice and the duty to do justice³. In the context of justice the Qur'an uses two concepts: ʿadl and ihsan. Both are enjoined and both are related to the idea of "balance," but they are not identical in meaning.

ʿAdl is defined by A. A. A. Fyzee, a well-known scholar of Islam, as "to be equal, neither more nor less." Explaining this concept, Fyzee wrote: "in a Court of Justice the claims of the two parties must be considered evenly, without undue stress being laid upon one side or the other. Justice introduces the balance in the form of scales that are evenly balanced" (Fyzee 1978, 17). ʿAdl was described in similar terms by Abu'l Kalam Azad, a famous translator of the Qur'an and a noted writer, who stated: "What is justice but the avoiding of excess? There should be neither too much nor too little; hence the use of scales as the emblems of justice" (Fyzee 1978, 17). Lest anyone try to do too much or too little, the Qur'an points

---

3. For instance, see Surah 5: Al-Maʾidah:8; and Surah 4: An-Nisaʾ:136.

out that no human being can carry another's burden or attain anything without striving for it (Qur'an 53:38–39).

Recognizing individual merit is a part of *'adl,* the Qur'an teaches that merit is not determined by lineage, sex, wealth, worldly success, or religion but by righteousness, which consists of both right "belief" (*iman*) and just "action" (*'amal*) (Qur'an 2:177). Further, the Qur'an distinguishes between passive believers and those who strive in the cause of God, pointing out that although all believers are promised good by God, the latter will be exalted above the former (Qur'an 4: 95–96).

Just as it is in the spirit of *'adl* that special merit be considered in the matter of rewards, so also special circumstances are to be considered in the matter of punishments. For instance, for crimes of unchastity the Qur'an prescribes identical punishments for a man or a woman who is proved guilty (Qur'an 24:2), but it differentiates between different classes of women: for the same crime, a slave woman would receive half, and the Prophet's consort double the punishment given to a "free" Muslim woman (Qur'an 4:25, 33:30). In making such a distinction the Qur'an, while upholding high moral standards, particularly in the case of the Prophet's wives whose actions have a normative significance for the community, reflects God's compassion for women slaves who were socially disadvantaged.

While constantly enjoining *'adl,* the Qur'an goes beyond this concept to *ihsan,* which literally means, "restoring the balance by making up a loss or deficiency" (Parwez 1977, 78). To understand this concept it is necessary to understand the nature of the ideal society or community (*ummah*) envisaged by the Qur'an. The word *ummah* comes from the root *umm,* or "mother." The symbols of a mother and motherly love and compassion are also linked with the two attributes most characteristic of God, namely, *rahim* and *rahman,* both of which are derived from the root *rahm,* meaning "womb." The ideal *ummah* cares about all its members just as an ideal mother cares about all her children, knowing that all are not equal and that each has different needs. Although showing undue favor to any child would be unjust, a mother who gives to a handicapped child more than she does to her other child or children, is not acting unjustly but is exemplifying the spirit of *ihsan* by helping to make up the deficiency of a child who needs special assistance in meeting the requirements of life. *Ihsan,* thus, shows God's sympathy for the disadvantaged segments of human society (such as women, orphans, slaves, the poor, the infirm, and the minorities)

Right to Freedom

As stated earlier, the Qur'an is deeply concerned about liberating human beings from every kind of bondage. Recognizing the human tendency toward dictatorship and despotism, the Qur'an says with clarity and emphasis in Surah 3: *Al-'Imran*:79 ('Ali 1994):

> It is not (possible)
> That a man, to whom
> Is given the Book,
> and Wisdom,
> And the Prophetic Office,
> Should say to people:
> "Be ye my worshippers
> Rather than Allah's"
> On the contrary
> (He would say):
> "Be ye worshippers
> Of Him Who is truly
> The Cherisher of all."

The institution of human slavery is, of course, extremely important in the context of human freedom. Slavery was widely prevalent in Arabia at the advent of Islam, and the Arab economy was based on it. Not only did the Qur'an insist that slaves be treated in a just and humane way (Qur'an 4:36), but it continually urged the freeing of slaves.[4] By laying down, in Surah 47: *Muhammad*:4, that prisoners of war were to be set free, "either by an act of grace or against ransom" (Asad 1980, 778), the Qur'an nearly abolished slavery because "the major source of slaves—men and women—was prisoners of war" (Parwez 1986, 346). Because the Qur'an does not state explicitly that slavery is abolished, it does not follow that it is to be continued, particularly in view of the numerous ways in which the Qur'an seeks to eliminate this absolute evil. A book that does not give a king or a prophet the right to command absolute obedience from another human being could not possibly sanction slavery in any sense of the word.

The greatest guarantee of personal freedom for a Muslim lies in the Qur'anic decree that no one other than God can limit human freedom (Qur'an 42:21) and in the statement that "judgment (as to what is right and what is wrong) rests with God alone" (Qur'an 12:40). As pointed out by Khalid M. Ishaque, an eminent Pakistani jurist:

> The Qur'an gives to responsible dissent the status of a fundamental right. In exercise of their powers, therefore, neither the legislature nor the

---

4. For instance, see Surah 2: *Al-Baqarah*:177; Surah 4: *An-Nisa'*:92; Surah 5: *Al-Ma'idah*:89; Surah 9: *At-Tawbah*:60; Surah 24: *An-Nur*:33; Surah 58: *Al-Mujadalah*:3.

executive can demand unquestioning obedience. . . . The Prophet, even though he was the recipient of Divine revelation, was required to consult the Muslims in public affairs. Allah addressing the Prophet says: "and consult with them upon the conduct of affairs. And . . . when thou art resolved, then put thy trust in Allah." (Gauher 1980, 157)

Because the principle of mutual consultation (*shura*) is mandatory (Qur'an 42:38), it is a Muslim's fundamental right and responsibility to participate in as many aspects of the community's life as possible. The Qur'anic proclamation in Surah 2: *Al-Baqarah*:256, "There shall be no coercion in matters of faith" (Asad 1980, 57) guarantees freedom of religion and worship. This guarantee means that, according to Qur'anic teaching, non-Muslims living in Muslim territories should have the freedom to follow their own faith traditions without fear or harassment. A number of Qur'anic passages state clearly that the responsibility of the Prophet Muhammad is to communicate the message of God and not to compel anyone to believe.[5] The right to exercise free choice in matters of belief is unambiguously endorsed by the Qur'an (Qur'an 18:29), which also states clearly that God will judge human beings not on the basis of what they profess but on the basis of their belief and righteous conduct (6:108), as indicated by Surah 2: *Al-Baqarah*:62 which says:

> Those who believe (in the Qur'an);
> And the Christians and the Sabians,
> Any who believe in God
> And the Last Day
> And work righteousness,
> Shall have their reward
> With the Lord: on them
> Shall be no fear, nor shall they grieve. (ʿAli 1994)

The Qur'an recognizes the right to religious freedom not only in the case of other believers in God but also in the case of non-believers in God (if they are not aggressing upon Muslims) (Qur'an 6:108).

In the context of the human right to exercise religious freedom, it is important to mention that the Qur'anic dictum, "Let there be no compulsion in religion" (Qur'an 2:25) applies not only to non-Muslims but also to Muslims. Although those who renounced Islam after professing it and then engaged in "acts

5. For instance, see Surah 6: *Al-Anʿam*:107; Surah 10: *Yunus*:99; Surah 16: *An-Nahl*:82; Surah 42: *Ash-Shura*:48.

of war" against Muslims were to be treated as enemies and aggressors, the Qur'an does not prescribe any punishment for nonprofession or renunciation of faith. The decision regarding a person's ultimate destiny in the hereafter rests with God.

The right to freedom includes the right to be free to tell the truth. The Qur'anic term for truth is *ḥaqq*, which is also one of God's most important attributes. Standing up for the truth is a right and a responsibility that a Muslim may not disclaim even in the face of the greatest danger or difficulty (Qur'an 4:135). While the Qur'an commands believers to testify to the truth, it also instructs society not to harm persons so testifying (see Parwez 1981, 34–35).

Right to Acquire Knowledge

The Qur'an puts the highest emphasis on the importance of acquiring knowledge. That knowledge has been at the core of the Islamic worldview from the very beginning is attested to by Surah 96: *Al'Alaq*: 1–5, which Muslims believe is the first revelation received by the Prophet Muhammad.

Asking rhetorically if those without knowledge can be equal to those with knowledge (Qur'an 39:9), the Qur'an exhorts believers to pray for advancement in knowledge (Qur'an 20:114). The famous prayer of the Prophet Muhammad was "Allah grant me Knowledge of the ultimate nature of things," and one of the best known of all traditions (*ahadith*) is "Seek knowledge even though it be in China."

According to Qur'anic perspective, knowledge is a prerequisite for the creation of a just world in which authentic peace can prevail. The Qur'an emphasizes the importance of the pursuit of learning even at the time, and in the midst, of war (Qur'an 9:122).

Right to Sustenance

As pointed out in Surah 11: *Hud:6*, every living creature depends for its sustenance upon God. A cardinal concept in the Qur'an, which underlies the socio-economic-political system of Islam, is that the ownership of everything belongs not to any person but to God. Because God is the universal creator, every creature has the right to partake of what belongs to God (Qur'an 6:165, 67:15). This means that every human being has the right to a means of living and that those who hold economic or political power do not have the right to deprive others of the basic necessities of life by misappropriating or misusing resources that have been created by God for the benefit of humanity in general.

Right to Work

According to Qur'anic teaching, every man and woman has the right to work, whether the work consists of gainful employment or voluntary service. The fruits of labor belong to the one who has worked for them, regardless of whether it is a man or a woman. As Surah 4: *An-Nisa':32* states:

> [T]o men
> Is allotted what they earn,
> And to women what they earn.
> ('Ali 1994).

Right to Privacy

The Qur'an recognizes the need for privacy as a human right and lays down rules for protecting an individual's life in the home from undue intrusion from within or without (Qur'an 24:27-28, 58; 33:53; 49:12).

Right to Protection from Slander, Backbiting, and Ridicule

The Qur'an recognizes the right of human beings to be protected from defamation, sarcasm, offensive nicknames, and backbiting (Qur'an 49:11-12). It also states that no person is to be maligned on grounds of assumed guilt and that those who engage in malicious scandal-mongering will be grievously punished in both this world and the next (Qur'an 24:16-19; 4:148-49).

Right to Develop One's Aesthetic Sensibilities and Enjoy the Bounties Created by God

As pointed out by Muhammad Asad, "By declaring that all good and beautiful things of life [i.e., those that are not expressly prohibited] are lawful to the believers," the *Qu'ran* condemns, by implication, all forms of life-denying asceticism, world-renunciation and self-mortification (Asad 1980, 207). In fact, it can be stated that the right to develop one's aesthetic sensibilities so that one can appreciate beauty in all its forms, and the right to enjoy what God has provided for the nurture of humankind are rooted in the life-affirming vision of the Qur'an (7:32).

Right to Leave One's Homeland
under Oppressive Conditions

According to Qur'anic teaching, a Muslim's ultimate loyalty must be to God and not to any territory. To fulfill his Prophetic mission the Prophet Muhammad decided to leave his place of birth, Mecca, and emigrated to Medina. This event (*Hijrah*) has great historical and spiritual significance for Muslims who are called upon to move away from their place of origin if it becomes an abode of evil and oppression where they cannot fulfill their obligations to God or establish justice (Qur'an 4:97–100).

Right to the "Good Life"

The Qur'an upholds the right of the human being not only to life but to the "good life." This good life, made up of many elements, becomes possible when a human being is living in a just environment. According to Qur'anic teaching, justice is a prerequisite for peace, and peace is a prerequisite for human development. In a just society all the earlier-mentioned human rights may be exercised without difficulty. In such a society other basic rights, such as the right to a secure place of residence, the right to the protection of one's personal possessions, the right to protection of one's covenants, the right to move freely, the right to social and judicial autonomy for minorities, the right to the protection of one's holy places, and the right to return to one's spiritual center also exist.[6]

6. In this context, reference may be made to several Qur'anic verses, for example, Surah 2: *Al-Baqarah*:229; Surah 3: *Al-'Imran*: 17, 77; Surah 5: *Al-Ma'idah*: 1, 42–48; Surah 9: *Al-Tawbah*:17; Surah 17: *Al-Isra'il*:34; Surah 67: *Al-Mulk*:15.

A Partial List of Organizations for Muslim Women's Rights, Advocacy, and Higher Islamic Education in the United States

KAREEMA ALTOMARE

International

International Association for Muslim Women and Children (IAMWC)
(formerly National Association for Muslim Women or (NAMW))

Undertakes projects to advocate and protect the message of Allah, the rights of Muslim women and children, and their security and well-being. Seeks to help Muslim women recapture the spirit and tradition of piety and service inherited from the wives of the Prophet through encouraging Islamic and academic education; challenging the innovations and stigmas that impede spiritual and material growth; and providing institutional, spiritual, and material support.

P.O. Box 7023
Reston, VA 22091
Phone: (703)941-3057
Fax: (703)941-1309
Contacts: Anisa Abd El Fattah, chair
Ruqiyyah Abdus-Salam, president

The International Network for the Rights of Female Victims of Violence in Pakistan (INRFVVP)

Established to mobilize and channel resources to help girls and women who have become victims of violence or who are vulnerable to it. Immediate objective is to provide direct help—humanitarian, medical, legal, and educational assistance—to female victims of violence in Pakistan.

> P.O. Box 17202
> Louisville, Kentucky 40217
> Phone: 502-637-4090
> Fax: 502-637-4002
> Contact: Riffat Hassan, president

International Union of Muslim Women (IUMW)

Implements the concept of "Muslim women making a difference" through a comprehensive approach to Islamic education, leadership training, and the initiation of special projects that involve young and elderly Muslim women in community activism.

> P.O. Box 181194
> Fairfield, OH 45018
> Phone/Fax: (513)887-882
> E-mail: aminah@fuse.net
> Contact: Aminah Assilmi, director of U.S. Services

Sisterhood Is Global, Institute (SIGI)

Works to improve women's rights on national, regional, and global levels by bringing together activists and academicians to identify issues that have priority in Muslim women's struggles and to develop effective strategies to empower women in Muslim countries.

> 4343 Montgomery Avenue
> Suite 201
> Bethesda, MD 20814
> Phone: (301)657-4355
> Fax: (301)657-4381
> Contact: Mahnaz Afkhami, executive director

Sisters in Islam (SIS)

Advocates a reconstruction of Islamic principles, procedures and practices in light of the basic Quranic principles of equality and justice through serious study of the sources of Islamic jurisprudence and the realities for women in the modern world.

Religious Studies Department
Virginia Commonwealth University
Richmond, VA 23236
Phone: (804)828-1224
Fax: (804)828-8714
Contact: Amina Wadud, U.S. coordinator

WAHAB: World Alliance for Humanitarian Assistance for Bosnia

Organizes professional and material assistance for Muslim victims of the holocaust in Bosnia (especially those women raped during "ethnic cleansing") through visits to the field; international networking; and lobbying of respective governments, agencies, and professionals.

P.O. Box 23091
Alexandria, VA 22304
Phone/Fax: (703)370-0714
Contacts: Beverly Britton El-Kashif, founder/director

Women's Global Film Project

850 N. Randolph, #1526
Arlington, VA 22203
Phone: (410)581-4208
Fax: (410)581-4338
Contact: Talat Shah

National

KARAMAH: Muslim Women Lawyers for Human Rights

Focuses on domestic and global issues of human rights for Muslims by increasing familiarity with Islamic, American, and international laws; providing advice and assistance on Islamic perspectives, and Muslim views on the proper observance of these rights.

T. C. Williams School of Law
University of Richmond
Richmond, VA 23173
Phone: (804)289-8466
Fax: (804)289-8683
Web: www.muntada.com/Karamah
Contacts: Azizah al-Hibri, president
         Asifa Quraishi, vice-president
         Arshi Siddiqui, treasurer

Muslim Communications Network (MCN)

Structures events to facilitate intracommunity communication that can lend support to Muslims who are single, incarcerated, or newly converted.

1440 V Street, NW, Apt. 203
Washington, DC 20009
Phone: (202)232-7849
Contact: Bahijah Abdus Salaam

Muslim Intercommunity Network (Muslim Internet)

Promotes understanding of Islamic traditions and seeks to provide relief to Muslim families with economic, social, psychological, and/or medical needs.

6911 Carlynn Court
Bethesda, MD 20817
Phone: (301)948-0817
Fax: (301)320-4683
Contacts: Maryum Funches
         Rumana Kazmi, M.D.

Muslim Peace Fellowship (Ansar as-Salam)

A gathering of peace and justice-oriented Muslims of all backgrounds dedicated to making the beauty of Islam evident in the world. All are welcome to join. Membership dues are $20.00 per year and include the newsletter, *As-Salamu ʿAlaykum*.

C/O FOR,
Box 271
Nyack, NY 10960
Phone: 914-358-4601

E-mail: *mpf@igc.apc.org*,
Web: http://www.nonviolence.org/mpf/ASA
Contact: Rabia Terri Harris, editor of *As-Salam 'Alaykum*

Muslim Women's League (MWL)

Seeks to disseminate accurate information about Islam and Muslims, particularly on issues pertaining to women; to promote social justice; to interact with all levels of government; and to cooperate with other religious, ethnic, and social organizations.

3010 Wilshire Blvd.
Suite 519
Los Angeles, CA 90010
Phone: (213)383-3443
Fax: (213)383-9674
E-mail: MPACMWL@aol.com
Contacts: Semeen Issa, president
        Lena al-Sarraf, vice-president
        Laila al-Marayati, MD, secretary
        Fatima Cash, treasurer

Muslim Women's Services (RAHIMA)

Carries out charitable activities including monthly brunch meetings; canned food collection for needy Muslim families; distribution of the Qur'an, *hadith* and *sunnah* of the Prophet; and collective *dua's* and "pennies for peace" *sadaqa* in support of afflicted Muslims worldwide.

Phone: (408)867-0421
Fax: (408)867-4716

North American Council for Muslim Women (NACMW)

Initiates programs and helps establish institutions that provide needed services to Muslim women and seeks to raise their level of Islamic conscientiousness and conformity.

902 McMillen Court
Great Falls, VA 22066
Phone: (703)759-7339
Fax: (703)759-9461

Contacts: Iman Elkadi, president
Sharifa Alkhateeb, vice-president

Sisters! The Magazine of Dialogue among Muslim Women

(*Sisters! LP*) Publishes a quality magazine focusing primarily on the Islamic life choices of Muslim women and works toward establishing a financial base for Muslim sisters in the United States

c/o Amica International, Inc.
1201 1st Avenue, South
Suite 203
Seattle, WA 98134
Phone: 800-622-9256
Fax: (206)467-1522
E-mail: AMICA@ix.netcom.com
Contacts: Rafiah Khokhar, vice-president Amica International, Inc.,
Partner, Sisters! LP
Tayyibah Taylor, editorial director

Local

American Muslim Women of Nevada (AMWON)

Hosts a variety of events, including seminars, Iftars, Muslim New Year celebrations, Sisters' night out, Qur'anic studies, "Saving Women and Children" fundraising, and an annual (now nationally advertised) conference.

P.O. Box 4151
Las Vegas, NV 89106
Phone: (702)648-5678
(702)649-1064
Contacts: Samesha Ramadan, president
Baheejah Abdus-Salaam, vice-president

Council for Muslim Women

Conducts a series of women's groups, seminars, and conferences to encourage the scholarly pursuit of Qur'anic knowledge and the Prophet's example in order to understand and apply the principles of Islam in women's lives and contribute to the improvement of Muslim communities and the society at large. Hopes to expand the concept of "council" to include the heads of all Muslim women's organizations and to produce an annual "State of Muslim Women Address" for consideration by the entire community.

Vineyard Square
7902 Gerber Road, #140
Sacramento, CA 95828
Phone: (916)689-6249
Fax: (916)689-5977
Contacts: Zakiyyah Muhammad, Ph.D.

Muslim Women's Association, Washington, DC

Holds monthly women's meetings, educational lectures, and cultural events with Muslim embassies and raises funds through an annual international bazaar for relief of Muslims in crisis areas and distribution to Muslim women applicants for academic scholarships.

11209 Hunt Club Drive
Potomac, MD 20854
Phone: (301)983-0405
Contact: Dr. Najat Arafat Khelil

Muslim Women's Georgetown Study Project

Provides alternatives to Western positions vis-à-vis human rights for women from the perspective of Islamic jurisprudence and conducts studies of specific grass-roots problems.

P.O. Box 3746
Georgetown Station
Washington, DC 20007-0246
Phone: (202)687-6118
Fax: (202)689-8000
Contacts: Sharifa Alkhateeb, co-coordinator
Kareema Altomare, co-coordinator
Maysam al-Faruqi, co-coordinator
Nimat Hafez Barazangi, co-coordinator

Muslim Women United

Encourages participation in solutions to humanities problems through improving the quality of life for Muslim women and all women; conducts community awareness programs and an annual conference; and has established a networking system for Muslims from New York to Georgia through the *Regional Gazette.*

P.O. Box 35486
Richmond, VA 23235
Contacts: Latish Abdul-Mumit

Al-Muslima Publishing Company

Produces an annual *Muslim Women's Business-Service Directory* that publicizes local Muslim women who are business owners or service providers, advertises other men and women in businesses or professions, encourages networking among business owners, and provides an educational and technical assistance guide for those starting or managing a business.

480 South Howard Street, SE
Atlanta, GA 30317
Phone/Fax: (404)377-0104
Contacts: Kareemah Hasan Rasheed, publisher

Nisaa as Salaam/Women of Peace

Organizes education and conducts a variety of activities by and for women, including an annual regional conference.

1427 Montrose Street
Philadelphia, PA
Phone: (215)476-7573
Fax: (215)476-7547
Contact: Alia Walker Abdur Rashied

Propagación Islamica para la Educación e Devoción a Ala' el Divino (PIEDAD)

Seeks to spread Islam by working one-on-one with Spanish-speaking non-Muslims and lending nonjudgmental, network support to new Muslims in the practice of their faith.

P.O. Box 41514
Washington, DC 20018
Phone: (202)529-9465
Contact: Fatima Jimenez

Sisterhood in Action

Encourages and supports Muslim women's leadership and participation in community services through mentoring, workshops, recreational/cultural activities, and outreach.

2213 M Street, NW
Suite 300
Washington, DC 20037
Phone: (202)861-8041
Fax: (202)293-9456
Contact: Iaesha Prime-Bray, president

Women in Islam

Reacting to the impact of the Bosnian tragedy, this coalition of professional and social activist Muslim women seeks to represent human rights interests, eliminate degrading practices that devalue Muslim women globally, cultivate Islamic scholarship and leadership among women and youth, provide a speakers bureau of professional Muslim women, highlight significant written works, and build bridges of understanding across the international, cross-cultural, and interfaith setting of New York City.

P.O. Box 814
Lincoln Street
New York, NY 10037-0814
Phone: (212)283-6264
Fax: (212)491-9185
Contacts: Aisha al-Adawiya, president

Al-Zaharaa Association of Muslim Women

Conducts social events for Muslim women and the community, including Sisters' Teas, monthly women's meetings, carnivals and bazaars, and an annual Al-Zaharaa convention; and prints a quarterly literary newsletter.

4420 SW 110th
Beaverton, OR 97005

Glossary

abaya: opaque, ankle-length coat or over-garment with wrist-length sleeves worn by some women in the Islamic world.

adab: literature; courteous behavior.

addaba: to impart a moral education; to educate, refine; to discipline, chasten.

ʿadl: the quality of being just.

ahkam (sing. **hukm**): literally, judgment; refers to those decrees in the Qurʾan deemed by the community as clear and unchangeable.

al-ahwat: that which is the safest, as in a course of action.

ʿAʾisha (alternative translits. **Aisha** or **ʿAisha**): one of Muhammad's wives. She is an important figure in the history of the early Islamic community and transmitted many of the *ahadith,* or narratives, of the Prophet Muhammad.

akhbar (sing. **khabar**): stories, accounts.

akhbirini: inform (or tell) me.

ʿalam ash-shahadah: the witnessable world.

ʿalim (pl. **ʿulama**): a scholar, one learned in religious knowledge.

ʿamal: right action, concomitant with right belief or faith (*iman*).

amr: a command.

an-nafs al-ammarah bi-suʾ: the evil-commanding self, or ego.

ʿaql: reason.

asatir: myths, legends.

asatir al-awwalin: tales of the ancients.

asatir al-nisaʾ: women's tales.

ashku ilaika (alternative translit. **ilayka**): literally, I complain to you; refers to the Qurʾanic chapter, Mujaddala.

awrah: taboo, prohibited to the public.

ayah (pl. **ayat**): Qurʾanic verse.

ayat muhkamat: those verses of the Qur'an deemed as clear and unambiguous.

al-'azl: coitus interruptus.

balagha (alternative translit. **balaghah**): the art of eloquent composition and style; rhetoric; classification of literature that includes religious history and literature.

balaghat al-nisa': the *balaghah* of women.

barza: one who has prominent merits; a dignified elder.

basmala: refers to the opening phrase and blessing of nearly all the Qur'anic verses, "In the Name of God, the Merciful, the Compassionate"; used by Muslims as a blessing preceding any work.

bima (alternative translit. **bi ma**): because.

dhikr: remembrance (refers to the act of remembering God); recital of words in remembrance of God; used by sufis to denote rituals of remembrance.

din (alternative translits. **deen** or **diin**): the Islamic belief system or worldview, encompassing religion and culture; a complete way of life.

din al-haqq: the religion of truth.

du'a: nonliturgical prayer; refers to prayers and blessings other than the five-times daily *salat* prayers.

faddala: to provide, to grant, to favor.

fadl: a favor, a grant.

faqih: one learned in *fiqh*, Islamic jurisprudence.

faskh: annulment.

fatwa: a legal opinion.

fiqh: Islamic jurisprudence.

fitna: mischief, strife.

fuhula: virility.

ghayb: that which is unseen, hidden; secrecy, privacy.

haddatha: to relate, to tell.

haddithini: tell me your account (story).

hadith (pl. **ahadith**): a saying, tradition, or narrative of the Prophet Muhammad.

hadith qudsi: a Divine Saying; traditional sayings understood as God's thoughts expressed in Muhammad's words. They have an exalted position between the Qur'an and the Prophetic *Hadith* materials.

haram: that which is forbidden.

hatk al-'arad: the attacking or raping of women.

hatk-il-harim: the rape of a woman.

haqq: truth.

Hawwa': Arabic/Hebrew counterpart for Eve. The term does not exist in the Qur'an.

haywan: animals.

Hedaya: guidance; also refers to a major Anglo-Indian text on legal issues in Islam.

Hijrah: the emmigration of Muhammad and his followers from Mecca to Yathrib (Medina); signifies the beginning of the Islamic community and calendar.

hiraba: the Qur'anic *hadd* crime of armed robbery or forcible taking.

hijab: the Muslim practice of veiling women. Depending on the cultural style and interpretation of modesty, it can include covering the hair or the entire head and face. It may include the *khimar*—fabric covering the throat in the way that a wimple does—along with a head-cover. It may include a long, loose-fitting coatlike dress that comes to the ankle and has long sleeves to the wrist.

hudud (alternative translit. **hudood**; sing. **hadd**): a legal term for the offenses and punishments that are defined in the Qur'an.

'id: a celebration; the feast day following Ramadan and the Hajj.

ihsan: to do right; to do what is beautiful.

ijtihad: jurisprudential interpretations; intellectual reasoning in Islamic *fiqh;* interpretation of Islamic law.

'illah (alternative translit. **'illa**; pl. **'ilal):** in law, the reason, the justification.

imam: the leader of ritual prayer for a particular occasion or as a regular function. He (traditionally, only men are imams) leads by standing in front of the rows of worshipers; if only two persons are praying, he stands to the left and slightly in front of the other. The basis for his office is knowledge, particularly of the Qur'an, age, or social leadership. The Shi'is hold a particularly exalted view of their imams. Every mosque has one or more imams.

iman: right belief, implying faith and determination, not to be separated from right conduct.

al-insan: the human being; a gender neutral word often translated as "man" or "mankind."

insan al-kamil: the perfect(ed) human being.

iqra': read, recite (command form); from the same root as Qur'an.

i'rad: shunning, avoiding.

Islam: engaged surrender (to the will of God).

istihsan: juridistic preference.

istislah: considering the public interest.

jadala: to coil or braid.

al-jadal: argumentation and skillful dispute.

Jahiliyah: the age of pre-Islamic history. It has a connotation of "the age of ignorance."

jalal: majesty (one of the divine attributes).

jalali: having a preponderance of *jalal* qualities. This word connotes qualities of power, courage.

jalda: sturdy in character.

jamal: beauty (one of the divine attributes).

jazala: lucidity, soundness.

jihad: effort, struggle, war.

al-jihad al-akbar: the greater war, or effort; refers to the Prophet's statement that the more difficult battle is the interior battle to control the lower self or ego.

al-jihad al-asghar: the lesser war; refers to struggle, or war against exterior threats of harm.

jilbab: Islamic modest dress, sometimes referred to as the *hijab*.

jirah: Islamic law of wounds (tort-like compensation for physical harm).

kaba'ir: the major sins.

kafir: an unbeliever.

kamal: perfection.

karahia: extreme dislike.

khabar: news, information.

khalifah: a trustee, vicegerent, moral agent.

kharajtu: I left; I went out.

khatib, khatiba: a male orator; a female orator.

khilafah: trusteeship vicegerency, moral agency.

khimar: a scarf worn by pious Muslim women that covers the head and hair fully and resembles the wimple formerly worn by the nuns or sisters of the Catholic Church.

khul': a form of divorce in which the wife returns the *mahr* to the husband to end the marriage.

khutba: a sermon.

kitab: a book, title of proprietorship.

kufr: disbelief, unbelief.

lin: tenderness, pliancy; an evaluative measure of poetry.

madhhab (pl. **madhahib**): refers to the schools (interpretations) of Islamic law.

Madinah: city in Arabia, location of the first Muslim community.

mahr: a tangible or intangible symbol of commitment and gesture of good will given by a Muslim man to a Muslim woman upon entering into marriage.

majazi khuda: God in earthly form.

makr: the divine ruse.

maqsurat mukhdirat: encircled and enchambered.

maslaha: commonweal, public interest.

maulid (alternative translit **mawlid**): in popular piety, a celebration in verse honoring the Prophet or other revered figure.

mufti: jurisconsult.

muhkam: precise. The word *muhkamah* means a definition. The word *muhkamat* is used to refer to the Qur'anic verses that are precise, clear, unambiguous.

mujadila (alternative translit. **mujadilah**): she who argues or disputes.

muqallidun: refers to those Muslims who emphasize following precedent behavior and interpretation over the Qur'anic mandate to reinterpret the text in time and space.

Muslimah: Muslim woman.

mutashabihah (pl. **mutashabihat**): a metaphor (as contrasted with a definition).

nafaqah: money owed by a husband to his wife for maintenance of her needs and those of the household.

nafs: self, or soul.

niyyah: intention.

nushuz: discord, disharmony, often interpreted as disobedience. (See chap. 4.)

nutfah: the life spark out of which God shapes human beings.

pbuh: stands for "peace be upon him," a blessing often said by Muslims after saying Muhammad's name.

q-t-l: the root of words denoting to slay or degrade.

qadi: an Islamic judge traditionally appointed by the ruler. The *qadi*'s judgment is binding, whereas the opinion of the *mufti* or *faqih* is advisory.

qasirat al-tarf: chaste-eyed.

qawa'idu buyutakum: biding in your houses.

qazf: slander.

qiwammah (pl. **qawwammun**): usually interpreted as meaning the position of boss or head of the family. See, for example, the chapters by Quraishi, al-Hibri, and Wadud for a more accurate meaning. The plural form of this word refers to men as advisors, protectors over women.

qiyas: analogical reasoning.

Qur'an: the revealed word of Allah.

al-Qur'an al-Karim: the generous/bounteous Qur'an.

Qutb: literally, the pole; the spiritual axis. *Sufis* (Islamic mystics) use the term to refer to the exalted person who stands at the head of the hierarchy of saints.

rahim: the compassionate (one of the most frequently recited names of God).

rahm: womb.

rahman: the merciful (one of the most frequently recited names, or attributes, of God).

rahmatan lil-'alamin: the quality of being a mercy to the world.

rasul: a messenger of God; usually denotes Muhammad.

sabaha (alternative translit. **sabahah**): refers to those who lived concurrently with the Prophet.

sabiqa: precedence, prominence coming from early conversion or service to the Prophet.

sadaq (pl. **Sadaqat**)**:** gift, may be monetary; in the Middle East the term is used interchangeably with *mahr*, the gift given to the wife upon marriage.

sahih: sound, reliable, authentic, canonical, as in the sound *hadith*.

saj': rhythmic prose.

sakana: a dwelling or abode.

sakina: the feminine quality of serenity, from *sakana*.

sariqa: theft.

sawm: fasting.

shahadah: the witnessing, affirming the creedal formula that there is no God but God and that Muhammad is His prophet; first of the five pillars (major duties) of Islam.

shari'ah: Islamic law, divine law. As with Jewish *halakhah*, there is no distinction between religious and secular law; the duties and commands derive from God and provide guidance for following the divine will in all areas of life.

shirk: blasphemy; a departure from the truth.

al-shu'ara al-fuhul: the virile poets.

shura: consultative democracy.

sufi: the Islamic mystic.

sultan: right, power, authority.

sunnah: traditions/practices of the Prophet Muhammad.

surah (alternative translit. **sura**)**:** a chapter of the Qur'an.

tafriq: judicial divorce.

tafsir: the science of Qur'anic commentary and exegesis.

takfir: proclaiming someone to be a nonbeliever.

taqwa: to balance the tension in human behavior, as the Qur'an intends in the first place when all human beings were entrusted with individual rights and responsibilities toward themselves, each other, and the universe. Piety.

tashabaha 'alayna: appearing as similar to us.

tashkiyah al-shuhud: the credibility of a witness.

tashtaki ila allah: she complains unto God

tawhid: the theological claim of the Oneness and transcendence of God.

tawhidi: principles that conform to the doctrine of *tawhid*.

ta'wil: interpretation; literally, to return something to its origins.

ta'zir: crimes created under Islamic law beyond those set out in the Qur'an.

ulama: religious scholars.

ulul-albab: people who have a pith, a core, and essence; people who have a point.

ummah: community.

umm: mother, source.

ʿurf: custom.

wali (pl. walis): a guardian, protector.

wilayah: in the context of Islamic law, a form of guardianship that a father (or one who has that authority) has over his daughter in matters of marriage. It is compulsory under some jurisprudential theories but merely advisory under others.

yuharibuna: from *haraba/hiraba*, a forceable taking; those who take by force.

zihar: a negative utterance of rebuke (usually referring to the husband's rebuke of the wife).

zina: adultery or fornication, punishable in Islamic criminal law.

zina-bil-jabr: *zina* by force; the term used in the Pakistani *Zina* Ordinance to refer to rape.

Works Cited

Abadi, al-Fairuz. 1993. *Al-Qamus al-Muhit.* Edited.by Muhammad Na'im al-'Irqsusi, et al. Beirut: Mu'assasat al-Risala.

'Abd al-Rahman, 'A'isha. 1958. *Sukaina bint al-Husain.* Cairo: Dar al-Hilal.

———. 1963. *Al-Khansa'.* 2d ed. Cairo: Dar al-Ma'arif.

———. 1970. *Qiyam Jadida li Adabina al-'Arabi.* Cairo: Dar al-Ma'arif.

Abou El Fadl, Khaled. 1991. "Law of Duress in Islamic Law and Common Law: A Comparative Study." *Islamic Studies* 30:305.

Abu Daud (or Dawud). 1990. *Sunan Abu Daud.* Translated by Ahmad Hasan. 2d ed. Lahore, Pakistan: Lahoti Fine Art Press.

Abu Shaqqa (or Shuqqa), 'Abd al-Halim. 1990. *Tahrir al-Mar'a fi 'Asr al-Risala.* Kuwait: Dar al-Qalam.

Abu Zahrah, Mahmud. 1957. *Al Ahwal al Shakhsiyah* (Personal status [in Islam]). Cairo.

———. 1963. *Usul al-fiqh al-Islami.* Cairo: Al-Majlis al a'la li Ri'ayat al Funun.

Afkhami, Mahnaz, ed. 1995. *Faith and Freedom: Women's Human Rights in the Muslim World.* Syracuse, N.Y.: Syracuse Univ. Press.

Afkhami, Mahnaz, and Haleh Vaziri. 1996. *Claiming Our Rights: A Manual for Women's Human Rights Education in Muslim Societies.* Bethesda, Md.: Sisterhood Is Global Institute.

Ahmad, Nausheen. 1995. "The Other Viewpoint." *Dawn* (Karachi), (weekly Tuesday rev. suppl.), Nov. 14–20, 8.

Ahmed, Leila. 1992. *Women and Gender in Islam: Historical Roots of a Modern Debate.* New Haven, Conn.: Yale Univ. Press.

Ajijola, A. D. 1981. *Introduction to Islamic Law.* 2d ed. Karachi: International Islamic Publishers.

Alexander, Dolly F. 1995. "Twenty Years of Morgan: A Criticism of the Subjectivist

View of Men's Rea and Rape in Great Britain." *Pace International Law Review* 7:207, 211.

Ali, ʿA. Yusuf, trans. [1989] 1991. *The Holy Qurʾan.* Commentary by ʿA. Yusuf Ali. Brentwood, Md.: Amana Corporation.

ʿAli, A. Yusuf. 1994. *The Meaning of the Holy Qurʾan.* Brentwood, Md.: Amana Corporation.

Ali, Ahmed, trans. *Al-Qurʾan.* 1984. Princeton: N.J.: Princeton Univ. Press.

Amin, Sayed Hassan. 1985. *Islamic Law in the Contemporary World.* Glasgow: Royston.

Amnesty International. 1992. *Amnesty International Report 1992.* New York: Amnesty International.

———. 1993. *Pakistan: Torture, Deaths in Custody and Extrajudicial Executions.* New York: Amnesty International

———. 1994. *Amnesty International Report 1994.* New York: Amnesty International.

———. 1995a. *Human Rights Are Women's Rights.* New York: Amnesty International.

———. 1995b. *Pakistan, The Pattern Persists: Deaths in Custody, Extrajudicial Executions, and "Disappearances" under the PPP Government.* New York: Amnesty International.

———. 1995c. *Women in Pakistan: Disadvantaged and Denied Their Rights.* New York: Amnesty International.

Apter, Terry. 1985. *Why Women Don't Have Wives: Professional Success and Motherhood.* New York: MacMillan Press.

Arkoun, Mohammed. 1994a. "Is Islam Threatened by Christianity?" In *Islam: A Challenge for Christianity*, a special issue of *Concilium* (1994/3), edited by Hans Kung and Jurgen Moltmann, 48–57. London: SCM Press.

———. 1994b. *Rethinking Islam: Common Questions, Uncommon Answers.* Translated and edited by Robert D. Lee. Boulder, Colo.: Westview Press.

Arnot, Madeline. 1993. *Feminism and Social Justice in Education.* London: Falmer Press.

Asad, Muhammad, trans. 1980. *The Message of the Qurʾan.* Gibraltar: Dar al-Andalus.

Asia Watch and Women's Rights Project, Human Rights Watch. 1992. *Double Jeopardy: Police Abuse of Women in Pakistan.* New York: Human Rights Watch.

"Asia: Pakistan." 1991. *Economist,* Dec. 14, 43.

al-ʾAsqalani, Ibn Hajar. 1907. *Al Isaba fi Tamyiz al Sahaba.* Baghdad: Maktabat al-Muthanna. Fourteenth century. Reprint.

al-ʾAsqalani, Ibn Hajar. 1909. *Al-Isaba fi Tamyiz al-Sahaba.* 4 vols. Cairo: Dar al-ʿUlum al-Haditha.

———. 1986. *Kitab al-Nikah min Fath al-Bari* (The book of marriage). Fourteenth dentury. Reprint. Beirut: Dar al-Balaghah.

AWAM and NWC. N.d. Pamphlet distributed in Malaysia. N.p.

Barazangi, Nimat Hafez. 1988. Perceptions of the Islamic Belief System: The Muslims in North America, Ph.D.diss., Cornell Univ.

———. 1989. "Arab Muslim Identity Transmission: Parents and Youth." *Arab*

Studies Quarterly (Spring/Summer): 65–82; and in *Arab Americans: Continuity and Change,* edited by Baha Abu-Laban and Michael W. Suleiman, 65–82. Belmont, Mass.: Association of Arab-American University Graduates.

————. 1993. "Worldview, Meaningful Learning and Pluralistic Education: The Islamic Perspective." *Religion and Public Education* 20, nos. 1, 2, 3:84–98.

————. 1995a. "Educational Reform." In *The Oxford Encyclopedia of the Modern Islamic World,* edited by John L. Esposito 420–15. New York: Oxford Univ. Press.

————. 1995b. "Religious Education." In *The Oxford Encyclopedia of the Modern Islamic World,* edited by John L. Esposito, 406–11. New York: Oxford Univ. Press.

————. 1996. "Vicegerency and Gender Justice." In *Islamic Identity and the Struggle for Justice,* edited by Nimat Hafez Barazangi, Raquibuz Zaman, and Omar Afzal, 77–94. Gainesville: Univ. Press of Florida.

————. 1997. "Muslim Women's Islamic Higher Education as a Human Right: The Action Plan." In *Muslim Women and the Politics of Participation: Implementing the Beijing Platform,* edited by Mahnaz Afkhami and Erika Friedl, 43–57. Syracuse, N.Y.: Syracuse Univ. Press.

————. Forthcoming. "Muslim Women's Education: Between East and West." In *Women in Islamic and Jewish Societies,* edited by Seth Ward. New York: Holmes and Meier.

al-Bardisi, M. 1966. *Al Ahkam al-Islamiya fi al-Ahwal al-Shakhsiya* (Islamic rules in personal status law). Cairo: n.p.

Bassiouni, M. Cherif. 1982. "Sources of Islamic Law, and the Protection of Human Rights in the Islamic Criminal Justice System." In *The Islamic Criminal Justice System,* edited by M. Cherif Bassiouni, 5.

Bat Shalom. 1997. Home page. Israel. tp://www.batshalom.org.

"Bengali Women: Tongues Untied." 1995. *World Press Review* (June): 48.

"Behind the Yashmak." 1989. *Economist* 313 (Oct. 28): 58.

Bennani, Farida. 1993. *Taqsim al-ʿAmal Bayn al-Zawjayn fi Dawʾ al-Qanun al-Maghribi wa al-Fiqh al-Islami* (Division of labor between spouses in light of Morrocan law and Islamic fiqh) (Silsilah Manshurat Kulliyyat al-ʿUlum al-Qanuniyah wa al-Iqtisadiyah wa al-Ijtimaʿiyah). Marrakesh: n.p.

Berkowitz, R. S., D. P. Goldstein, and M. R. Bernstein. 1991. "Evolving Concepts of Molar Pregnancy." *Journal of Reproductive Medicine* 36:1.

Bokhary, Ashfaq. 1979. *Law Relating to Hudood Cases.* Lahore, Pakistan: Khyber Law Publishers.

Bowen, D. L. 1991. *Islam and Family Planning.* Population and Human Resources Division. Technical Department. Europe, Middle East, and North Africa Region, 1, no. 1 (Feb.).

Branion, John. 1992. "Recent Development: A World of Rape." *UCLA Women's Law Journal* 2:275.

al-Bukhari, Abu ʿAbdullah I. N.d. *Sahih al-Bukhari bi Hashiat al-Sindi*. Ninth century. Reprint. Vol. 3. Beirut: Dar al-Maʿrifah.

al-Bukhari, Imam. 1985. *Sahih al-Bukhari*. Translated by Muhammad Muhsin Khan. Madinah: Islamic Univ.

al-Bukhari. 1994. *Sahih Bukhari*. Translated by Muhammad Muhsin Khan. Madinah: Islamic Univ.

Carroll, Lucy. 1982. "Nizam-I-Islam" Processes and Conflicts in Pakistan's Programme of Islamization, with Special Reference to the Position of Women." *Journal of Commonwealth and Comparative Politic* 20, no.1(Mar.): 57–95.

Cornell, V. J. 1994. "Tawhid: The Recognition of the One in Islam." In *Islam: A Challenge for Christianity*, a special issue of *Consilium* (1994/3), edited by Hans Kung and Jurgen Moltmann, 61–66. London: SCM Press.

Coulson, Noel J. 1994. *A History of Islamic Law*. Edinburgh: Edinburgh Univ. Press.

Crone, Patricia, and Michael Cook. 1977. *Hagarism*. Cambridge, U.K.: Cambridge Univ. Press.

Curtius, Mary. 1994. "Report Blasts Global Abuse of Women's Rights; 'Conflict Zone' Governments Found to Be Worst Offenders." *Boston Globe*, Mar. 8, 2.

al-Dabbi, al-ʿAbbas bin Bikar (attrib.). 1983. *Akhbar al-Wafidat min al-Nisaʾ ʿala Muʿawiya bin Abi Sufyan*, edited by Sakina al-Shihabi. Beirut: Muʾassasat al-Risala.

Daif, Shawqi. 1965. *Al-Balagha Tatawur wa Tarikh*. 6th ed. Cairo: Dar al-Maʿarif.

———. 1992. *Al-Shiʿr wa al-Ghinaʾ fi al-Madina wa Makka*. Cairo: Dar al-Maʿarif.

al-Dakhil, Said F. 1989. *Mawsuʿat Fiqh ʿAisha Umm al-Muʾminin*. Vol. 4. Beirut: Dar al-Nafaʾis. vol. 4.

De La Mothe, Cassandra M. 1996. "Liberta Revisited: A Call to Repeal the Marital Exemption for All Sex Offenses in New York's Penal Law." *Fordham Urban Law Journal* 23:857.

Doi, ʿAbdur Rahman I. 1984. *Shariʿah: The Islamic Law*. London: Ta Ha Publishers.

———. 1989. *Women in Shariʿah* (Islamic law). London: Ta Ha Publishers.

Dripps, Donald A. 1992. "Beyond Rape: An Essay on the Difference Between the Presence of Force and the Absence of Consent." *Columbia Law Review* 92:1780.

Dugger, Celia W. 1996. "A Refugee's Body Is Intact, but Her Family Is Torn." *New York Times*, Sept. 11, sec. B6.

El-Awa, Mohammed S. 1976. "Taʿazir in the Islamic Penal System." *Journal of Islamic and Comparative Law* 6:41.

———. 1982. *Punishment in Islamic Law*. Indianapolis, Ind.: American Trust Publications.

Engineer, A. A. 1992. "Islam and Family Planning." *Progressive Perspectives* 1, no. 4 (Oct.). Bombay: Institute of Islamic Studies.

Esposito, John. 1982. *Women in Muslim Family Law*. Syracuse, N.Y.: Syracuse Univ. Press.

————. 1993. *The Islamic Threat: Myth or Reality?* New York: Oxford Univ. Press.

————. 1995. *The Oxford Encyclopedia of the Modern Islamic World.* New York: Oxford Univ. Press.

Fadel, Mohammad. 1997. "Two Women, One Man: Knowledge, Power and Gender in Medieval Sunni Legal Thought." *International Journal of Middle East Studies* 29: 185–204.

Farrukh,ʿUmar. 1984. *Tarikh al-Adab al-ʿArabi.* Vol. 1, *Al-Adab al-Qadim.* 5th ed. Beirut: Dar al-ʿIlm li al-Malayin.

al Faruqi, Ismaʿil Raji. 1981. *Al-Tawhid: Its Implications for Thought and Life.* Herndon, Va.: International Institute of Islamic Thought.

————. 1982. *Islamization of Knowledge: General Principles and Workplan.* Washington, D.C.: International Institute of Islamic Thought.

————. 1986. *The Trialogue of the Abrahamic Faiths.* Washington, D.C.: New Era.

Fineman, Mark. 1988. "Pakistan Women Fear New Islamic Law May Blunt Struggle for Rights." *Los Angeles Times,* July 2, pt. 1, 5.

Funk, Rus Ervin. 1994. *Stopping Rape: A Challenge for Men.* Philadelphia: New Society Publishers.

Fyzee, A. A. A. 1978. *A Modern Approach to Islam.* Lahore, Pakistan: Universal Books.

Gauher, A., ed. "Islamic Law—Its Ideals and Principals." 1980. In *The Challenge of Islam,* edited by A. Gauher. London: Islamic Council of Europe.

Ghadbian, Najib. 1995. "Islamists and Women in the Arab World: From Reaction to Reform?" *American Journal of Islamic Social Sciences* 12:19.

Ghandur, A. 1972. *Al-Ahwal al-Shakhsiyyah fi al-Islam.* Kuwait: Matbuʿaat Jamiʿat al-Kuwait.

Gharib, George. 1984. *Shaʿirat al-ʿArab fi al-Jahiliya.* Vol. 39 of *Al-Mawsuʿa fi al-Adab al-ʿArabi.* Beirut: Dar al-Thaqafa.

————. 1985. *Shaʿirat al-ʿArab fi al-Islam.* Vol. 40 of *Al-Mawsuʿa fi al-Adab al-ʿArabi.* Beirut: Dar al-Thaqafa.

al-Ghazali, Abu Hamid. 1939. *Ihyaʿ Ulum al Din* (Reviving religious sciences). Fifteenth century. Reprint. Vols. 2, 3. Cairo: Mustafa al-Babi al-Halabi wa Awladuh. 15.

———— (authorship listed as al-Ghazzali, Imam). 1984. *Marriage and Sexuality in Islam; Chapter from Ihya-Ulum-Ud-Din.* Translated by Madelain Farah. Salt Lake City: Univ. of Utah Press.

Graham, William A. 1977. *Divine Word and Prophetic Word in Early Islam.* The Hague: Mouton.

Haddad, Yvonne. 1985. "Islam, Women and Revolution in Twentieth Century Arab Thought." In *Women, Religions, and Social Change,* edited by Yvonne Haddad and Ellison B. Findley. Albany: SUNY Press.

Haeri, Shahla. 1995. "The Politics of Dishonor: Rape and Power in Pakistan." In

Faith and Freedom: Women's Human Rights in the Muslim World, edited by Mahnaz Afkhami, 161–74. Syracuse, N.Y.: Syracuse Univ. Press.

Hale, Matthew. 1778. *History of the Pleas of the Crown*. London: Assigns of Richard Atkins and Edward Atkins. Esq.

al-Hariri, Abdur Rahman. 1986. *Kitab al-Fiqh ʿAla al-Madhahib al-ʾArbaʿa.*

Hasan, Husain al-Haj. 1992. *Adab al-ʿArab fi Sadr al-Islam.* Beirut: Al-Muʾassasa al-Jamiʿiya li al-Dirasat wa al-Nashr wa al-Tawziʿ.

Hassan, Riffat. 1982a. "On Human Rights and the Qurʾanic Perspective." *Journal of Ecumenical Studies* 19 (summer): 3, 51–65.

———. 1982b. "On Human Rights and the Qurʾanic Perspective." In *Human Rights in Religious Traditions*, edited by Arlene Swidler. New York: Pilgrim's Press.

———. 1992. "On Human Rights and the Qurʾanic Perspective." In *Muslims in Dialogue*, edited by Leonard Swidler. Lewiston: Edwin Mellen Press.

———. 1994. "Women in Islam and Christianity. A Comparison." In *Islam: A Challenge for Christianity*, a special issue of *Concilium* (1994/3), edited by Hans Kung and Jurgen Moltmann, 18–22. London: SCM Press.

———. N.d. *Women's Rights and Islam: From the I.C.P.D. to Beijing.* Self-Published by author.

Hawting, G. R. 1986. *The First Dynasty of Islam: The Umayyad Caliphate A.D. 661–750.* London: Groom Helm.

The Hedaya or Guide: A Commentary on the Mussulman Laws. 1982. Translated by Charles Hamilton. Delhi: Islamic Book Trust.

Heise, Lori. 1991. "When Women Are Prey; Around the World, Rape Is Commonplace—and the Victims Can't Fight Back." *The Washington Post*, Dec. 8, sec. C1.

Henderson, Mae Gwendolyn. 1994. "Speaking in Tongues: Dialogics, Dialectics and the Black Woman Writer's Literary Tradition." In *Colonial Discourse and Post-colonial Theory: A Reader*, edited by Patrick Williams and Laura Chrisman, 257–67. New York: Columbia Univ. Press.

al-Hibri, Azizah. 1982. "A Study of Islamic Herstory: Or How Did We Get into This Mess?" In *Women and Islam*, edited by Azizah al-Hibri. New York: Pergamon Press.

———. 1985. "Women In Islam." *Hypatia* (Special issue no. 2). New York: Pergamon Press.

———. 1992. "Islamic Constitutionalism and the Concept of Democracy." *Case Western Reserve Journal of International Law* 24:9–10.

———. 1993a. "Panel on Religious and Ethical Perspective on Population Issues." The Religious Consultation on Population, Reproductive Health, and Ethics. Washington, D.C.

———. 1993b. "Prenuptuial Agreements." Symposium on Religious Law: Roman Catholic, Islamic, and Jewish Treatment of Familial Issues, Including Education, Abortion, In Vitro Fertilization, Prenuptial Agreements, Contraception, and Marital Fraud. *Loyola of Los Angeles International and Comparative Law Journal.* 16: 10.

———. 1997. "Islam, Law, and Custom: Redefining Muslim Women's Rights." *American University Journal of International Law and Policy* 12, no. 1:1–44.

Hodkinson, Keith. 1984. *Muslim Family Law: A Source Book.* London: Croom Helm.

Hodson, Peregrine. 1994. "Bhutto Appeals for Reward over Moderate Stand." *Times* (London), Nov. 26, 16.

al-Hufi, ʿAbd al-Salam. N.d. *Al-Khansaʾ: Sharh Diwanaha.* Beirut: Dar al-Kutub al-ʿIlmiya.

al-Hufi, Ahmad. 1972. *Al-Marʾa fi al-Shiʿr al-Jahili.* Cairo: Nahdat Misr.

Husain, Taha. 1991. *Min Tarikh al-Adab al-ʿArabi.* Vol. 1. 4th ed. Beirut: Dar al-ʿIlm li al-Malayin.

Ibn ʿAbd al-Birr (Abu ʿUmar Yusuf bin ʿAbdullah al-Nimri al-Qurtubi). 1969 *Al-Istiʿab fi Maʿrifat al-Ashab.* 4 vols. Edited by Ali Muhammad al-Bakhawi. Cairo: Nahdat Misr.

Ibn al-Athir. N.d. *Asad al-Ghaba fi Maʿrifat al-Sahaba.* edited by Muhammad Ibrahim al-Banna and Muhammad Ahmad Ashur. Cairo: Kitab al-Shaʿb.

Ibn Majah, M. 1998. *Sunan Ibn Majah.* 2 vols. Beirut: Dar al-Kutub al-ʿIlmiyah. Ninth century. Reprint.

Ibn Qutaiba (Abu Muhammad ʿAbdullah bin Muslim bin Qutaiba). 1925. *Kitab ʿUyun al-Akhbar.* Beirut: Dar al-Kitab al-ʿArabi.

Ibn Saʿd. 1957. *Al-Tabaqat al-Kubra.* 9 vols. Beirut: Dar Sader.

Ibn Taifur (Abi al-Fadl Ahmad bin Abi Tahir). 1987. *Balaghat al-Nisaʾ,* ed. Ahmad al-Ulfi. Beirut: Dar al-Hadatha.

Iqbal, Anwar. 1995. "Bhutto Seeks Laws Against Rape." United Press International, Aug. 1.

Iqbal, Muhammad. 1971. *The Reconstruction of Religious Thought in Islam.* Lahore, Pakistan: Muhammad Ashraf.

Islamic Council. 1994. "Universal Islamic Declaration of Human Rights." In *Islam: A Challenge for Christianity,* a special issue of *Concilium* (1994/3), Hans Kung and Jurgen Moltmann, 141–50. London: SCM Press.

Ismaʿil, ʿIzz al-Din. N.d. *Al-Masadir al-Adabiya wa al-Lughawiyya fi al-Turath al-ʿArabi.* Cairo: Dar Gharib.

Jabbar, Bushra. 1991. "The Reality of Rape." *Economic Review* (Pakistan), July, 7–8.

Jalal, Ayesha. 1991. "The Convenience of Subservience: Women and the State in Pakistan." In *Women, Islam and the State,* edited by Deniz Kandiyoti, 102. Philadelphia: Temple Univ. Press.

al-Jawsi, Jamal al-Din Ibn. 1985. *Tarikh Omar Ibn al-Khattab* (History of Omar (ʿUmar) Ibn Khattab). Reprint. Beirut: Dar al-Raʾid al-ʿArabi.

al-Jaziri, ʾAbd al-Rahman. 1969. *Kitab al-Fiqh ʿala al-Madhabib al-Arbaʿah* (The Book of fiqh on the four schools of jurisprudence). Vol. 4. Beirut: Dar ʿIhyaʾ al-Turath al-ʿArabi.

———. 1986. *Kitab al-Fiqh ʿala al-Madhabib al-Arbaʿa.* Cairo: Dar al-Irshad lil Taʾif wa al-Tabʿ wa al Nashr.

Jehan Mina v. the State. 1983. PLD Federal Shariat Court 183 (Pak.) [Mina v. State].

Jilani, Hina. 1992. "Whose Laws? Human Rights and Violence Against Women in Pakistan." In *Freedom From Violence: Women's Strategies from Around the World,* edited by Margaret Schuler, 63. New York: Widbooks.

Johnson, Richard William. 1989. "Wars of Religion." *New Statesman and Society* 2: 13–14.

Kabbani, Rana. 1986. *Europe's Myths of Orient.* Bloomington: Indiana Univ. Press.

Kahhala, ʿUmar Rida. 1991. *Aʿlam al-Nisaʾ.* 10th ed. Beirut: Muʿʾassasat al-Risala. 5 vol.

Kamali, Mohammad Hashim. 1991. *Principles of Islamic Jurisprudence.* 2d ed. Cambridge, U.K.: Islamic Texts Society.

Kandiyoti, Deniz, ed. 1991. "Women, Islam and the State," *Middle East Report* 21, no. 173:9–14.

———. 1995. "Reflections on the Politics of Gender in Muslim Societies: From Nairobi to Beijing." In *Faith and Freedom: Women's Human Rights in the Muslim World,* edited by Mahnaz Afkhami, 19–32 Syracuse, N.Y.: Syracuse Univ. Press.

al-Kawamila, Fathi. 1988. *Fi Rihab al-Khansaʾ,* Damascus: Dar al-Jalil.

Khadduri, Majid. 1984. *The Islamic Concept of Justice.* Baltimore: John Hopkins Univ. Press.

Khalid, Khalid M. and Min Hina Nabda. 1953. *Our Beginning Wisdom.* Translated from the Arabic by Ismaʿil al-Faruqi. Washington, D.C.: American Council of Learned Societies.

Khalidi, Ramla, and Judith Tucker. N.d. "Women's Rights in the Arab World." Special report of the Middle East Research and Information Project (MERIP), 2–8.

Khalidi, Tarif. 1994. *Arabic Historical Thought in the Classical Period.* Cambridge Studies in Islamic Civilization. Cambridge, U.K.: Cambridge Univ.

Khalif, Mayy Yusuf. 1991. *Al-Shiʿr al-Nisaʾi fi Adabina al-Qadim.* Cairo: Maktabat Gharib.

Khan, Aslam. 1985. "Zia's Islamic Democracy. Leading Pakistan into the Past." *Nation,* June 29, 791.

Khan, Shahid Reman. 1986. "Under Pakistan's Form of Islamic Law, Rape Is a Crime—for the Victims." Los Angeles *Times,* May 25, sec. 1.

al-Khansa. N.d. *Diwan al-Khansaʾ.* Beirut: Dar Sader.

Kung, Hans and Jurgen Moltmann, eds. 1994. *Islam: A Challenge for Charistianity.* A special issue of *Concilium* (1994/3). London: SCM Press.

Lorber, Judith. 1994. *Paradoxes of Gender.* New Haven, Conn.: Yale Univ. Press.

Ma'badi, Muhammad Badr. 1983. *Al-Nisa' fi al-Jahiliya wa al-Islam: Al-Nathr.* Cairo: Al-Matba'a al-Namudhajiyyah.

Maghniah, M. 1960. *Al-Fiqh 'ala al-Madhahib al-khamsah* (Jurisprudence based on the five schools [of thought]). Beirut: Dar al-'Ilm Li al-Malayin.

Mahdi, Muhsin. 1990. "Orientalism and the Study of Islamic Philosophy." *Journal of Islamic Studies* 1:72–98.

Mahmassani, Sobhi. 1962. *Muqaddimah fi Ihya' 'Ulum al-Shari'ah.* Beirut. Dar al-'Ilm li al-Malayin.

———. 1987. *Falsafat al-Tashri' fi al-Islam* (The philosophy of jurisprudence in Islam). Translated by Farhat J. Ziadeh. Malaysia: Malaysia Penerbitan Hizbi.

———. 1965. *Al-Awda' al-Tashri'iyah fi al-duwal al-'Arabiya* (Legal conditions in Arab countries). Beirut: Dar al-'Ilm Li al-Malayin.

The Major Acts. 1992. Lahore, Pakistan: Lahore Law Times Publications.

Malik, Imam. 1982. *Al-Muwatta'.* Translated by 'A'isha 'Abdarahman at-Tarjumana and Ya'qub Johnson. Norwich, U.K.: Diwan Press.

Malti-Douglas, Fedwa. 1991. *Woman's Body, Woman's Word: Gender in Arabo-Islamic Discourse.* Princeton, N.J.: Princeton Univ.

al-Maqdisi, Muhammad Ibn Quddamah. 1994. *Al-Mughni 'ala Mukhtasar al-Kharaqi.* Vol. 8. Cairo: Dar al-Kutub al-'Ilmiyyah.

Maududi, A. A. 1974. *Birth Control.* Translated and edited by K. Ahmad and M. I. Faruqi. Lahore, Pakistan: Islamic Publications Limited.

Mayer, Ann. 1991. *Islam and Human Rights.* London: Westview Press.

McCloud, Aminah Beverly. 1995. *African American Islam.* London: Routledge Press.

McIntosh, Peggy. 1994. Review of *The Politics of Women's Education. Women's Book Review,* Oct.

Mehdi, Rubya. 1990. "The Offence of Rape in the Islamic Law of Pakistan." *International Journal of Society and Law* 18:19.

———. 1994. *The Islamization of the Law in Pakistan.* London: Curzon Press.

Mehmet, Ozay. 1990. *Islamic Identity and Development.* London: Routledge.

Menon, N. R. Madhava. 1981. "Islamic Criminal Jurisprudence and Social Defence [sic] in the Modern World: An Appreciation." *Islamic and Comparative Law Quarterly* 1:232.

Mernissi, Fatima. 1987. *Beyond the Veil: Male-Female Dynamics in Modern Muslim Society.* Bloomington: Indiana Univ. Press.

———. 1991. *The Veil and the Male Elite: A Feminist Interpretation of Women's Rights in Islam.* Reading, Mass.: Addison-Wesley.

———. 1992. *Islam and Democracy—Fear of the Modern World.* Reading, Mass.: Addison-Wesley.

———. 1996. *Women's Rebellion and Islamic Memory.* London: Zed Books.

Mishkat al-Masabih. 1990. Translated by James Robson. 2d ed. Lahore, Pakistan: Sh. Muhammad Ashraf.

Moghadam, Valentine. 1993. *Modernizing Women: Gender and Social Change in the Middle East.* Boulder, Colo.: Lynne Rienner.

Moore, Kathleen. 1991. "Muslims in Prison: Claims to Constitutional Protection of Religious Liberty." In *The Muslims of America,* edited by Yvonne Y. Haddad. New York: Oxford Univ. Press.

————, ed. 1994. *Identity Politics and Women: Cultural Reassertions and Feminisms in International Perspective.* Boulder, Colo.: Westview Press.

Mubarak, Mazen. 1981. *Al-Mujaz fi tarikh al-balagha.* Damascus: Dar Al-Fikr.

————. 1996. Telephone interview with Mohja Kahf, United Arab Emirates, Nov. 29.

Muhaiyaddeen, M. R. Bawa. 1987. *Islam and World Peace: Explanations of a Sufi.* Philadelphia: Fellowship Press.

al-Mundhiri, Zaki al-Din ʿAbd al-ʿAzim bin ʿAbd al-Qawiy. 1977. *Mukhtasar Sahih Muslim,* edited by Muhammad Naser al-Din al-Albani. 3d ed., Damascus: Al-Maktab al-Islami.

Murata, Sachiko. 1992. *The Tao of Islam: A Sourcebook of Gender Relationships in Islamic Thought.* Albany, N.Y.: SUNY Press.

Muslim, Ibn al-Hajjajal-Qushairi. 1976. *Sahih Muslim.* Translated by A. H. Siddiqi. Lahore, Pakistan: H. Muhammad Ashraf.

Mussallam, B. F. 1983. *Sex and Society in Islam.* Cambridge, U.K.: Cambridge Univ. Press.

An-Naʾim, Abdullahi Ahmed. 1990. *Toward an Islamic Reformation: Civil Liberties, Human Rights, and International Law.* Syracuse, N.Y.: Syracuse Univ. Press.

Nasr, Seyyed Hossein. 1993. *A Young Muslim's Guide in the Modern World.* Chicago: Kazi.

New York Times. 1985. June 19, sec. 2, 6:1, June 25, sec. 3, 6:1.

"O. J. Simpson Fits Stereotype: Religious Fundamentalism Appears to Breed More Violence Toward Women." 1995. *Business Wire,* Jan. 30.

Omran, A. R. 1992. *Family Planning in the Legacy of Islam.* London: Routledge.

Osman, Fathi. 1960. *Al-Fikr al-Islami wa al Tatawwur.* Cairo: n.p.

Pakistan Legal Decisions [PLD]. 1979. Central Statutes. Lahore, Pakistan: Law Publishing Company.

Pakistan Penal Code. 1860. [Repealed 1979]. 375. Reprinted in R. A. Nelson. 1975. *The Pakistan Penal Code.* Lahore: PLD Publishers.

Papanek, Hanna. 1984. *Women-in-Development and Women's Studies: Agenda for the Future.* Working paper no. 55. E. Lansing: Michigan State Univ. Press.

Parliamentary Human Rights Group. n.d. *Iran: The Subjugation of Women.* Pamplet circulated at the NGO Forum at FWCW. N.p.

Parwez, G. A. 1961. "Lughat al-Qurʾan." *Idara-e-Tuluʾe-Islam.* 3. Lahore, Pakistan: n.p.

———. 1977. Tabweeb-ul-Qurʾan (Urdu). *Idara-e-Tuluʾ-e-Islam.* 1. Lahore, Pakistan: n.p.

———. 1981. "Bunyadi Haquq-e-Insaniyat" (Urdu). *Idara-e-Tuluʾ-e-Islam.* Lahore, Pakistan: n.p.

Patel, Rashida. 1991. *Socio-Economic Political Status and Women And Law in Pakistan.* Karachi, Pakistan: Faiza Publishers.

Qadri, Anwar Ahmad. 1982. *Justice in Historical Islam.* Lahore, Pakistan: Sh. Muhammad Ashraf.

Rahman, Anika. 1994. "A View Towards Women's Reproductive Rights: Perspective on Selected Laws and Policies in Pakistan." *Whittier Law Review* 15:981.

Rahman, Fazlur. 1972. " Religion and Planned Parenthood in Pakistan." In *Muslim Attitudes Toward Family Planning,* edited by Olivia Schieffelin. New York: Population Council, New York.

———. 1980. "A Study of Modernization of Muslim Family Law." *International Journal of Middle East Studies* 2:451

———. 1982. *Islam and Modernity.* Chicago: Univ. of Chicago Press.

———. 1989. *Health and Medicine in the Islamic Tradition.* New York: Crossroad.

———. 1996. "Islam's Origin and Ideals." In *Islamic Identity and the Struggle for Justice,* edited by Nimat Hafez Barazangi, Raquibuz Zaman, and Omar Afzal., 11–18. Gainesville: Univ. Press of Florida.

Rashid, Ahmed. 1991. "Rape Scandal Rocks Pakistan: Ahmed Rashid in Islamabad on a Gang Attack that Is Exposing a Rotten State Machine." *Independent* (London), Dec. 29, sec. 14.

al-Razi, Fakhr al-Din. 1992. *Al-Mahsul fi ʿilm ʿusul al-fiqh* (The substance in the foundations of jurisprudence). 5 vols. Twelfth century. Reprint. Beirut: Muʾassasat al-Risalah.

Renard, John. 1994. "Islam, the One and the Many: Unity and Diversity in a Global Tradition. In *Islam: A Challenge for Christianity,* a special issue of *Concilium* (1994/3), edited by Hans Kung and Jurgen Moltmann, 31–38. London: SCM Press.

Rida, M. R. N.d., *Tafsir al-Qurʾan al-Hakim.* Vol. 2. Beirut: Dar al-Maʿrifah.

———. 1984. *Huquq al-nisaʾ fi al-Islam* (The rights of women in Islam). Beirut: al-Maktab al-Islam.

———. N.d. *Tafsir al-Manar.* Vol. 2. Beirut: Dar al-Fikr.

Robinson, Melissa. 1992. "Unveiled: Rape in Pakistan." *New Republic,* Mar. 9, p. 11.

Roded, Ruth. 1994. *Women in Islamic Biographical Collections: From Ibn Saʿd to Who's Who.* Boulder, Colo.: Lynne Rienner.

Sabbah, Fatna A. 1984. *Woman in the Muslim Unconscious.* Translated by Mary J. Lakewood. New York: Pergammon.

Saadatmand, Yassaman. 1995. "Separate and Unequal—Women in [the] Islamic Republic of Iran." *Journal of South Asian and Middle Eastern Studies* 18, no. 4 (summer: 1–24.

Sabiq, Sayed. 1993. *Fiqh-al-Sunnah.* Vol. 2. 10th ed. Mecca: Bab al-Loq.

Safia Bibi v. the State. 1985. PLD Federal Shariat Court 120 (Pak.) [Bibi v. State].

Salama, Ma'amun M. 1982. "General Principles of Criminal Evidence in Islamic Jurisprudence." In *The Islamic Criminal Justice System,* edited by M. Cherif Bassiouni, 109. London: Oceana Publications.

al-Saleh, Osman 'Abd-el-Malek. 1982. "The Right of the Individual to Personal Security in Islam." In *The Islamic Criminal Justice System,* edited by M. Cherif Bassiouni, 5. London: Oceana Publications.

al-Sarkhasi, Shams al-Din. 1986. *Kitab al-Mabsut.* Vol. 5. Reprint. Beirut: Dar al-Ma'rifah.

Sarwar, Beena. 1995. "Pakistan-Women: Bhutto Campaigns Against Domestic Violence." Inter-Press Service, July 12.

Schacht, Joseph. 1953. *The Origins of Muhammedan Jurisprudence.* Oxford, U.K.: Clarendon Press.

Scroggins, Deborah. 1992. "Playing the Power Game with Rape Series: Women of the Veil." *Vancouver Sun,* July 13, A10.

Seminar. 1982. "Adultery and Fornication in Islamic Jurisprudence: Dimensions and Perspectives." *Islamic and Comparative Law Quarterly* 2:267.

al-Shafi'i, Al-Imam Muhammad ibn Idris. 1987. *Al-Risala [Treatise on the foundations of Islamic jurisprudence].* Translated by Majid Khadduri. 2d ed. Cambridge, U.K.: Islamic Texts Society.

Shalabi, Muhammad Mustafa. 1960. *Al-Fiqh al-Islami bayn al-mithaliya al-waqi'iyah.*

Shawkani, Muhammad. A.H. 1344. *Nayl al-Awtar Sharh Muntaq al-Akhbar.* Cairo.

Siddiqi, Muhammad Iqbal. 1985. *The Penal Law of Islam.* 2d ed. Lahore, Pakistan: Kazi.

Smith, J. I., and Y. Y. Haddad. 1982. "Eve: Islamic Image of Women." In *Women and Islam,* edited by Azizah al-Hibri, 135–44. New York: Pergammon.

Sobhan, Salma. 1993. "Political History in the Indian Subcontinent." Paper read at seminar, Women, Islam, and Development, sponsored by the Foreign Ministry of the Royal Netherlands Government, Sept. 15.

Sonn, Tamara. 1996. "The Islamic Call: Social Justice and Political Realism." In *Islamic Identity and the Struggle for Justice,* edited by Nimat Hafez Barazangi, Raquibuz Zaman, and Omar Afzal. 64–76. Gainesville: Univ. Press of Florida.

Spellberg, D. A. 1994. *Politics, Gender, and the Islamic Past: The Legacy of 'A'isha bint Abi Bakr.* New York: Columbia Univ. Press.

Spender, Dale. 1980. *Man Made Language.* London: Routledge and Kegan Paul.

Stowasser, Barbara Freyer. 1994. *Women in the Qur'an, Traditions, and Interpretations.* New York: Oxford Univ. Press.

al-Tabari, Abu Ja'far. 1910. *Jami' al-Bayan 'an Ta'wil al-Qur'an.* Ninth century. Reprint. Cited in D. A. Spellberg. 1994. In *Politics, Gender, and the Islamic Past: The Legacy of 'A'isha bint Abi Bakr.* New York: Columbia Univ. Press.

————. 1989. *The History of al-Tabari.* Translated by Gautier H. A. Juynbull. Albany: SUNY Press.

————. 1992. *Jami' al-Bayan fi Tafsir al-Qur'an.* 30 vols. Beirut: Dar al Ma'rifah. Ninth century. Reprint.

al-Tanir, Salim. [1408] 1988. *Al-Sha'irat min al-Nisa': A'lam wa Tawa'if.* Damascus: Dar al-Kitab al-'Arabi.

al 'Umari, Akram Diya. 1991. *Madinan Society at the Time of the Prophet.* Vol. 2. Translated by Huda Khattab. Herndon, Va.: International Institute of Islamic Thought.

United Nations. 1994. "The Convention on the Elimination of All Forms of Discrimination Against Women." U.N. Publications.

United Nations Education Scientific and Cultural Organization. 1995. "Muslim Women in the Middle East." Sources no. 71, July–August. UNESCO Publications.

United States Department of State. 1994. *Country Reports on Human Rights Practices for 1993.* Washington, D.C.

USC-MSA Hadith Database. http://www.usc.edu/dept/MSA/reference/searchhadith.html.

Wadud, Amina (authorship listed as Wadud-Muhsin). 1992. *Qur'an and Woman.* Kuala Lumpur: Penerbit Fajar Bakti. SDN.BHD.

————. 1999. *Qur'an and Woman: Rereading The Sacred Text from a Woman's Perspective.* 2nd ed. New York: Oxford Univ. Press.

Walther, Wiebke. 1995. *Women in Islam.* Princeton, N.J.: Marcus Wiener Press.

Wensinck, A. J., and J. P. Mensing. 1943. *Concordance et Indices de la tradition Musulmane.* Leiden: E. J. Brill.

Whitehorn, Katharine. 1994. "The Apartheid of Gender." *Observer* (London), June 19, p. 23.

Wolkstein, Diane, and S. N. Kramer. 1983. *Inanna: Queen of Heaven and Earth. Her Stories and Hymns from Sumer.* Quoted in Eisler, Riane. 1995. *Sacred Pleasure: Sex, Myth, and the Politics of the Body.* San Francisco, Calif.: Harper San Francisco.

Women's Centre for Legal Aid and Counseling. 1995. *Towards Equality: An Examination of the Status of Palestinian Women in Existing Law.* Jerusalem: Women's Centre.

Zaidan, Abdul-Karim. 1994. *Al-Mufassal fi Ahkam al-Mar'ah wa al-Bayt al-Muslim fi al-Shari'ah al-Islamiya* (detailed in laws pertaining to women and the Muslim household in Islamic Shariʿah). Vols. 4, 6, 7, 8, 9, 10. Beirut: Muʾassasat al-Risalah.

Zia, Afiya Shehrbano. 1994. *Sex Crime in the Islamic Context: Rape, Class and Gender in Pakistan.* Lahore, Pakistan: Asr Publications.

al-Zirkili. Khayr al-din. N.d. *AlʿAlam. Damascus: al-Zirkili.*

al-Zuhayli, Wahhab. 1984. Al-Fiqh al-Islami wa Addillatuh. Vol. 7. Damascus: Dar al-Fikr.

———. 1986. *Usul al-fiqh al-ʿIslami* (The foundations of Islamic jurisprudence). Damascus: Dar al-Fikr. vol. 1, no. 662.

Index